GOOD MEASURE

Introduction
My personal path to understanding fit

I have been happily employed as a freelance knitwear designer for over 30 years, creating garments of every type for women, men, and children of all ages. I enjoy designing not just for small-yet-tall models, but for people of all other dimensions: those of "average" build as well as larger individuals.

No matter the size, I always strive to make my garments fit well: to me, fit is an indispensable part of designing. Good fit enhances and supports my materials, the knitted fabric and pattern stitches, and my design details. Good fit makes all the effort of bringing a garment to life and the cost of my valuable materials pay off.

I consider myself a serious garment-maker. I love to create knitted clothing, and I have explored this area with wide eyes for decades, gathering information about size and fit, one project at a time. It's not difficult—it just takes practice and a modicum of information. Skill at fashioning good fit comes with experience.

Two-pronged approach
I learned early in my career that understanding garment shape is an inextricable part of achieving a good fit. Yes, we need to consider individual measurements when adapting a pattern or designing a knitted piece for ourselves or someone else, but not all garments are shaped the same way—and wearers, too, come in a variety of shapes and sizes. Separating fit from the specifics of garment shape would be putting the proverbial cart before the horse.

I have studied the structure of all kinds of garments within the context of knitting, and I've come to a clear understanding of how to merge that knowledge with the need to make my designs fit and look good on a human body.

Of course, we want to achieve good fit for aesthetic reasons. I always remind my students in workshops (and they readily agree) that—unfortunately!—our eyes seek out imperfections in a garment. Even if we've worked with wonderful materials and exquisite pattern stitches, poor fit will prevent a sweater from being something special in our eyes. Without good fit, a garment looks dowdy and sloppy. When the fit is perfect, all elements shine equally.

Fit is a curious aspect of a garment—more complex than most people realize. Here are just a few of the factors we will consider:

1. Good fit contributes to comfort in addition to beauty. Sometimes certain body characteristics—narrow or broad shoulders, or heavy arms, for example—need to be accommodated for comfort. Most standard patterns do not offer choices to change the design for our personal fit issues and preferences.

2. Fit can be very personal. When we buy a ready-made garment off the rack, we often choose a size based not on the tag, but on how we like clothes to look on us. Of course, cultural norms tell us what looks good, but our own individuality and personal style can also lead us to our own look. Likewise, when making things fit for someone else, we need to consider what distinguishes that person from another.

3. Fit is related to what I call "garment integrity." Certain kinds of garments, as well as their parts, need to be structured a certain way to fit well. For example, a raglan sleeve is not shaped the same way as a cap-style sleeve. A flowing cape is not shaped the same way as a body-conscious jacket. Understanding the many types and shapes of garments, each with unique characteristics and parameters, is very important.

4. Yarn type and fiber, stitch pattern and texture, all factor into fit. As knitters, we need to understand the qualities of our yarn: Is it heavy, hairy, slick, or slinky? And the characteristics of pattern stitches—flat or clingy, firm or stretchy—need to be considered when we plan our garments.

Starting on the path to good fit

So, how do you accomplish good fit, considering all of the above—and enjoy the process? Answering that question was my goal in this book.

As a professional designer for magazines, yarn companies, and online marketplaces, I strive to create sweaters that can be sized for a range of body types, in all kinds of materials and shapes. I want my designs to look good on a waif-like model as well as someone who is sturdily built. Finding a balance among these elements—some more personal than others—happens before a sweater is started. Often before I even cast on!

Whether you are following a pattern to knit for yourself, making gifts for family and friends, or designing garments as a professional, you need ground rules to ensure that good fit will be a given result of your hard work, not a question mark.

Don't worry if the elements I have listed are daunting at first! Achieving good fit in knitted sweaters was easier for me than for most knitters, because I came from a sewing background, where adjusting patterns is common. Often, guidelines for fitting sewn garments are part of purchased patterns—a helpful extra, uncommon in knitting patterns. In this book I will encourage you to look at patterns with an eye for necessary changes, to achieve the fit you require before you begin to knit.

My many years in theater also made me fearless about adapting a pattern. In the costume shop, working with a talented designer, I draped and sewed garments from every era—historical and modern-day. I learned to measure correctly and assess these measurements. I learned to adjust ready-made, store-bought garments and to make garments from scratch. One of my first jobs, for a historical production, was to take a man's tailcoat from the 18th century and make a pattern to fit three different-sized cast members. For a production of Rodgers and Hammerstein's *Cinderella*, we created patterns for close-fitting corseted dresses for many sizes, from a child-sized woman to a much taller, broad-shouldered actress. Nothing was impossible!

All these experiences prepared me for designing knitted garments. When I began to knit, I realized that the same rules applied—perhaps with a little more relaxation, because knits are inherently stretchy and require less perfection in fit than many sewn garments. As I progressed to designing, I relied on lessons from sewing and theater, but I also learned by observing knitted fabric and studying other knitted garments. Here, after years of testing these methods, I present them as they apply to knitwear and garment types, for you to study and follow.

Even if you have never sewn, never imagined re-creating a garment from the past, you can still absorb and understand the basic rules of fit! I will take you step-by-step through all you need to know to design knitted garments for real people.

What I said about my love of finishing in my book *Finishing School* I can say with regards to establishing perfect fit: you need to consider yourself more than just a person who knits! You belong to a long tradition of garment-makers who have considered how to use fabric to conform to the body. I encourage you to approach each project with this mindset, integrating the aspects of design that contribute to making one-of-a-kind knitted garments that fit well.

Let me be your guide and share my experience, so you can enjoy this process as much as I do.

Deborah Newton
2015

Here are some themes presented throughout *Good Measure*:

SCHEMATIC DRAWINGS

I depend on a schematic for every project I make, and I explain many ways to use these.

PROJECTS

Using projects as examples, I go into more depth on the main topics. At the back of the book you'll find all the patterns with instructions given for many sizes.

PRACTICAL MATTERS

I share tips and tricks I have picked up throughout my years of designing to make planning for a good fit easier.

WHAT IF?

Sometimes we want to change things up with a pattern! I offer suggestions for how to personalize designs to suit your body type and preferences.

IT'S IN THE DETAILS

Learn how to add flattering extra details to any sweater to expand upon basic good fit.

CHAPTER 1

The Good Fit Mindset

If you have entered the world of knitted garments, you have concerns about fit. Maybe, despite strong knitting skills, you made a sweater—or multiple projects—that didn't fit successfully, and as a result you've strayed from knitting garments. Let's start by changing that mindset: from taking our chances with fit to understanding it as a garment-maker should.

What Is Good Fit?

Fit is different from—yet related to—what flatters us. We want both! Any style of garment should encircle our body without strain, while at the same time having a shape that flatters who we are. As a designer, I like to think most garments can be planned to accommodate most body shapes. The archetypical "hourglass shape" or "waif-like model" frame does not belong to all of us. But with the correct adjustments, a garment that looks good on a curvaceous figure or a narrow frame can look good on almost any figure.

It doesn't matter how you knit your sweaters: in pieces, in the round, from the top down, or side-to-side! You want good fit to be an element of every project. No one sets out to knit a sweater that is uncomfortable or unflattering, too small or too large. But things happen: for example, a garment fits well in one area but not as a whole. Many of us have encountered this—often more than once.

Many hand-knitters face disappointment after the pleasure of knitting is over and the details of finishing complete. Instead of a feeling of accomplishment and success, there is sadness, and the sense of a waste of time and expensive materials.

How do we approach this dilemma of poor fit? Or, more positively, how do we ensure good fit? The path to understanding how to make knitted garments fit well is accessible, if you break it down into easy-to-navigate sections. When you gain familiarity with each area that affects fit, you can begin to make projects with confidence and control. Instead of waiting to see if something will fit and be flattering after it is knitted and finished, you can plan ahead and be reliably pleased with the results.

Getting a good fit is more complicated than just adding or subtracting stitches at the sides of pieces! Some garments require complex adjustments—and in this book I will explain all of the concerns you must learn about and address when seeking a good fit. You should also develop an awareness of details that flatter your personal shape and size, which is helpful both in choosing patterns and in altering them. Keep these concepts in mind as you enter this territory, and your sweater-making will never be the same.

An important note: although the designs and guidelines in this book are for women, the process of getting a good fit is the same for men, women, and children!

A Course of Study

As a professional designer, I encounter the challenges of new concepts on a regular basis. When meeting the needs of editors and others I design for, I've often had the opportunity to explore new ideas that, on my own, I might not have pursued. Sometimes I think my design career has been one long course of study: I've gained a wealth of knowledge from problem-solving, working on new kinds of garments, and developing new knitted fabrics.

In workshops I always present this question to my students: Why not consider an interesting and revelatory course of study, self-directed, that includes working with new ideas on a regular basis? Lightbulbs go off in students' heads when I suggest that after every two or three "pleasure" projects, they try working with a new—and possibly daunting—aspect of their knitting. Learning new techniques will expand your vision of what your craft has to offer and make it even more rewarding.

Understanding how to make garments fit better is a pursuit that you should consider making a regular part of your knitting life—especially if you have avoided knitting garments because finding the right fit has been challenging.

Topics We'll Cover

The following areas of concern about fit are all interconnected. I list them here to introduce you to the concepts; in the chapters that follow, I present each topic in detail. Also, I have designed projects for this book that correspond to these topics and, I hope, illuminate the issues at hand.

I feel it is most useful to read this book chronologically. However, you may, according to your experience, jump around among the subjects listed above. But don't dismiss any one section, thinking you already know what it contains. Each is important and is connected thematically to the others. Strive to have a grasp of ALL of these areas, and become an expert about your own fit concerns and those that affect the gifts and garments you make for others.

YOUR OWN MEASUREMENTS, EXPERIENCE, AND REVELATORY GARMENTS
• Know your own measurements and body shape.
• Identify the fit issues you have had in the past.
• Review garments that fit you well: analyze their characteristics and how they relate to your body.
• Learn how to work with sweaters that fit you well.
• Develop an annotated schematic of your body for your own reference and use.

UNDERSTANDING SILHOUETTE, EASE,
AND FABRIC CHARACTERISTICS
• What is silhouette?
• Ease and fabric weight—how do they work
together?
• How do the characteristics of fiber and yarn
weight affect fit?

HIGHLIGHTING YOUR FEATURES
• In what ways can you use line, color, and
proportion to make a sweater suited to your
figure type: your own size and shape?

THE WORLD OF GARMENT SHAPES
• Familiarize yourself with the range of garment
types, from basic to complex, and learn their unique
characteristics.
• What makes one type of garment different from
another: Do the same rules for adjustments apply
to each?
• What garment types look best on which
figures—and why?

CHANGING KNITTED GARMENT PATTERNS
• Learn how to study a pattern before knitting to
assess whether you want to alter the pattern to
achieve a better fit.
• Using your newfound knowledge from the previous
sections, learn to analyze and adjust a pattern for
your own body issues.
• Master new techniques for altering patterns.

THE KNITTING ITSELF
• Learn how to best alter and shape different kinds
of knitted fabrics to achieve better fit with fabric that
still looks good.

What Makes a Sweater Fit—or Not?

Think about it: What does it mean for a garment
to fit well?

1. IT FEELS GOOD! A sweater should feel good when
you wear it. It should cover the body without being
uncomfortably tight or being too large, bulky, or full
in areas where it shouldn't be. When you wear something comfortable, there is no tugging or pulling.
Strive for that feeling!
2. SHAPE AND FABRIC WORK TOGETHER. The
garment shape and the knitted fabric of the sweater
must work well together. This is important to keep
in mind when substituting one yarn for another. The
same knitted fabric worked in two different yarns can

vary greatly in drape and thickness, and thus affect
the fit of a garment.
3. IT ENHANCES THE WEARER. A good-fitting sweater
should enhance and flatter the body. It should not
be distorted by being too tight, nor droop or be too
full. The openings and what I call the "perimeters"—
neckline, lower edges, armholes—should not be
strained so the fabric pulls or stretches, nor be too
loose so they flare in a way that does not conform to
the design of the sweater.

Although there are cultural guidelines for what
looks good, our preferences are also based on personal taste. A garment should draw attention to the
features the wearer herself would like to enhance.

Some features work for everyone, no matter their
size or shape. For example, a well-framed face is always wonderful: this means fit in shoulders and neckline should be considered, and detail applied there.
Also, knowing what lengths work well for you—and
look good—is crucial to good fit.

Ways a Garment Can Fit

Good fit is always essential: it both goes along with
and transcends the style of the time you live in.
Culturally, from a fashion point of view, clothing fits
a certain way in a given space in time. Some decades
are notable for large, oversized garments; other times
the silhouette tends to hug the body.

The choice is yours, too. We are all different—even
though we follow the same patterns! How do *you*
like—or would you like—a sweater to fit? You may
be used to a certain fit when purchasing ready-made
garments, but you need not accept that in garments
you make for yourself.

There are many common ways a garment can fit
poorly. Take a hard look at the way clothes fit you.
In addition to being too tight or too loose, they may
have issues people often do not see. Do any of the
following elements apply to you?
1. The fronts of a cardigan should fall straight,
perpendicular to the ground. They should not flare
toward your sides, unless the style is a "cut-away"
design. I see this frequently: it might mean that (a)
the wearer has made the measurements of the upper
body the deciding factor, or (b) the wrong size has
been chosen. It might mean that the garment fits
in the neckline and armhole areas, but that the fit is
poor in the lower body, and perhaps the bust as well.
2. Unless the shape of a sweater is deliberately asymmetrical, the front and back should be even and parallel to the ground. In other words, the front should
not hike up, nor should the back.

FIT TIP

Shopping for Fit Ideas

*When you shop for
clothing, try this new
approach: observe how
clothing fits you, not
how much you like it.
A few ideas:*

1. *Try on items you would
never think to buy, and
see how they hang on
your body. Choose shapes
that are not your normal
preference, and see
how they look.*

2. *Try on multiple sizes
of a garment or sweater
you like. Identify the
elements that work, and
those that don't.*

3. *Because you knit,
you may not often try
on manufactured
machine-knit sweaters.
See how they are made
and how they fit next time
you shop, noting how
different brand names
have a different cut.*

4. *I have a friend who
repurposes large men's
shirts to make dresses for
little girls. Why not visit
your nearby secondhand
store and find large men's
sweaters that you can cut
and sew into shapes as
"test knits"? This may seem
like a lot of work, but it is
a good way to gain a new
perspective on making a
sweater that fits well, or
to explore a new shape
before knitting a sweater.*

Practical Matters Don't Take Knitting Basics for Granted!

Maybe the two most important hands-on knitting basics that contribute to a garment's fit are gauge and proper seaming.

Gauge

Laying the groundwork for a successful garment means knitting it well and to the appropriate gauge. Before we even get into the issues of fit, I want to stress this point as a given: all adjustments to achieve fit are a total loss if you do not get the knitted fabric right!

So at the outset of any project, be sure you obtain the correct gauge and understand the pattern stitch.

Even if you have achieved the gauge in a swatch, I encourage you to start with a smaller piece of a garment—a sleeve can be perfect—and measure gauge on it before moving on to the body parts that require a more careful fit. Knitters often loosen up after working their swatch, so the pieces of a garment are not always the same gauge as the original swatch.

What if you are making a one-piece or sleeveless garment, like a vest? Then work a very large swatch—at least 8" square—to be sure your gauge will be correct when you get to the actual project. You might even find a fun way to use your swatch in the project itself: I reused the swatches for the geometric poncho on page 31 as cuff-like sleeves.

Good finishing affects good fit, too! Learn the basics of good finishing, including seaming, and you'll improve your garment-making experience.

Simple Seams

Assembly is a big part of garment-making, so you should want your seams to be perfect. Seams that create bulk on the inside of your garments can contribute to poor fit.

In my early days of designing, I was frustrated by attempts to seam pieces that featured textured patterns. Often my seams were knobby and irregular. Even simple reverse stockinette—the background for many pattern stitches—posed a problem. No matter how neat I tried to be, seaming this purl-faced fabric to itself always created an indentation on the right side of the fabric that looked "scar-like" to me. Sometimes, especially in stiffer fabrics, this "scar" actually stole width from the garment, negatively affecting the fit.

Then, a "Eureka" moment: I realized that I could add extra stitches at difficult-to-seam edges. With two (smoother) stockinette stitches at each edge, I could

I repurposed my initial swatches into matching sleeves for this poncho.

more easily seam them.

You can add these "seam stitches" at sides, at cardigan edges to neatly outline the fronts, and at armholes. Check your pattern to see if the fabric at the edges might be difficult to seam. If so, add two stockinette stitches at each edge. When you seam, sew between the two edge stitches. Always have the right side of the fabric facing, so you can see how your seam looks as you sew.

If you add a significant number of edge stitches in a heavier yarn, you may have to eliminate some in an adjacent pattern to avoid adding width to your sweater and affecting the fit. With a fine-gauge yarn, additional stitches will be inconsequential. ∎

3. As mentioned earlier, the neckline should be without flaw—it frames the face, and the viewer's eye goes there first! I have seen sweaters with beautiful fabric and good fit that still suffer if the neckline pulls or fits sloppily.

4. The armhole of a sweater should not constrict: there should be room to move. Since the neckline edge, the cross shoulder (front and back), and the armhole are related, fit-wise, you need to identify which of these areas is the culprit and needs to be adjusted.

5. The sleeves of a sweater should end where you want them to end, and not be overly long or too short. This differs from design to design—no one measurement works for every sweater.

6. No sweater should pull, gap, or strain in any area!

These are just a few very important highlights. You might have other pet peeves when it comes to how a garment should surround your body, or specific fit problems you have encountered. Turn your eyes to how different kinds of sweaters fit you and other people: not in a judgmental way, but in a scientific appraisal of what can go wrong. An awareness of all kinds of problems, not just those that affect you, will make you a better garment maker when it comes to adjusting patterns.

The Garment-Maker's Mindset

In our culture we often take great care in our professional lives, when we are being paid to make or do something. But when knitting "for pleasure" we tend to drop our troubleshooting mind and plow ahead for the sheer joy of the work in our hands.

It takes a particular mindset to enter into the complex and challenging terrain of garments. Some knitters get caught up in what I call the "finish-line mentality": as soon as a project is begun, their sights are set on the end. Other knitters encounter one type of project with a detail that does not work out, and then avoid that type of project forever! This confines knitters: they repeat a successful project over and over, with no creative growth. And since today's knitting culture inundates us with small, quick-to-knit projects—which of course are fun, comfortable, and rewarding—we often don't realize that we have limited ourselves.

There is nothing wrong with knitting for the joy of it, or with a desire to complete your current project and move on to the next. And often people want to avoid projects that require facing issues of fit. But if you are armed with skills and preparation, with eyes wide open to the areas you need to address, you can have both pleasure and speed even in those larger, more complex projects that once seemed daunting.

The fact is, when you want a garment to fit well, you often need—for a little while during the planning—a more attentive mind! The more fitting work you do, the easier and more automatic it will become. In my workshops, whenever I explain my simple approach to adjusting sleeve caps (completely related to fit!), I look around the room to see faces lit up with recognition and relief. Once you know how to approach a problem that once flummoxed you, you are empowered. Decisions become easier in all your work. If you have avoided certain kinds of projects due to a lack of success in the past, it's time to change your mindset.

I find what I call a "garment-maker's mindset" very useful, and I encourage you to embrace this concept. Knitters often see themselves only as knitters, but we are also makers of sweaters—knitted garments!—and we are often not as well versed as garment-makers should be in the areas of fit and garment structure. We take our knitting seriously, but we often approach the garment-making aspect with less planning and care than we should.

I have always envisioned myself as part of the long tradition of people who make garments. Do you see yourself in this way? From the first person who fashioned a needle to sew skins together, to the couture garments of our 21st century—with our knits we are walking a well-trodden path. See yourself in a grand tradition of people who create one-of-a-kind

garments, and you will feel a subtle shift in the way you approach making sweaters.

Like the designers of the past century whose work I love, I wanted a special, dedicated place to work, albeit on a humble scale, where my knitting was the focus and my creativity could blossom. My studio space contains a large library table that I use as a desk and workspace, shelves of reference books and yarn, and a dress form. My walls are a changing gallery: fashion inspiration of the moment, images that interest me, and some that just make me happy. For years I worked in two large rooms, but when I moved to a smaller space, I personally felt more content, less distracted.

Everyone needs a dedicated space in which to work. You may already have a "knitting corner" or even a "knitting room," but why not consider it more than that? The less tangible qualities of positive attitude and patience are a part of that physical space. "A room of one's own," Virginia Woolf called it! Surround yourself with the things you love, have the necessary tools, and give yourself enough room to spread your work out and look at it.

Even though my workspace is tiny, it is a "studio" of sorts, with all the tools I need for the planning stages of my work. I expect to spend a certain amount of time planning and preparing for a successful garment. As a professional, I strive to meet my clients' needs, and over the years I have developed the skills to make complex, one-of-a-kind garments that fit well in a very short time, without glitches or disappointment. But even when I knit gifts for people who are close to me, I take the same care with preparation, so they will fit well and honor the materials I've used.

Here's the best by-product of having done your homework and planning: when the up-front work is over, your knitting proceeds with ease and pleasure. With fewer concerns about fit, you can simply enjoy the work in your hands.

1. My office is just a small hallway between rooms, but has enough space for me to work in. My cocker spaniel, Brownie, is a constant visitor.
2. I collect my favorite plastic and wooden knitting needles.
3. My table is big enough for day-to-day paperwork and for laying out sweater pieces.
4. I have a large collection of knitting and design books, for inspiration.

Practical Matters
Materials and
Supplies

Add a few items to your regular knitting tools to become a master of fit! Here's what I rely on:

1. Computer: even though it is not essential—I could very reluctantly replace it with a notebook!—I do use my computer to record my pattern-writing efforts.

2. Measuring devices: gauge ruler, straight rulers of various sizes, tape measures, yardstick

3. Graph paper of various sorts:

• 5 X 5 grid for schematics (the smallest grid you should use for analyzing the shapes of pieces). My personal favorite is 8½" X 11" from Rhodia.

• Large sheets of 8 X 8 or 10 X 10 grid for plotting large pieces of knitting

• Good quality (not tissue-thin) tracing paper, 8½" X 11"

4. Pencils, erasers, markers, etc.

5. Calculator

6. T-pins, straight pins, a variety of needles for seaming

7. Masking tape for the measuring process ▪

Identifying Your Personal Fit Needs

Before we get into the study of the elements of fit, and the gradual path to understanding how to alter patterns to improve it, this might be a good time to consider what you feel are your biggest concerns, both in sweaters you have knitted and in ready-to-wear clothes.

Put aside measurements and think about how clothes fit you. Focus on generalities of fit, not the quirks of a particular design or an individual piece of clothing. What issues arise for you over and over again, across a spectrum of clothing?

Identifying these issues will prepare you to study the concepts that lie ahead. As you become more fluent in the language of fit, you can be more specific about how to address your issues. For now, just noting the areas that need attention is a good way to begin.

Widths

• Are certain areas of garments often tight or loose for you, widthwise?

• If the bust fits, does the hip area seem loose or tight?

• Or vice versa: If the hip fits, does the bust area seem loose or tight?

• Do sleeves ever feel too tight?

Lengths

• Are particular parts of garments perennially too long or short for you?

• Do you find that garments that accentuate the waist are too long above the waist?

• Or perhaps garments are too short to meet the waist?

• When something is fitted below the bust, is there too much fabric, or not enough, to cover from the shoulder to below the bust?

• Are sleeves ever too long or too short for you?

• Are you tall enough that you feel garments could be a bit longer to suit you?

Proportion

• If you have a large frame, do details of garments seem too small in scale?

• If you are petite, do you ever feel garments are oversized, and in what areas?

• Do you ever feel the details of a garment are too overpowering for you?

Armholes

• Is the place where the sleeve attaches to the body ever problematic for you?

• Even if the body fits, do you ever feel a tightness, or looseness, at the underarm or in the general circumference of the armhole area?

Shoulders

• Do you notice that garments that fit in other parts of the body do not fit across the shoulders—either too loose or too tight?

Neckline Area

• Do you ever wish for more ease than a garment offers in the neckline area?

• Do you ever feel that necklines are awkwardly or uncomfortably large?

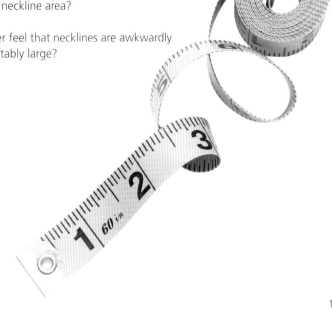

> Know, first, who you are;
> and then adorn yourself
> accordingly.
> – EPICTETUS

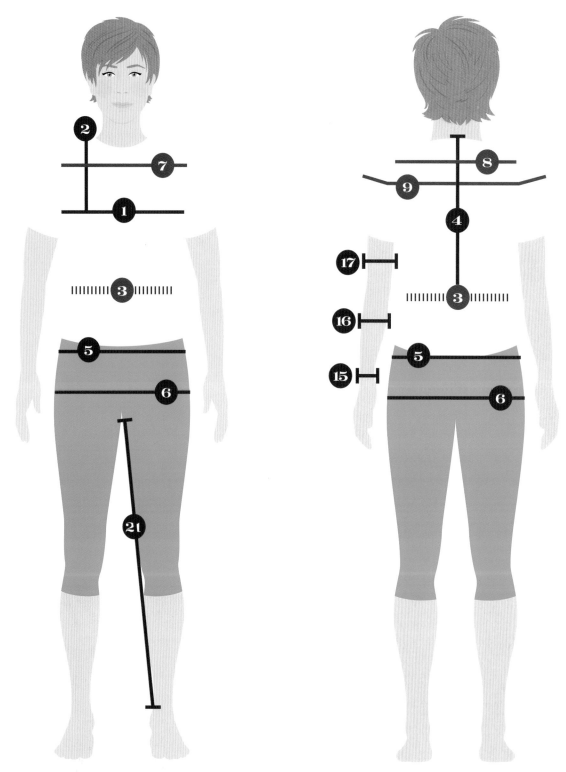

Your Own Measurements

We've come to the first important step toward good fit: whether planning to make a flat shawl or a shaped garment, you will need a record of your body measurements. Here I present a full range of measurements, including some you may never have considered. This information will help you face any project, and allow you to utilize the "Math Magic" equations that appear throughout the book to achieve a personalized fit.

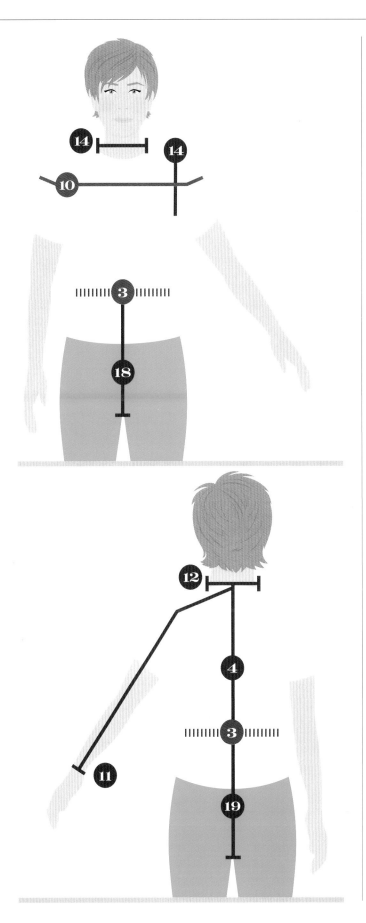

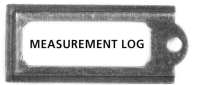

MEASUREMENT LOG

PHOTOCOPY THIS LIST AND RECORD YOUR MEASUREMENTS FOR EASY REFERENCE.

1. Bust _____

2. Bust point _____

3. Waist _____

4. Back neck to waist _____

5. High hip _____

6. Full hip _____

7. Cross shoulder front _____

8. Cross shoulder back _____

9. Around shoulders, arms down _____

10. Around shoulders, arms at 45 degrees _____

11. Mid back to wrist, arm at 45 degrees _____

12. Back neck width _____

13. Neckline depth _____

14. Neck circumference (at base of neck) _____

15. Armhole depth _____

16. Armhole circumference _____

15. Wrist circumference _____

16. Lower arm circumference _____

17. Upper arm circumference _____

18. Front crotch depth _____

19. Back crotch depth _____

20. Full crotch depth = #18 + #19

21. Inseam _____

Record Keeping

As a professional designer, I keep a "hard copy" folder of all the information that goes into a project: my sketch and swatch, any "tear sheets" that helped inspire the project, notes about materials, suggestions from the editor or client, the measurements, schematic drawing, yarn labels, yarn and color samples, and my full printed-out instructions. When my project is successfully completed, I might scan some of the material (always the schematic!) to have a digital record.

While working toward an understanding of fit—not an overnight process!—you, too, should keep records of your projects. You can look back and refresh your memory about fabric, measurements, and other details. Make it a habit to have a folder ready at the beginning of every new project!

Given that we all vary from the averages, assigning a "size" to an individual person can be very inaccurate. What is most important is understanding your own measurements. Body and garment measurements must be considered together: this allows you to determine whether a pattern can fit or be altered to fit you better.

Despite this, few knitters know any measurements other than their bust, and maybe their hips. Many other measurements are crucial to good fit, but I've realized, with surprise, that my students rarely consider these when planning their projects.

Before you can learn to use your own measurements, let's talk about how to take and record them.

Keeping records means not having to take the same measurements over and over. Measure other people you knit for, too, so you have numbers to refer to when they are not around! On page 21 is a chart that you can photocopy and fill in. Not all garments require all these measurements, but keep them on record just in case. Note: I have included some measurements not often seen on standard charts. Let's concentrate here on gathering the numbers— more about how to use them in the pages ahead.

Measuring Mindset

First, let's go over some issues that come up when taking body measurements.

A word to the wise: make no judgments about the measurements you take; look at them with a neutral, scientific eye! They are not admonitions to lose weight, not reasons to find fault with your figure or make negative comparisons with the "average" or with other people. They are tools to make garments that fit well, and learning how to utilize them will help you achieve the best results from your efforts. If you measure other people, impress upon them that you are an impartial recorder of information: these numbers have no bias inherent in them.

Also, when you take measurements you should be capturing the body the way it moves and stands naturally—not in a frozen, stiff pose. Try to relax, and help relax the person you are measuring!

Move methodically through the list, and do not leave out measurements because you think they are not essential. Each project is different, so keep an open mind to the ways each measurement might affect dimensions in the body of a sweater.

How to Take Measurements

Recently I held up a tape measure in a workshop and asked who knew what it was and how to use it. I got blank stares. Granted, it might have sounded like a trick question, but the response was revealing. After a discussion, I found that people were vague on how to take measurements—and why! And I came to realize that most knitters don't really know how to use measurements.

Knowing the correct way to measure is essential. First, use a soft fabric or plastic tape measure. Don't try to take measurements with a metal or wooden ruler, which can't conform to a body's curves.

Measuring yourself is difficult, so arrange for a friend to help. With someone else taking the measurements, you can stand straight, but not stiff, at all times (not possible when using both hands) and also get true vertical lengths, especially along your back.

Wear thin, non-bulky clothing—like a lightweight, close-fitting T-shirt and close-fitting tights or lightweight pants—that will reveal the body's shape and will not add inches. Try to wear a style of T-shirt whose seams reflect your body's lines: one that conforms to the base of the neck where the neck meets the torso, with armhole seams that encircle the arm where the arm meets the torso.

Be sure to measure wearing the undergarments you most commonly wear and that give the look you are most comfortable with.

Be sure the measuring tape is parallel to the ground when you are taking girth—or horizontal—measurements. When taking length measurements, such as back neck to waist, hold the tape perpendicular to the floor.

A roll of masking tape—the kind that peels easily from clothing without damage—will make your measuring session easier. Lacking that, you can also use several straight or safety pins for marking.

PREPARATION TIPS

To be sure you are taking vertical measurements from the same place every time, tie pieces of yarn around the fullest part of the bust, the waist, and the fullest part of the hip. Keep these yarn markers in place until you are done. Use masking tape in a few spots to hold the yarn in place, if necessary.

To measure torso lengths, first tie a yarn marker around the bust and waist. Tie another marker horizontally 7–9" below the waist, at the widest part of the hips. When measuring from the back neck, start at the point on the spine where the base of a shirt collar would sit.

Also, be sure the side seams of the T-shirt are vertical, not skewed. In a few cases you will be using these as markers. If your T-shirt has no side seams, attach a safety pin centered under the arm and another at the lower edge on the same side. Tie a yarn marker between these two pins.

If your T-shirt follows the lines of the neck and armholes, where these areas meet the torso, then use the neckline and seams as markers. If not, attach safety pins as markers at the back neck and outer shoulders, to keep those points secure during the measuring process.

Take these measurements and record as you proceed. Do not measure tightly; just let the tape measure lie flat: touch the body without tugging.

Note that certain vertical and horizontal lines are dependent on each other, so you need to note their measurements together. For example, take bust and bust point at the same time, as well as waist and back neck to waist. If you were to take only two measurements—bust and hip—you might be able to muddle along and choose patterns, but the additional numbers will be very helpful in refining a garment for the fit that works best for you.

Rather than just listing the areas to be measured, I have included a little information about each, so you can begin to see how these measurements might be used. All of this knowledge contributes to your "garment-maker's mindset."

Upper Body

BUST: Take the bust circumference around the body, parallel to the waist or floor, at its widest point. Don't be surprised if this is the largest girth of the body. If larger than average, the bust area often proves more challenging for good fit than the hips, since it is related to armholes, shoulder width, and neckline.

BUST POINT: Take this crucial but less commonly known measurement at the same time as the bust. This depth measurement is taken from the point on the shoulder directly above the point of the bust, down to the bust point, parallel to the midline of the body.

On some bodies, the point of the bust falls directly under the center of the shoulder; on bodies with wider shoulders it might be a little closer to the neck and farther from the outer shoulder. For those with a wide or full neck, this vertical line can fall closer to the neck than to the center of the shoulder. Note generally where this is: it will be helpful when plotting this measurement on your body schematic in the section to come.

Add the following measurements, especially if you are very full-busted:

FRONT BUST WIDTH: Take the measurement from side seam to side seam across the front. This is especially

helpful if you are fuller in the front, but is useful even if you are perfectly symmetrical from front to back.

BACK BUST WIDTH: When measuring a fuller front bust, also take the measurement across the back.

WAIST: The waist is a crucial measurement that you should know even if you are not planning to make garments that are fitted in that area. If this measurement is larger than bust or hip, you can determine whether you have a "Diamond" or "Round" body shape and take note of the challenges that type presents for good fit as we proceed.

BACK NECK TO WAIST: When you measure the waist, also record the distance from the back neck to the waist. This will be useful when planning garments with a defined waist: if you are longer than average, you can check to see if your patterns are long enough to accommodate you; if you are short-waisted (shorter than average), this number will help you plan where to position the waist.

Also, if a pattern has shaping that must be done over a given length, this measurement—combined with your row gauge—will tell you if you have to adjust the pattern to accommodate the increases or decreases. More about this in Chapter 5.

If your back is curved and sweaters tend to be shorter for you in the back than in the front, this is a crucial measurement to know. If this is the case, also measure from the side of your neck to the side waist, parallel to the spine, and from the side of the front neck to the front waist, parallel to the center front line. Then you will be able to compare these measurements.

CROSS SHOULDER: The cross-shoulder measurement is a must-have. Measure from your T-shirt armhole seam to armhole seam, at the top of the shoulders, or from pin to pin if you have placed them as markers. For curiosity's sake and to learn something about your own body, take this measurement on both front and back. The numbers are often the same, but for some people they differ by more than 1–2". Be sure to record both.

AROUND SHOULDERS, ARMS DOWN; AROUND SHOULDERS, ARMS AT 45 DEGREES: These two measurements are not listed on standard charts, but I find them useful—obviously, with garments that encircle the upper body, as with a circular yoke, but also when determining if a sleeve cap needs to be widened or narrowed for a better upper-body fit.

This is an example of what I like to call "composite measurements." Several smaller body measurements can be added up to equal one composite measurement, as in many of the "Math Magic" equations in this book. This "around-shoulder" measurement will tell you how wide the upper part of a sweater needs to be to encircle the body without strain or extra fabric.

If you subtract the cross-shoulder measurements for front and back from the around-shoulder measurement, the result (divided by two) tells you how wide each sleeve needs to be in this area.

We will look more at composite measurements in Chapter 4 when we talk about garment shapes, as they can be useful when analyzing schematics with an eye to good fit.

Both of these encircling measurements are taken 5–6" down from the outer tips of the shoulders, with the tape measure parallel to the waist or floor. If the tape hikes up in the back, your measurement won't be accurate.

"Reference" Measurements

Though very useful, these measurements can be hard to take or to envision on the body. Why? Because although the body has dimension, many of these measurements are taken as straight lines.

Even though you are working with a curved body, the straight-line measurements need to be taken as such. Some are what I call "reference measurements," which I rely on when in doubt. They can add extra information to your equation when calculating or altering the measurements of a piece, or the combined measurements of pieces.

BACK NECK WIDTH: This is not the width of a sweater neckline, and not a curved measurement—which would be longer than a straight line! It is the width of the base of the neck itself, at the neck's widest point. I do not curve the tape measure when taking this measurement.

Look from behind at the widest part of the neck, at its base. Draw a line with your finger from one side of this part of the neck down to a flat part of the back, place a pin (or a piece of masking tape) vertically along this line, and repeat on the other side. Then measure between the pins or tape.

Sometimes the neckband of a close-fitting T-shirt can help you see where the base of the back neck actually is. This measurement varies greatly from person to person, and knowing it will allow you to plan for the correct width of any type of neckline.

NECKLINE DEPTH: From the widest part of the neck, measure straight down to the base of the neck (the point where your neck meets the upper chest), parallel to the midline of the front body.

This measurement will help you plan necklines as well, especially rounded styles, such as a classic crew neck.

NECK CIRCUMFERENCE: This not-often-used "reference" measurement can be very helpful on occasion. Turn the tape on its side and measure along the base of the neck, where the neck meets the front upper chest and the upper back, holding the tape loosely. This is also a "composite measurement." Compare it with the combined widths of the front and back necks, as well as the back neck alone, to see how many inches go into forming the curve of the neckline. More about this when we look at necklines in Chapter 4.

ARMHOLE DEPTH: This is a crucial measurement, especially if you have heavy arms. It is also a straight-line measurement—not curved—taken from the outer shoulder, along the armhole seam of your close-fitting shirt, down to an invisible line that emerges from the underarm, parallel to the floor. This emerging line should not hug the crease of the underarm, but clear the underarm by at least an inch below. This is not the armhole depth of a sweater, but a general measurement of the depth of the connection between the arm and the torso.

Use masking tape on the body to signify the emerging line described above: note that this horizontal tape line may fall below the underarm seam on your close-fitting T-shirt. Measure straight down to the tape from the outer shoulder. If you are large busted, this measurement might be easier taken on the back than the front. But try taking both and see how they compare. Keep the tape in place for the next measurement.

ARMHOLE CIRCUMFERENCE: This reference measurement is also not used often, but might prove pertinent. I call upon it when I need more information: when calculating a complexly shaped cap sleeve or other shaping that must conform to the upper body, or when room is needed for extra movement.

Take your tape and follow the line of the seam that encircles the armhole, but bring it down to the marker line, not the crease of the underarm.

Lower Body

The following two measurements are among the most useful and often-referred-to. They not only aid with body fit, but are indispensable when calculating the best length for a sweater, or skirt measurements.

FULL HIP CIRCUMFERENCE: This measurement is usually taken 9" down from the waist, parallel to the ground or the waist: this is often the widest part in the body. However, if 9" down is not the widest point on your lower body, then note how far down from the waist that point is. Mark with masking tape. Then take the full hip measurement at this point, noting on the chart both depth (from the waist) and the circumference at this widest point.

HIGH HIP: Take this measurement halfway between the waist and the fullest part of the hip. Obviously, this measurement can help in determining sweater length, but it is also useful when planning the width of sweaters that fall around this point, or when planning shaped sweaters where increases or decreases need to be plotted within a given length. More about this in Chapter 5.

CROTCH DEPTHS: Although these three measurements are not commonly used for knits, they might just come in handy one day for making a pair of stretchy pants or shorts (see pages 106–107). It will help if your close-fitting pants have seams along the crotch line, from front to back.

With the tape measure passing between the legs, measure from back waist to front waist for the total crotch measurement.

For most people, the front length will be shorter than the back, so for a good-fitting garment you will need to capture both measurements. For the front crotch depth, measure from the waist to where the inner leg seam meets the center crotch seam. For the back, measure from the waist to the same point. Record all three of these crotch measurements.

INSEAM: While you are measuring the crotch depth, take the inseam as well by measuring from where the inner leg seam meets the center crotch seam, down to the anklebone. Your project will have to be checked and adjusted based on whether the pants or shorts are meant to be tight or loose.

Arms

LOWER AND UPPER ARM CIRCUMFERENCES: Measure these parts of the arm at their widest points.

WRIST CIRCUMFERENCE: Encircle your wrist, not too tightly.

MID-BACK TO WRIST: This is an essential measurement for determining sleeve length. See the equations related to sleeve length on page 72 for more info on how to correctly use this number in conjunction with others.

Locate the center back neck, and mark it. Then extend one straight arm to the side at an angle of approximately 45 degrees away from the body. Place the tape measure at the center back neck edge, then bring it along the shoulder and down the arm to the wrist. For a sewn garment with no stretch—like a man's shirt—it is traditional to measure over a slightly bended elbow, but in my experience measuring over the extension of the arm is more accurate for most stretchy knits. If you ever use a dense, firm knitted fabric, you may want to measure over a slightly bended elbow. As an experiment, bend your elbow and see how much longer the measurement is!

Note that this measurement is not arm length or sleeve length! We will calculate these measurements based on the mid-back to wrist, taking into account the kind of sweater you are making, as well as the fabric you choose.

MATH MAGIC!

$$e = mc^2$$

Throughout this book you will see some equations I have devised over the years related to the body and issues of fit for sweaters. I find these little calculations very useful: they can help you "add up" measurements to make sure the parts of your sweater relate well to your body. I hope those of you who shudder at the memory of math class will use and enjoy them as much as those who are "math geeks"!

What Is a Schematic Drawing?

The schematic drawing is one of our most useful tools when planning for good fit. You will most often be looking at (and creating) schematic drawings of garments you are making, but I will also show you how to create a body schematic based on the measurements you just took.

FIT TIP

Using Body and Garment Schematics

As you gain experience, you can draw the lines of your sweater schematic right on a copy of your body schematic sheet, for a permanent record of how it corresponds to your body. As changes are made to the sweater pieces for better fit, you can erase and redraw the lines of the sweater schematic.

If you want the final sweater schematic to stand alone, without a body outline, draw it onto a piece of tracing paper that has been taped to your body schematic. After making any changes for fit, remove the tracing paper, tape it over a plain grid sheet of the same size, and photocopy it.

A schematic drawing shows the individual body pieces of a pattern in flat form, in one size, usually the smallest, and gives the actual measurements, ranging from small to large, in order.

BEWARE: some patterns may have schematics that are not drawn to scale. These do not reflect the true shape or silhouette of the garment! In such cases, you might want to create your own schematic for your size (see below). If you are not sure whether the scale is correct, find a length and a width measurement for a particular size given in the pattern, and compare their ratio to the scale of those areas within the drawing.

Note how the schematic represents basic widths and lengths. A simple garment will have a few; a complex, fitted garment may have many. But choosing the right measurements for a garment is just as important! I always tell my editors that it is as difficult to design an easy sweater as a complicated one: all areas of the garment must still be considered.

If a pattern you want to follow does not have a schematic drawing, I highly suggest that you draw one yourself before beginning. It may seem time-consuming, but it can be saved for reference to save you time with similar projects in the future. You will see, as this book progresses, many reasons to refer to schematics to achieve a perfect fit.

How to Make a Schematic Drawing

If you have never drawn a schematic, first try drawing one for a pattern you have made or are familiar with—even a pattern that already has a schematic drawing, so you can check your own practice one against it. This is such a valuable garment maker's tool, it is worth taking the time to learn it.

For a pattern that includes a schematic drawing, creating your own for the size you plan to make is very useful—I consider it a necessity—when you are altering the pattern for fit. Whether this is the case or you're drawing a schematic for a pattern that does not include one at all, you first need to read the pattern and locate all the stitch counts for the size you are considering.

If the gauge is given over 4", prepare by dividing this number by 4. This equals the gauge per inch.

Draw the garment divided into pieces, starting with the back. After the back is drawn, draw in one front

separately if it is a cardigan; or you can draw a full front over the back, but only if they share the same shaping.

Always divide the number of stitches given for any width by the gauge per inch.

For example, if the cross-shoulder width, above the armhole shaping, is 75 stitches, and your gauge is 5 stitches per inch, then:

75 sts divided by 5 sts/inch = 15" cross shoulder

1. Determine the widest point: find the fullest point on the body in the pattern, and divide this number of stitches by the number of stitches per inch. Be sure to use the stitch count above any edge or ribbing, since those might not share the same gauge as the main sections of the sweater.

2. Find the length from the shoulder to the lower edge of the garment.

3. Using the widest point of the body piece and the length, draw a rectangular box on 5X5 grid paper.

4. Within this rectangular box, add the additional length and width measurements, including armhole depth, length to the armhole, cross shoulder width, and any shaping below the armhole, as well as neck width.

5. To find the width of any part of the garment, just divide the number of stitches for that part by your gauge.

6. Draw in any curved edges for neckline, armhole, or sleeve cap.

7. Do the same thing for a sleeve: use the widest point and longest length to create a box, then fill in the shape of the sleeve based on its measurements.

This finished schematic can be used in comparison with your own measurements and body schematic, in ways we'll learn about later.

Drawing your own body schematic

When you have all your body measurements recorded, I suggest you commit them to paper, schematic style. You can capture a basic body outline this way—very useful even if it is not three-dimensional.

This schematic will represent the unique qualities of your figure. Most important, you can refer to your

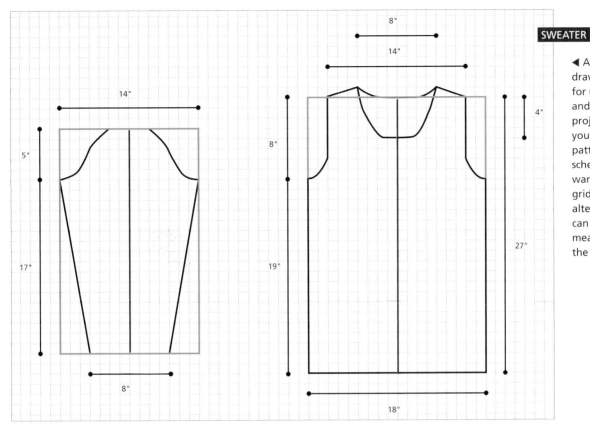

SWEATER

◀ A schematic drawing is a useful tool for understanding fit and envisioning a project's pieces before you begin. If your pattern includes a schematic, you might want to redraw it on a grid for note-taking and alteration. If not, you can create one based on measurements given in the pattern.

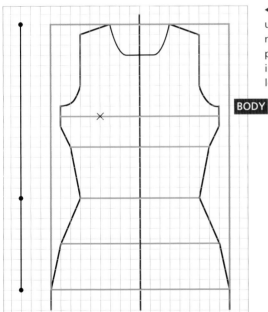

◀ This body schematic creates a useful outline that reflects the actual measurements of the body itself. The points of reference are your most important body measurements, both lengths and widths.

BODY

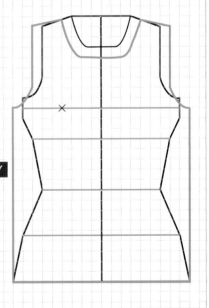

SWEATER OVER BODY

Look at how the outline of your own body relates to the lines of the sweater you hope to make. You can see where they seem well placed, leaving enough room between body and sweater for the desired silhouette and ease. ▶

body schematic in comparison with the schematic of a sweater you hope to make, to see how the basic proportions correspond. Be sure to use grid/graph paper with lines dark enough to be photocopied. Work with pencil and eraser to start—you can ink in the lines when the drawing is complete if you like.

Stage 1

Refer to the graph paper at left above, which has these important lines drawn in:

1. A central vertical line, representing the midline of the torso.

2. A horizontal line, representing the waistline.

Choose your widest measurement—bust or hip, usually—and divide it in half. Then refer to the length from back neck to the hip at its widest point. Use these measurements to form a box.

Stage 2
Draw in other vertical and horizontal lines that represent other important markers on the body.
Vertical lines:
• Back neck to waist
• Waist to high hip
• Waist to full hip
• Armhole depth

Horizontal lines:
• Waist
• Cross shoulder
• High hip
• Full hip
• Back neck width

When all of these vertical and horizontal lines have been plotted on your graph, then you can draw curves to connect them in the following ways:

CURVED BACK NECK: Starting one inch (one square of the grid) above each side of the neck edge, make a curved line, the same width as the neck measurement, to indicate the shape of the back neck edge.
ARMHOLES: Draw a gradual curve from the lower armhole, at the widest point of the bust, to the cross shoulder width, ending the curve about halfway up the armhole.
WAIST TO FULL WIDTH OF BUST: Connect at sides, about 3" down from underarm.
WAIST TO HIGH HIP: Connect at sides.

HIGH HIP TO FULL HIP: Connect at sides.
Add these other measurements:
BUST POINT: Plot this point straight down from the shoulder where you took this measurement.
FRONT NECK DEPTH

Stage 3
The illustration at bottom right on page 27 shows how I have overlaid a simple sweater schematic over a body schematic. We will use this technique more in the future; here let's look at how the body schematic allows you to see your measurements in relation to a particular project.

Remember that the sweater schematic you use for this purpose should be the schematic for the particular size you are planning to make.

Note the ways the lengths and widths differ between body and sweater schematics. At first glance, I observe that the bust of the sweater is large enough to cover the body beneath, but that the width of the hip on the body is very close to the measurement for the hip of the sweater.

How do you overlay a schematic? Simply attach a piece of tracing paper to a copy of your body schematic. Draw the schematic for your project on the tracing paper, aligning the central lines and following the grid that shows through the tracing paper.

Reserve your body schematic for future reference. In Chapter 3, we will look at the ways we can interpret these measurements as they relate to ease, silhouette, and fiber. In Chapter 4, we'll refer to juxtaposed schematic drawings like this to learn more about how garment shapes can be altered for better fit.

FIT TIP

My Favorite Paper
I am lucky to live near a wonderful art supply store. I always browse for new paper, pencils, and pens. For years I used blue grid graph paper for my schematics, but it did not photocopy or scan well: the copies of my schematics were without grid lines.

Then I discovered Rhodia brand paper, which is now my favorite grid paper. It has distinct gray lines, which copy and scan very well. It is available in small pads, perfect for drawing small pattern stitch charts, and larger pads that are great for schematics. I always make my first draft of a schematic with pencil, then finalize in ink later.

Modular and Simply Shaped Projects
Before we look at the ways more complex shapes make up specific kinds of sweaters, let's start with garments that are not sophisticated, that cover the body with little or no attention to shaping or to the issues of ease and silhouette that we will look at in other chapters.

Even very simple body coverings need attention to measurement. Flat shawls might not conform to particular parts of our three-dimensional bodies, but they must be planned to cling or drape or wrap in a specific way. As a designer, I am often inspired by peasant-style garments made from simple rectangles, squares, or triangles. Japanese kimonos, shapeless peasant smocks, and the hooded cloaks of African desert nomads are examples of very boxy garments, and these shapes still emerge in fashionregularly. They are generally oversized, and can be perfect for coats and other garments that are showpieces for patterning as opposed to shape.

If there is no schematic for the type of pattern you're working on, or one that is suggestive rather than accurate, I encourage you to create one.

TWO DIMENSIONS TO THREE
Oversized Wrap • Poncho Pullover

Project
Oversized Wrap
SEE PAGE 124

Shawls and wraps are flat, two-dimensional pieces, but they, too, often have issues related to fit. Fabric that falls from the shoulders needs to be planned for both length and width. Curved shawls that overlap or tie at the front need to be the best length for those styles.

I designed the rectangular shawl at left to be very long—an oversized fit!—so it can wrap the body like a huge scarf. Before the knitting began, I played with a large piece of scrap fabric, cut to my desired width, to plan the final length. I have also been known to pin bath and beach towels together to simulate a shawl.

If you want a smaller shawl to cover the shoulders alone, you will want a more body-conscious fit. Use a tape measure to wrap around the shoulders and arms as you envision the best length for your body. A larger person is going to need more fabric to cover shoulders than a smaller person, so measurement is essential.

I thought it would be an informative experiment to take flat, unshaped rectangular pieces—with the same pattern stitches as my large shawl—and make a 3-D garment out of them, with no shaping. What would be the concerns for good fit? Let's look at some traditional garments made out of squares and rectangles. Obviously, the body underneath is curved and has complex shape, but these simple, boxy garments drape in an unstructured way.

I decided on a poncho-like shape made up of two connected pieces. Having no similar garment to measure, I worked with a couple of pieces of fabric to determine widths and lengths. Here's what I did:

1. Draped one rectangle so it angled across the body and formed a point at the lower center front.

2. Draped a second rectangle of the same width to meet the piece already in place, then adjusted to make the neckline large enough.

3. Transferred all my measurements to a schematic.

I knew my final knitted pieces would stretch more than the woven test fabric, which seemed to fit. I trusted that the measurements would be fine and transferred them to a schematic, drawn on grid paper.

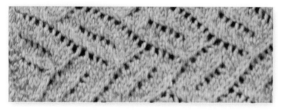

The pieces were knitted to the schematic measurements, as close as gauge and pattern would allow.

Since my shawl featured two pattern stitches, I wanted the poncho-like garment to incorporate both. The border, worked with "yarn over" elements on both RS and WS rows, was textured and elegant. The allover lace was scalloped at the sides, an uncommon feature in knitting patterns. I wanted to highlight, not hide, these edges, so when sewing the garment together I overlapped the pieces where they met and sewed through both layers, instead of seaming them together side by side. The opening for the neck was not shaped; it was just a diamond that allowed the head to pass through, similar to what I had pinned in the test fabric.

After the pieces were sewn together, I noticed the two test swatches for the project on my desk. Eureka! Could these pieces be used to make a sleeve-like extension, expanding on the three-dimensional nature of my design? I seamed each swatch into a tube, along the straight side, and sewed them to the outer edge on each side to line up with the shoulder line.

While the poncho alone, made from two adjacent pieces alongside each other, could drape in any alignment over the body, the little tubular sleeves allow it to be worn in a more garment-like way, with more connections to the body beneath.

I offer this poncho in just two sizes, since it is intended to have a loose, oversized fit and does not conform to the torso below the shoulders. ▨

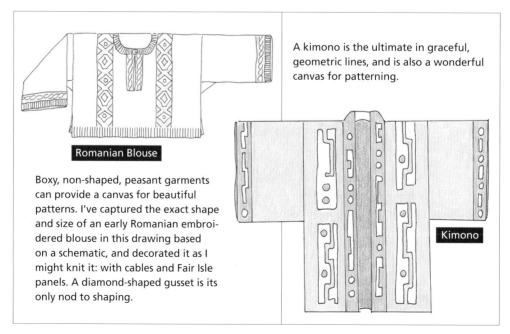

Romanian Blouse

Boxy, non-shaped, peasant garments can provide a canvas for beautiful patterns. I've captured the exact shape and size of an early Romanian embroidered blouse in this drawing based on a schematic, and decorated it as I might knit it: with cables and Fair Isle panels. A diamond-shaped gusset is its only nod to shaping.

A kimono is the ultimate in graceful, geometric lines, and is also a wonderful canvas for patterning.

Kimono

Project
Poncho Pullover

SEE PAGE 125

CHAPTER 2

Considering
The Body

Factors That Affect Sweater Fit

Having taken time to prepare—by adopting
the garment-maker's mindset, learning to take
measurements and create schematic drawings,
and starting to think about fit with simply shaped
projects—we are ready to consider the issues
of the body and how they relate to the
knitwear that covers it!

Body Types: What Looks Good?

Rather than focusing on one kind of body, I encourage you as you absorb this material to expand your awareness of all types. Whether you're knitting for others or for yourself, the more you know when planning, the better your decisions will be.

We want to understand not only fit and garment construction, but also what looks good on the various body types. One goal in sweater/garment making is to choose a pattern that flatters our shape and/or accentuates our preferred features. We might also use a particular pattern (or alter one) to create an illusion, such as looking leaner or taller.

Let's start with the basic body shapes, shown in the illustration on the opposite page. Although we don't all fit neatly into these categories, they are a useful starting point for identifying our own unique considerations in planning sweaters. Be aware that these shapes are general and address only the body/torso, not the other crucial features, like armholes or neckline width, that we saw in Chapter 1 when we took our measurements.

Most garments are designed for the "average" figure—often a far cry from who we are. If we know how our body type veers from the "average," we are better prepared to alter our patterns and sweaters to fit our specific shape.

We can also choose to consider cultural "guidelines" for what looks good on which type of body when planning our garments. This is an area of personal preference, so I leave it to you to decide. I present these guidelines here as a way of beginning to look generally at how shapes can affect fit.

What do these "types" tell us about good fit?

Although body-type charts tend to emphasize "what looks good" on various types, they also provide a way to recognize the issues we must consider when choosing and altering a pattern. They can also help us find a style of sweater that flatters us—more on that later.

After examining various depictions of body types, I have come up with a set of guidelines for how these types relate to fit. Most charts show five body types, but this seems too simplistic, especially since there are so many of what I call "hybrid" types. Also, as I mentioned, these figures represent only the torso. I have made my own suggestions for additional areas of fit as they relate to these charts.

I chose the analogy for my chart that describes our body types as geometric shapes, rather than various kinds of fruit (banana, strawberry, apple, etc.), as some charts do. I have to laugh at that, since food is so often what alters our shapes! But for our purposes, geometry feels more "scientific" and useful, and it relates to our discussion of two- and three-dimensional shapes in the last chapter.

Please read about all the types, not just your own. Let my comments inspire you to think about fit in general, and start to develop a mindset that leads to better decision-making.

Rectangle

This type is basically straight up and down, with measurements for bust, waist, and hip that are similar to one another. As a professional designer, I am very familiar with this type, since it is the shape of most fashion models. Many standard knitting patterns assume this as a neutral zone, so a person with this body type might not need to make many adjustments—if so, they would most likely be to the neckline or lengths.

I think we can agree that most designs will flatter this type, especially those with simple lines. A common cultural suggestion for this body type is to accent the waist and have fullness above and below, to suggest a more shapely look.

Triangle

This shape has a wider hip measurement than bust. The goal for flattering this figure type is to try to balance the narrower upper body with the wider hips below. Aim for more attention to the upper body in terms of detail and focus: wider necklines and empire waists are good choices. Darker colors below and brighter or lighter above can create balance.

This type can confound knitters when it comes to certain types of patterns: Should you choose a size to accommodate the wider hip? If so, the upper body of the pattern may be too large. If you choose a size to accommodate the bust or upper body, then the lower body may be strained and not fit well. You will probably also need to adapt sweater patterns that are fitted at the waist.

The goal is to look at each pattern individually to see which area would be easier to adjust, and base your size choice on that. The bust area is complex, since it includes armhole and neckline, and the lower body less complex. So it is wise to base your choice on the bust and avoid having to make changes there.

Inverted Triangle

This shape has a wider-than-average cross shoulder

or larger-than-average bust, topping off a narrower lower body—the reverse of the previous type.

If the bust is large, you might choose a pattern to accommodate this measurement; but without alteration, the lower body of the sweater might be loose in an unattractive way. Also, if you're an Inverted Triangle type your shoulders might be larger than most patterns allow for. If so, the fit in the armhole, upper sleeve, and even the neckline can be strained, as the fabric tries to accommodate the shoulder width.

You may find it easy to wear a garment that is fitted at the waist without making alterations, since the area below the waist is narrower than above. Large upper sleeves will tend to widen you as a whole and should probably be avoided. Bell sleeves, on the other hand, which are wide at the lower edge and narrow at the upper arm, might provide balance.

A common hint for this body type is to wear a V-neckline, to elongate the upper body and create the illusion of a smaller bust. This works best, in my opinion, with a close-fitting armhole and shoulder, not with an oversized garment.

Hourglass

This shape has a small waist, with both benefits and difficulties in aiming for good fit, based on the kind of garment. If this is your shape, you will find patterns for fitted sweaters that accentuate the waist easy to wear and necessary adjustments minimal, if any.

Since yours is a traditionally desirable shape, don't drape fabric over the narrowest part of your figure. Looks that elongate the body, rather than shorten it, will accent the waistline.

Even within this shape there are variations: if your bust is much larger than the hips, or vice versa, you might share some issues with the Triangle or Inverted Triangle types.

Diamond

The waist is predominant, and the hips and upper body are narrow. I found that many systems of depicting the body exclude this type, and wondered why: because the Diamond is similar to the Round body type?

I decided that this shape indeed is different, with its own qualities to be aware of. It has girth or bulk just at the waist, and not in the upper body or at the hips. If you are a Diamond, you benefit from a garment that fits the upper body well and flares to accommodate the waist. Any section from the waist

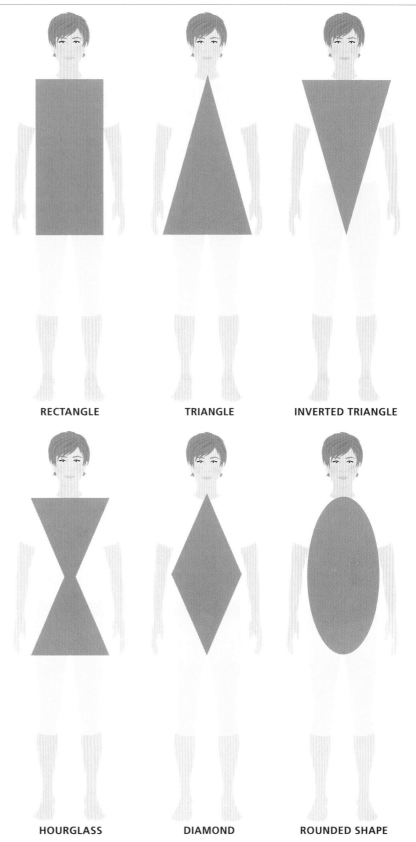

RECTANGLE   **TRIANGLE**   **INVERTED TRIANGLE**

HOURGLASS   **DIAMOND**   **ROUNDED SHAPE**

Although "types" exist that fall between these traditional shapes, or are hybrids of them, these common body types have characteristics that we should consider when choosing or altering a pattern for good fit.

downward should be flared or straight, unless you desire a "blouson" effect.

Rounded

To be rounded can mean several things. One may be rounded everywhere—in the upper arms, upper body, waist, and hips—or in the torso, but not in the arms, shoulder, or armhole area. Since this is a complex shape, we need to consider many areas for good fit.

The first rule is to elongate the look of the body. Emphasize your upper body or neckline area, and avoid accentuating to the midsection with belts or other lines. An empire waist flatters by drawing attention to the upper body and bustline. Avoid large or wide sleeves, which tend to widen you as a whole.

Hybrids—and the Details

Since the above shapes are simple, each of us is more likely a hybrid of more than one. The additional elements of arms, armholes, shoulder width, and armhole depth interact with the torso in ways that are important for good fit.

Here are some thoughts to consider:

1. An hourglass can veer closer to a rectangle, or vice versa. Both types tend to require adjustments in patterns in the areas of neckline and length, rather than in the torso shape.

2. A rounded person might be more of a triangle than an inverted triangle, or vice versa. So we should consider what works for each of these types.

3. In any of these types, excepting the Inverted Triangle, narrower-than-average shoulders can cause poor fit in the upper body, looseness in the armhole,

and a flaccid upper sleeve, even if the bust is accommodated.

4. Wider-than-average shoulders in any type might cause poor fit in the upper body, with a strain on the neckline, upper sleeve, and even armhole depth.

5. All body types above reflect mostly issues of width: they imply that our fronts and backs are relatively even, which of course they are not. Often people are much wider in front than in back, or vice versa. You might be curved more widthwise at back, with a small bust. You might have a large bust and a narrow back, affecting the fit in the shoulders and armholes. We touched on this in the section on measurements in Chapter 1.

6. For all types, torso length can vary, presenting issues that need to be considered:

a. One might be very short-waisted, with a shorter-than-average distance from the neck to the waist.

b. Conversely, a long-waisted person has a longer-than-average distance from the neck to the waist. Either of these possibilities—(a) or (b)—can create fit problems if a crucial length in a pattern does not correspond.

c. A curved back can make the back considerably longer than the front, even taking the bust into account.

7. For all body types, we should consider the neck and arms when studying a pattern, since each can have its own "type." These areas influence fit much more than people realize. For instance, someone who has a rounded, or thicker-than-average, neck might need to adjust neckline width and/or neckline depth. Also, wide upper arms can affect armhole fit. More on this to come.

GETTING GAUGE

Achieving the right gauge is a necessary foundation for good fit.

STITCH GAUGE
Number of stitches over 4" ÷ 4 = stitches per inch

ROW GAUGE
Number of rows over 4" ÷ 4 = rows per inch

WIDTH OF PIECE
Number of stitches in piece ÷ GAUGE = width of piece

NUMBER OF STITCHES NEEDED FOR A GIVEN WIDTH
Width of piece X STITCH GAUGE = number of stitches

NUMBER OF ROWS NEEDED FOR A GIVEN LENGTH
Length of piece X ROW GAUGE = number of rows

FIT LAB	# BORROWING A FAVORITE SWEATER Detachable-Cowl Pullover

Project
Detachable-
Cowl Pullover

SEE PAGE 126

We can learn a lot from a ready-to-wear sweater that fits us well! Working with a sweater like this is a way to compare measurements and practice drawing a schematic. I encourage you to choose a sweater that you love for the way it feels and looks on you, and commit its measurements to paper. I decided to take this a step further—and I encourage you to do this, too: I created a project of my own, based on one of my favorite commercially made, machine-knit sweaters.

To re-create a sweater according to its actual measurements, it is best to use a yarn that knits up to a fabric with the same drape and weight. If you use a heavier or lighter yarn, you will have to make other decisions about ease and fabric weight.

My inspiration for this design? A friend and I encountered some inexpensive "buy one, get one free" sweaters at an international chain store, and a long pullover with a large cowl collar appealed to her. I am often amazed at the great designs made with the cheapest of materials! My friend, a non-knitter, bought one pullover and gave me the extra one.

I was unprepared to love the sweater as much as I did. It was a cheap acrylic machine knit, but was made with great proportion in both body and details, and I wore it all winter even as it pilled and shredded. It fit me so well and was so comfortable, I had to make it in a better yarn!

I did not want to guess at any of the shaping: I wanted to re-create the outlines of the actual sweater, with all its details, even the curve of the shaped areas. This was a valuable approach for understanding this particular sweater, seeing the actual measurements, and learning something I could apply to both my design work and future sweaters for myself.

Even if you don't plan to re-create a store-bought sweater, as I did, take the time to draw a schematic for one or two that fit you well. This will become part of your tool kit when you analyze patterns for yourself.

Here's the process I followed:

1. First I placed my sweater on a flat surface. I had a pencil and eraser, a piece of 5 X 5 squares-to-the-inch graph paper, and a tape measure.

2. I measured the length of my sweater, from lower edge to shoulder, and its width at the widest point, and made a rectangle on my graph paper based on these measurements. I drew a central line down the

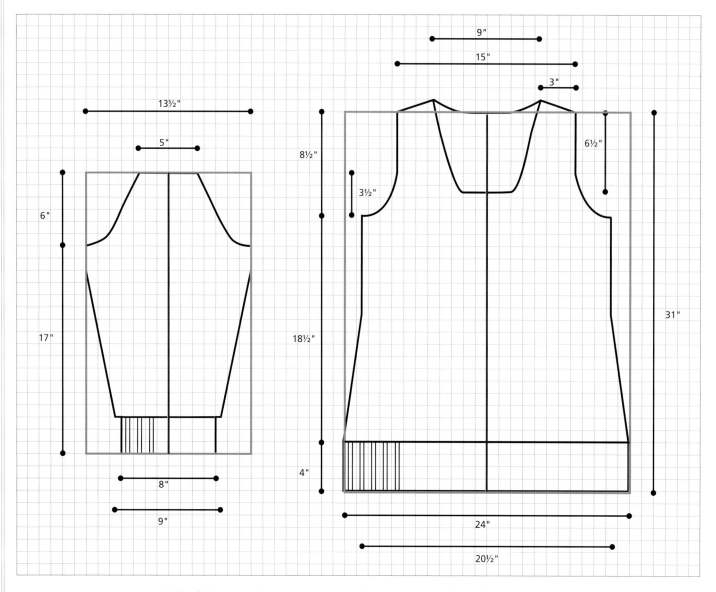

▲ I recorded the measurements of a favorite manufactured sweater on grid paper, replicating the shaping so I could make my own version using hand-knit pattern stitches. This is an almost foolproof way to make a sweater that fits you well!

middle of the rectangle to aid me in counting squares and drawing. This is similar to the guidelines for the body schematic in Chapter 1 (page 26). I could have drawn this over my own body schematic, but here I show the sweater alone, to be as clear as possible.

3. I measured each area of my sweater, working from the largest to smaller, more detailed areas:

a. WIDTHS: waist; bust; cross shoulder above the armhole shaping, neck width, and shoulder sections

b. LENGTHS/DEPTHS: side seam; armhole; neckline

c. LENGTHS WITHIN SMALLER AREAS: points where shaping began and ended, such as in the waist area

I transferred the measurements to lie within the perimeters of the rectangular outline. Note that I connected perpendicular lines for widths and length, and along the neckline edge and armholes, in order to draw the curves for the shaping.

Note: When you measure curved or shaped lengths, such as the armhole or neckline, do not measure the curved line itself. Measure the depth of that area, parallel to an invisible central line.

4. After I'd drawn all the lengths and widths, I repeated the process for the sleeve:

a. WIDTHS AND LENGTHS: I formed a rectangle with the measurement of the sleeve at its widest point, and the total length, from lower edge to top of cap.

b. SMALLER AREAS: length of the lower sleeve; height of the cap; width of the sleeve at upper cap.

c. SHAPING: I refined the shape of the sleeve by connecting the width at lower edge to the full width at upper arm. Then I drew in the cap shaping, paying attention to the shape on the sleeve itself.

Other garment shapes might not be as simple to plot on paper, but the process is the same.

The Next Step

Having plotted the shape and measurements of my sweater, I could now consider the yarn and fiber characteristics. I chose a lightweight, soft wool that shared a similar gauge and weight with the original sweater's yarn. My purchased sweater was in plain Stockinette stitch, but I wanted my new fabric to be more fun to knit. I chose a simple knit/purl pattern, and since I wanted a slimming effect on the lower body, I created some vertical "lines" using a graceful lace panel at the center front and back.

Since my yarn choice yielded a very similar-weight fabric to the original, I did not have to make any alterations to the shape to achieve the same fit. I decided to make the collar separately, like a cowl, to give me more wearing options. The original design used a thicker fabric for the neck than the body, so I used a slightly heavier yarn for the cowl.

Comparisons

Compare your body schematic with the sweater's schematic and answer the following questions. What you learn will help you with other knitted garments—after all, comfort is a given in a favorite sweater!

1. How many inches' difference is there between the two sets of measurements, in important areas?

2. How does the armhole depth of the sweater relate to your measurement in this area?

3. Does the neckline measurement relate at all to your body neckline? Much larger—or similar? ▪

▲ The photo at upper left shows the sweater's neckline without the cowl. At right, note the vertical panel from the front repeated on the back.

The Aesthetics of Fit

"Body types" help us begin to envision the issues involved in choosing and altering a pattern. But they also offer cultural guidelines for what "flatters"— which shapes and proportions work best for us.

What is "flattering"? These ideas are culturally current and can help us settle on shapes and proportions that look "good" on us, but when you come down to it, what looks good is a matter of personal choice. I have read through many versions of these guidelines and have culled the ones I feel work best with our discussion of fit.

I take things I read about what is "flattering" with a grain of salt. For instance, some guidelines claim that wide shoulders are a detriment and should be deemphasized. I don't necessarily agree, since I am of the mindset that we are who we are, and making clothing that covers our bodies without strain is most important. If you do find wide shoulders an issue, you might try to diminish the area through color choice.

In some guidelines I sense a cultural bias in favor of the Hourglass figure—which is fine if you possess it! One suggestion for this body type is to never accent the shoulder area, since it would draw attention away from the waist. This makes little sense to me: I think the neckline and framing the face are as important as accenting the waist.

Absorb from these guidelines what works for you. You may care deeply about what looks good on you from a cultural point of view—or you may not. Wearing what is "fashionable" may be of great concern, or may hold no interest for you. Even though I keep only a loose grip on these concepts myself—I like to wear what I like!—I still see some pointers here, cultural guideposts, that support developing a good-fit mindset.

Note: these guidelines for what is flattering for different body types converge with issues of fit, as well as with your own preferences. For example, if you are a Round type, full in the waist, you might want—and choose!—to make a garment with focus at the waist, even though it's not culturally suggested. You can still create a successful garment that feels good, by planning so it will not be strained in fit or appearance. This is working toward good fit while listening to your own desires.

Also, as knitters, we may fall in love with a pattern because of a technique used in the design or a curious detail we would like to explore. Wearing such a garment is a badge of success, a talisman of our pleasure and exploration of an idea, even though its proportions or shape may not be "right" for us. We can still analyze the pattern ahead of time to make it

work as well as possible for our figure.

I feel very democratic about clothing: anyone should wear what she or he wants to wear. However, I still encourage you to strive for the best fit for your individual viewpoint! Use these guidelines as suggestions, rather than rules.

In Focus: Upper Body

The upper body is a focal point, both visually and structurally. These guidelines can help you choose the most flattering shapes and details for your garment.

• If you are large-busted or bulky in the upper body, extra fabric in this area will emphasize that. A garment style with a lot of fabric at the underarm, such as a dropped shoulder, dolman, or kimono, can add bulk, and details such as ruffles, or large collars, pockets, or yokes can add volume to your silhouette. An expanse of fabric in the upper body and neckline area can create focus there. Try to avoid shortening the torso—a long line will accent your figure. Lower any waist accents, such as a belt or pockets, to sit at the high hip rather than the actual waistline, to elongate the line of the upper body.

• A wide, broad, or high neckline can add an illusion of width and bulk. And a close crewneck or bateau neckline tends to widen and add extra fabric in the upper body. Instead, a V-neckline, or crossover V-neckline, is flattering for all body types and adds the illusion of vertical length, as do deeper and narrower scooped necklines.

• Sleeves can be chosen to accent a full figure in the upper body. A cap or short sleeve that ends at the line of the bust-point will visually widen that area— no sleeve at all might be more flattering. Alternately, a three-quarter sleeve, or one that approaches the elbow, has a longer visual line that does not widen the upper torso. Narrow sleeves add visual length, so avoid sleeves that are full at the upper arm and cap.

• On the other hand, if you are small in the upper body, you can wear fuller garment shapes with success. Look for details in the upper body, and embrace elements that add extra fabric, such as fuller and shorter sleeves. A high, fitted neckline works in figures that are less bulky in the upper body.

• Framing the face is one tip that works for all figure types, and can be achieved in many ways. Consider the choices you have for edgings, trims, and shaping. Think about "knitterly" ways—maybe

FIT TIP

Necklines Rule!

Never underestimate the power of a neckline to make a garment attractive and flattering. Before beginning any project, ponder the neckline and be sure you like its proportions. After you have knitted the sweater, draw attention to this area with a great edging or collar. As a designer, I always see the neckline as a place to frame the face.

different from what your pattern suggests—to add a flattering detail to your garment.

Lines of Sight

The most obvious and acknowledged guidelines for what is flattering have to do with lines, both vertical and horizontal. We have all heard the admonition to avoid horizontal stripes, and to use long vertical lines, if we want to look slim. Consider what your own features are and how you want to highlight them with each design you consider. There are exceptions to these "rules," as for all the others!

For our purposes as knitters, this relates to the topic of fabric as well. Lines can be stripes of color, or columns or bands of texture, such as cables. Here I offer a few thoughts about how to use pattern stitches for specific visual effects.

VERTICAL LINES

As we have heard over and over, vertical stripes have a slimming, narrowing effect. They can be an allover feature of a garment or be planted in sections. Vertical lines can occur as areas of color or of patterning: cables occur in a vertical arrangement naturally and are a good choice to elongate the look of a fabric. Individual motifs can also be arranged in a vertical way, as I did in my sweater project on page 62. I took the eyelet element of an allover pattern and arranged this element in vertical columns at the center front of the garment, which I hoped to visually "narrow."

HORIZONTAL LINES

Another well-accepted rule is that horizontal lines, including stripes, tend to widen the look of a garment and the body. If you are tall and/or thin, it is easy to draw a line across the body without creating an adverse effect. But for those who are short, with bulky figures, a horizontal line can cut the body in half and make it look wider.

CUT-OFF LINES

Consider the best length to emphasize or diminish a part of the body. Where a garment's lower edge falls can call attention to that area, so we don't generally end a sweater at our widest point. This doesn't mean a sweater needs to be longer than the widest part of the body, especially if that part is the hips: a short sweater, which might end above the waist, can draw attention away from the lower body.

COMBINATION OF LINES

Vertical and horizontal lines combined in the same piece can create visual tricks. For a Triangle shape, combining horizontal lines in the upper body with vertical lines below the bust or waist might be very flattering. And the reverse is true: a person who is narrow in the hips might wear a garment with strong horizontal lines below the waist, if the upper body fits well and/or has strong vertical lines.

To diminish the waist, ribbing or other vertical patterning can provide a visual trick. If this vertical patterning doesn't cling or fit very close to the body, it can also be flattering for the Diamond and Rounded shapes, even if they are wider in this area.

DIAGONAL LINES

Diagonal lines moving in both directions from a central line, upward or downward, can be a flattering way to accent one area of the body. Upward-moving diagonal lines can draw the eye away from the lower

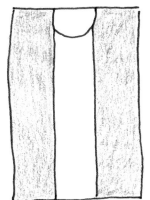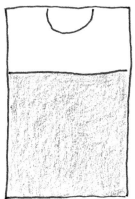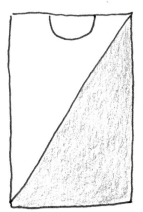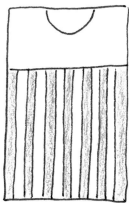

Color placement, or contrast between dark and light, can lend a flattering look to a sweater. Vertical stripes or dark areas at the sides or in lower sections can narrow the line. Diagonals tend to draw the eye upward.

body and create focus in the upper body, or frame the face. Those with Hourglass figures can successfully wear lines in both directions, and they may accentuate that shape even more. To draw attention away from the upper body or a large bust, diagonal lines moving from the center outward from below the bust or waist can widen the lower body and create balance from top to bottom.

Shaped Areas
Flattering lines can also derive from garment shaping.

FLARED AREAS
A garment can flare, ruffle, or pleat in many ways. This type of feature, well chosen, can provide flattering detail for a range of figure types.

Generally, if you are wide on the bottom, the flared part of a sweater—in front and/or back—is best started higher on the upper body, either above the bust or just below the bust, rather than near the waist. This way the fabric can skim your hips, rather than accentuate them. Fullness in the form of a pleat falling from the upper back or upper body creates gradual width, good for those with Rounded, Diamond, or Triangle shapes.

Flaring that starts at the waist will call attention to the hips. For those with a narrow waist and/or lower

body, this can create fullness in the hips; if you want to downplay the hip area, it might be best to avoid this shape.

A garment that skims the body and flares from the lower hip is a good choice for all types, especially if the fit is good in all other areas. It provides detail at the lower edge without flaring at the widest part of the body.

DRAWING IN
Allover fitted sweaters look best on narrow or curvy bodies. But fitted sections of a garment can suit all figure types, if you consider where best to place them.

To flatter Triangular bodies with wider-than-average hips, a fitted upper bodice or an area that draws in below the bust brings focus to the shoulders and neckline, especially if the garment flares below and skims the lower body.

Those with bulk in the waist should allow the fabric to skim rather than cling. Often a slightly larger body of a garment is more flattering than one that conforms closely.

Rectangular figures may want to create an illusion of shapeliness by giving a boxy garment a more hourglass-like shape, with a belt to provide a focal point.

FIT TIP

Real Experience
Many years ago I wrote an article for Threads magazine about making sweaters for larger-than-average women.

I spent time with two wonderful women, taking measurements, asking them what they liked, and talking about how ready-to-wear clothing and other sweaters fit them.

I decided to make "mock-up" sweaters for them before planning their actual sweaters. I made schematics based on their measurements. Then I bought knitted fabric and made a paper pattern for each, cutting the pieces slightly larger than their body measurements. I "draped" the pattern pieces on them, pinning to adjust for fit, and cut the neckline shapes into the fabric. I adjusted my schematic drawings: both garments ended up being slightly wider at the lower edge than anticipated.

I swatched to get gauge and planned the designs. The sweaters fit perfectly according to the measurements that came out of our fitting sessions—a great investment of time to know that future sweaters could rely on these measurements.

Practical Matters
Visual Tricks

Although these elements are not related to fit in terms of measurements or garment shaping, they are related to our focus on making a flattering garment.

Using Color to Shape
Dissecting a garment in terms of color can shift emphasis.
• A bright upper body and dark lower body shift the focus to the shoulders and face, diminishing the lower body.
• Placing a darker color at the sides of the body—easy when working a garment side to side—narrows the silhouette.

Focal Points
Accents, either knitted in or external, can be planned to draw or divert attention. For example, areas of ribbing below the bust can narrow the silhouette.

Choosing the Right Length
• Avoid placing ribbing, or a strongly horizontal trim, at the lower edge when it hits at the widest point of the hips.
• Shorter sweater lengths, ending above the waist, can be flattering for all sizes, since they bring the focus upward.
• Longer lengths, covering the hips, should skim rather than cling. ■

USING LINES OF SIGHT
Striped Blocks Pullover

In this sweater I designed for *Vogue Knitting* Spring/Summer 2014), I arranged the stripes of the hood placket and the pocket to be vertically aligned, to create a lengthening effect.

▲ Good fit at the shoulder and armhole enhances the crisp, geometric look of stripes.

Project Striped Blocks Pullover

SEE PAGE 128

Everyone loves stripes, but many people tell me they like them better on kids or other adults—they are loath to wear horizontal stripes themselves. I employed a visual trick with this striped sweater, interrupting the strong horizontal lines with a side section of the same patterns placed vertically. This not only serves to break the strong tendency of stripes to widen the look of the body, but also lends another layer of visual interest to the design. ■

Standard Industry Measurements and Sizing

Now that you have taken your own measurements, and examined the measurements of a ready-to-wear sweater, let's look at what is considered "average" in the knitting industry. Here is a chart of standard industry measurements, from the Craft Yarn Council, which represent a full range of body measurements (not garment measurements) given for sizes X-Small (bust 28–30") to 5X (bust 60–62"). Some yarn companies, magazines, and independent designers refer to these standards to create sizing for their patterns.

Note that these measurements have been compiled for sweaters and the yarn industry. They are not necessarily the same numbers used by Seventh Avenue or manufacturers of ready-to-wear clothing. In fact, sizing varies so much from maker to maker of ready-to-wear that it is almost impossible to define a size "Small," etc. In one system it might fit a person with a bust of 32"; in another, a 34–36" bust.

Even though it is desirable—and democratic!—for all sizes to be represented in every pattern, not every design concept can be adapted for every "standard size." Often you will see only three or five sizes given, instead of the full range suggested by the Craft Yarn Council. Some garments are just not designed to be worn by every figure, or the the range of sizes is limited for another reason. If you like the concept but are smaller or larger than the size range offered, you may have to take matters into your own designer's hands and adapt the pattern for your size. More about that in Chapter 4, when we discuss garment types.

The notion of assigning a set of measurements to a single size is, frankly, not as useful as we would like. Rarely do a person's actual dimensions correspond to those given for a certain size. Sizing, at best, reflects only an "average" and rarely the "actual." As we discussed in Chapter 1, knowledge of your own measurements is the best foundation for creating a garment that fits you the way you want it to.

The best use of actual "sizes" is to simply have an awareness that they can vary from pattern to pattern, and that not all magazines, publishers, or designers present sizing in the same way. Many patterns you encounter may not reflect these "standard" measurements at all! Make a point of seeing how "sizing" is presented in any pattern you might consider.

I always encourage knitters to ignore all numerical sizes in patterns of interest and jump right to the measurements, either in the up-front material or in the schematic drawing. The best use of measurements is for comparison. When a size is given in a pattern you are considering, be sure to note what body measurement is given for that size. Does this measurement reflect your body measurement? And, as you'll see in the next chapter, you must also factor in fabric weight and ease.

I present these charts as only one industry version of the measurements assigned to given sizes. Study all the sizes and acquaint yourself with the range of numbers possible for any given sweater. This can be humbling for someone who wants to design for a full range of figures—given the differences!—and illuminating for individuals who want to see where they fall within the range of "average."

It is useful to compare the body measurements you took in Chapter 1 with these numbers. Why? Even though not all patterns adhere to these measurements, a comparison can give you an idea of where you stand with regards to the "average." The knowledge that a certain measurement is larger or smaller than average can enlarge your personal lens, so you can anticipate where you might make changes to a pattern even before you begin to knit.

The difference in inches between sizes, in either lengths or widths, is called an increment. This increment is also present in the sizing of patterns.

In the chart at right, you will see a rough increment of 4" between the bust measurement sizes, and varying distances in other parts of the body. Many patterns use the same incremental approach, so these standard body measurements are often the basis for sizing.

However, if you study schematics for different designs, you will see that increments can differ from the chart and can vary from pattern to pattern. Why? Increments between pattern sizes, and pieces, can also change based on the different sizes and shapes of pattern stitches and arrangements. So even though standard sizing is the basis of pattern increments, fabric matters can change that—one reason that sizing is not standard among knitting patterns.

A wise knitter considers these many details before beginning any project. We want to look our best, as well as respect our investment in time and materials, and be sure that our up-front planning sets us up for happy knitting. ∎

In this system, some of your measurements may relate to one size, others to another: this is why general sizing can be only a guideline. Note the increment, in inches, between sizes for various areas of the body. ▶

 # Woman's Sizing Standards

WOMAN'S SIZE	X-SMALL	SMALL	MEDIUM	LARGE
1. BUST (IN.) *(CM.)*	28–30 *71–76*	32–34 *81–86*	36–38 *91.5–96.5*	40–42 *101.5–106.5*
2. CENTER BACK NECK-TO-CUFF	27–27½ *68.5–70*	28–28½ *71–72.5*	29–29½ *73.5–75*	30–30½ *76–77.5*
3. BACK WAIST LENGTH	16½ *42*	17 *43*	17¼ *43.5*	17½ *44.5*
4. CROSS BACK (SHOULDER TO SHOULDER)	14–14½ *35.5–37*	14½–15 *37–38*	16–16½ *40.5–42*	17–17½ *43–44.5*
5. SLEEVE LENGTH TO UNDERARM	16½ *42*	17 *43*	17 *43*	17½ *44.5*
6. UPPER ARM	9¾ *25*	10¼ *26*	11 *28*	12 *30.5*
7. ARMHOLE DEPTH	6–6½ *15.5–16.5*	6½–7 *16.5–17.5*	7–7½ *17.5–19*	7½–8 *19–20.5*
8. WAIST	23–24 *58.5–61*	25–26½ *63.5–67.5*	28–30 *71–76*	32–34 *81.5–86.5*
9. HIPS	33–34 *83.5–86*	35–36 *89–91.5*	38–40 *96.5–101.5*	42–44 *106.5–111.5*

WOMAN'S PLUS SIZES	1X	2X	3X	4X	5X
1. BUST (IN.) *(CM.)*	44–46 *111.5–117*	48–50 *122–127*	52–54 *132–137*	56–58 *142–147*	60–62 *152–158*
2. CENTER BACK NECK-TO-CUFF	31–31½ *78.5–80*	31½–32 *80–81.5*	32½–33 *82.5–84*	32½–33 *82.5–84*	33–33½ *76–77.5*
3. BACK WAIST LENGTH	17½ *45*	18 *45.5*	18 *45.5*	18½ *47*	18½ *47*
4. CROSS BACK (SHOULDER TO SHOULDER)	17½ *44.5*	18 *45.5*	18 *45.5*	18½ *47*	18 ½ *47*
5. SLEEVE LENGTH TO UNDERARM	17½ *44.5*	18 *45.5*	18 *45.5*	18½ *47*	18½ *47*
6. UPPER ARM	13½ *34.5*	15½ *39.5*	17 *43*	18½ *47*	18½ *49.5*
7. ARMHOLE DEPTH	8–8½ *20.5–21.5*	8½–9 *21.5–23*	9–9½ *23–24*	9 ½–10 *24–25.5*	10–10½ *25.5–26.5*
8. WAIST	36–38 *91.5–96.5*	40–42 *101.5–106.5*	44–45 *111.5–114*	46–47 *116.5–119*	49–50 *124–127*
9. HIPS	46–48 *106.5–122*	52–53 *132–134.5*	54–55 *137–139.5*	56–57 *142–144.5*	61–62 *155–157*

Practical Matters Using a Dress Form

A professional dress form is a wonderful tool for working with in-progress knitted garments and dealing with issues of fit and design. Look for one that works with your space and your budget.

Over the years I have seen what measurements work in different situations for different sizes, and I employ my instincts based on experience. If you become a serious garment-maker, you will observe each completed project with an eye for the numbers and measurements that proved successful. This information builds up in your "garment-maker's mind," allowing you to anticipate similar results in the future—and make those results happen!

But for a variety of reasons, I sometimes use a dress form—a substitute for a real person, or for the model who will wear my design. A professional dress form has solidity and a padded surface into which you can pin your pieces in progress, as well as the capacity to be raised and lowered for ease of use.

Standard dress forms have limitations, though: most have no arms! Look down at your own body: your upper arm extends beyond the torso and has its own dimensionality that contributes to the fit of a garment. Since fit in the upper body is related to how the upper arm interacts with the torso, this dressmaker's tool is best used for the body sections of a sweater, rather than for often-crucial sleeve and armhole issues.

A new dress form is a big investment, but I have never regretted purchasing one. If you are lucky enough to find and be able to afford a dress form in your size, that's great, but a less expensive alternative is to search for an older, used one, which can be padded to your measurements with batting or layers of fabric, then covered with cotton fabric to make it smooth, shapely, and easy to pin into.

If you do plan to make the investment, consider a form with small extensions that replicate the girth of the upper arms. If you have a dress form without this detail, it is possible to sew (or knit!) padded and shaped extensions and pin them in place for a more accurate upper-body shape.

There are also lightweight, modular dress forms that stand on a table or are held by a pole, and have parts that expand and contract. What they lack in weight and solidity, they make up for in flexibility of measurements.

I have never done this, but techniques exist for making a "body double" by wrapping yourself—with the help of an assistant!—using duct tape, then removing the form and filling it in to hold the shape. This type of body cast closely replicates your own measurements: a huge plus! I cannot attest to its solidity, an essential feature for weighty pieces, but it seems like a worthy, less expensive alternative that is perhaps more accurate than padding an older dress form.

Ways to Use Your Form

1. With a form that is your double, you can view a garment in progress from a distance, rather than surveying the effects on yourself in a mirror.

2. Analyze the fit of the front or back before a sweater is done. For instance, you might hang the back of your sweater, pinning it in place along the armhole and shoulder, to check the drape, width, and length before beginning the front.

3. I often pin my pieces—or place the completed garment—on the form to be steamed, so I can "set" the patterns in the way they will hang on the body itself.

4. My favorite use of the dress form is to assemble a three-dimensional part of a garment. The form fills out the garment as I seam it together, so it is shaped the way it will hang on the body. For instance, I might place the finished body of a sweater on the form and then sew the lower half of the sleeve cap into the armhole. At that point, I can see if the cap is going to fit or needs adjustment. Or I might pin my seams in place to see the drape of the garment before I sew it together.

5. A dress form is indispensable for determining the placement of sewn-on collars or other small elements, like pockets, ruffles, flaps, belts, buttons, or applied details. I have learned that details can end up oddly placed if I arrange them when the sweater is flat, whereas pinned on the form, I can see how they relate to the body beneath. I can even seam small details while the pieces are held by the form with the right side of the fabric facing.

6. Before making a sweater, I check the neckline shape by taking a length of yarn, arranging it on the dress form in the position I like, and pinning it in place. (See the illustration on page 81.) Then I take the measurements of the yarn outline and transfer them to my schematic. This never fails to be successful: if you don't have a form, try this neckline planning on your own body.

7. Occasionally, and with great success, I have made a "mock-up" of a garment shape that is new to me and checked it for fit on the dress form. I buy a length of machine-knit fabric that has the weight and drape of my anticipated garment. Then, working from the measurements on my schematic, I cut out pieces, adding a little extra for seams. I baste the pieces roughly together, then stand back and look. I can alter the pattern pieces to my liking, then redraw my schematic to the new measurements. If I am unsure of the shape of a piece, I won't bother to cut it out. Instead I just drape the fabric on the dress form and trim it to shape, then transfer the measurements to my schematic.

When you own a dress form, you tend to find uses for it, and it often inspires creativity beyond your expectations. ∎

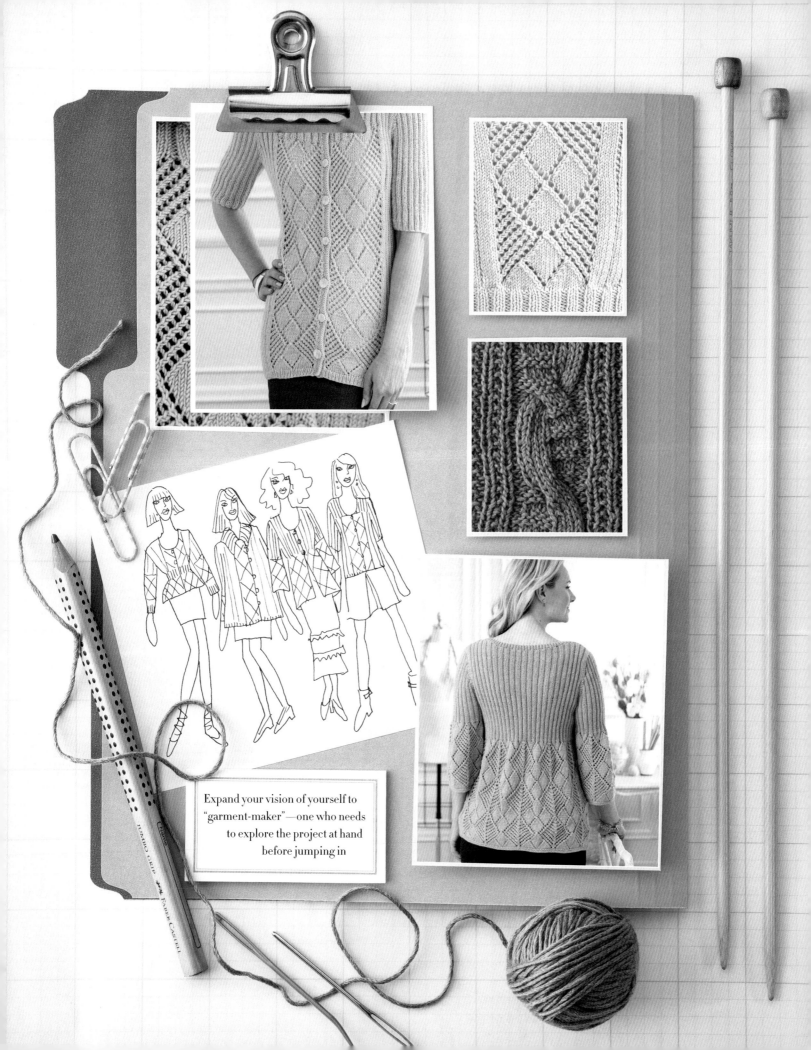

Expand your vision of yourself to
"garment-maker"—one who needs
to explore the project at hand
before jumping in

CHAPTER 3

The Dynamic Trio

Ease, Silhouette, and Fabric

Once you have recorded your measurements
(and memorized them, as I do!), and recognized
the fit issues of the body, you can choose
patterns and adapt them to fit you.
But, as a garment-maker, you must also first
consider three crucial, interconnected elements—ease,
silhouette, and fiber/fabric characteristics.

Understanding the Elements

These three elements—ease, silhouette, and fiber characteristics—apply to any type of garment, any shape or size. If you understand and consider all three—and how they work together—you will lay the foundation for good fit every time.

Ease, silhouette, and fabric always need to be considered when you do the following:

1. Choose a pattern.
2. Choose a size for a pattern.
3. Choose a yarn for a pattern.
4. Substitute a yarn for one suggested in a pattern.
5. Choose to alter a pattern for better fit.

In this chapter I'll explain each of these crucial issues, and we'll see how they interact with and affect one another. If you are new to making garments, you might find this information daunting. Don't worry: it's not rocket science! You will easily learn to apply it to your projects. On the other hand, if you are experienced, these points might seem obvious or unimportant—but beware of dismissing them. Experienced knitters should know to consider ease, silhouette, and fabric (and how they work together) automatically at the outset of every project.

Ease

The concept of ease may be understood as the amount of fabric beyond body measurements required to achieve the fit you want in a garment AND/OR the best look for your body shape. Of course, as we've seen already, these two goals are very much interconnected.

There are many ways a garment can fit, based on how much extra fabric—if any!—is allowed beyond the actual shape and size of our bodies. You're innately familiar with the concept of ease, even if you don't realize it: all of us consider it when buying clothing. For different kinds of sweaters, you need to choose an amount of ease that will produce the kind of fit you want.

Over the years, many people have asked me to explain ease. Often knitters are confused by what size to choose, and when a pattern mentions ease, they find it difficult to understand. Here are a few thoughts about ease, as it relates to fit.

Important Related Facts

1. *Body measurements* are the first step in determining the size of the various parts of your sweater.
2. Body measurements reflect the *body* itself, *not the garment's measurements*.
3. Ease must be added to, or subtracted from, body measurements to choose the size and fit you desire.
4. If another garment with bulk is going to be worn under the sweater, you will need to add extra ease to accommodate it.

Put simply: if you made every sweater with the same measurements as *your body*, then every sweater would cling to you. Different kinds of sweaters require more or fewer inches to achieve their look—a loose sweater will need more inches beyond your body measurements than a close-fitting sweater.

MATH MAGIC! EQUATIONS FOR EASE

By identifying your fabric weight and knowing your measurements, you can calculate the best width for the parts of a garment.

THE BASIC EQUATION:
Body Measurement + EASE (to accommodate yarn and silhouette) = Measurement of Garment Part
To be more specific about the width of your sweater pieces, work these separate equations for the most important parts of the body.

In most cases, this simple equation will work:
Bust Measurement + EASE = Garment Measurement at Bust

If you are very different at front and back, you may want to calculate these areas separately:
Front Width at Bust + EASE = Garment Measurement at Front Bust

Back Width at Bust + EASE = Garment Measurement at Back Bust

The term "ease" is often misunderstood: it refers not only to the amount of extra fabric needed to make a garment fit well, but also to a *specific type of fit or silhouette*. Garments come in all shapes and sizes, and not all are meant to fit the same. Most are designed to conform to the body in a certain way.

A garment's "ease"—whether it is larger than the body or smaller—creates a certain kind of look and fit, regardless of size. Ease can be designed for function, warmth, or sheer drama! And personal choice has a lot to do with determining the amount of ease that is added to pieces.

Ease is often incorporated into sweater patterns. If you choose too small or too large a size, the design will not fit you as the designer intended. Additionally, if you are altering a pattern to your measurements, you must take into account the extra ease needed to suit you and maintain the integrity of the design.

Ease and Fit

For a general guide to ease, with fit in mind, refer to the following descriptions. These generally relate to torso measurements, but consider the ease of sleeves, too, especially if they are meant to fit the arms differently than the pieces for the body do.

The pieces of a garment can all share the same ease: they all fit the same way. Or the sleeves can have a different ease from the torso pieces: the torso piece might fit loosely while the sleeves are close-fitting. Or vice versa: a garment may have a close fit in the body but have dramatic, voluminous sleeves.

If you want to alter a pattern to suit your measurements, consider the ease for all parts of the project.

Note that the inch measurements in these descriptions are appropriate for the "average" size. They refer, generally, to the fit of a sweater body based on the bust or hip measurements. If you are smaller than "average"—fine-boned and thin—your ease requirements may be at the low end, or smaller than the suggested ease for each kind of fit. Likewise, if you are larger than average, your ease might be at the upper end of the suggested numbers, or perhaps even more, depending on the fit you desire.

Very simply, a small-framed person will require less ease than a larger person, in relation to the volume of the body. So the numbers here are suggestions to consider.

TYPES OF EASE

Choose your size based on the kind of fit a sweater is meant to have in relation to the body.

TIGHT FIT: A tight-fitting sweater clings closely to

the body, and is often made from a pattern stitch/fabric that expands, like ribbing. The sweater itself is smaller than the body measurements and stretches to accommodate the body. A tight sweater might, for example, correspond to the fit of a leotard, measuring from 2" to as much as 4" smaller than the body.

The term "negative ease" can be confusing. This simply means that the measurements of the sweater are smaller than the measurements of the body: the finished sweater will have to stretch. Conversely, "positive ease" refers to the extra inches needed beyond body measurements to create a certain fit.

CLOSE FIT: A close-fitting sweater can be slightly smaller, the same as, or up to 2" larger than the body measurements, depending on the thickness of the fabric and the elasticity of the pattern stitch. A close-fitting sweater often has shaping to conform to the body's dimensions, but it does not cling.

CLASSIC OR "REGULAR" FIT: This common type of fit skims the body or is slightly larger—generally 2–4". A classic garment stands away from the body and does not conform or cling.

▲ Ease can be the same in all parts of a garment, as in an oversized silhouette (second from left). Or it can have different ease in different parts, as in the sweater at left with extra ease above a fitted waist. The third sweater has a close fit in the upper body and slightly oversized fit below, whereas the cardigan at far right is fitted at the sides and sleeves for a more classic fit.

What's in an inch?

A single inch means a lot when it comes to fit. An extra inch in front and in back can make a sweater fit in a very different way. In a smaller area, like the neckline or wrist, an inch can totally change the look.

An inch in a heavy fabric counts less than in a fine-gauge material. Why? The bulk in a thick fabric requires adding more inches to change the way it wraps around a body. Because a fine, thin fabric can lie against the body more closely, it will be greatly changed by one inch. It's like the difference between a thick potholder and a tissue of the same size: try wrapping each around your wrist and see how they are different.

A sock knitted in a very thin yarn, at a gauge of 8 stitches per inch, would fit the foot closely at a certain measurement. A sock knitted in a thick yarn, say 4 stitches per inch, would need to be larger to fit in the same way.

SLIGHTLY OVERSIZED FIT: This type is looser than classic but not swimmingly large. A slightly oversized sweater can be 4–8" larger than body measurements: large enough to drape slightly, covering the shape of the body beneath.

Classic and slightly oversized garments might have a closer fit in the armhole areas than in the rest of the body, depending on the type of sleeve cap.

OVERSIZED FIT: An oversized garment is much larger than body measurements, anywhere from 8" upward, depending on the drama of the design. I always say that very oversized garments draw attention to the garment itself, and away from the body.

In addition to defining a design, ease should also reflect the way you personally want a garment to fit—not necessarily how it is depicted in a pattern. Recently a knitter asked my advice: she loved the design of a sweater that was shown to be between close-fitting and classic fit. But she wanted to wear it over a heavy winter shirt, with a loose fit over that

underlayer. Given that, we decided she should go up not just one size but two. I also pointed out that she might want to lower the armhole, for comfort and ease of movement—more about that in Chapter 4!

When you are planning a sweater, it is useful to have a little dialog with yourself about *how* you will wear your sweater. Think beyond simply altering a pattern to correspond to your measurements. You have a choice as to how you want a garment to fit your own body, and whether it needs to fit over an underlayer.

EASE IN THE ARMHOLE AREA

Although we most often think of ease with regards to the width of body pieces, for good fit the armhole area must have ease as well. This means the armhole depth of the sweater must be longer than the armhole depth measurement of the body. And the sleeve cap, if any, must have enough depth and width to cover the upper arm. This is related to how wide the cross shoulder area is. More about this in Chapter 4.

IS THE SLEEVE WIDE ENOUGH?

A tight sleeve can be constricting.

Upper Arm Measurement + EASE = Upper Sleeve Circumference
Considering the silhouette of the sleeve and your yarn choice (EASE), this equation can be useful for those who need to accommodate larger upper arms more comfortably.

Silhouette

"Silhouette" refers to the outline or specific shape of a garment itself. It does not refer to *your silhouette*, but to the shape a garment has when it is worn over your body. An individual part of a garment—torso, sleeve, even collar—can also have its own silhouette.

SILHOUETTE describes a specific shape of a garment—and this shape can have variations based on EASE! This is one reason the complex notion of ease is often hard for knitters to understand.

"Silhouette" is a term derived from a kind of black-on-white illustration from the past that showed the outline of a person, scene, or shape. Sometimes we refer to historical garments by their silhouette: bustle dresses of the late 19th century had a distinct lower-body outline, as did the slender, columnar shapes that defined the dresses of the Empire period.

Why do we need to discuss silhouette? An awareness of garment shaping methods is important when planning for fit. All of the silhouettes I mention are created by adding or subtracting ease in different parts of a garment. We can alter for good fit while keeping—or changing—the integrity of a silhouette.

Allover Silhouette

When a sweater's silhouette is the same throughout its parts, I call it an *allover silhouette*: no part of the garment is distinguished by a special shape. A basic "shift" dress is a tube that varies little in width from armpit to lower edge. For our purposes, the sleeves fit the arms in the same way the body relates to the torso. A simple pullover or "boyfriend sweater" has no variation in shape from area to area. A simple shape is easy to alter, and fabric or color is the garment's primary focus.

Varied Silhouette

When different parts of the body have different silhouettes or outlines, with shapes that vary from the average, I call this a varied silhouette. This adds a layer of visual interest beyond fabric and color.

Here are some varied silhouettes, where one part of the garment diverges from the body beneath and creates a distinctive shape.

A-LINE: This shape flares slightly either below the bust or from the waist to the lower edge.

HOURGLASS: The waist is small and close-fitting, and the areas above and below are flared or more oversized.

TENT or SWING: The fit in the shoulders is close; the fabric flares from above the bust or from the bust point.

BLOUSON: The upper body is full and/or drapey and meets a band or close-fitting area of fabric above or below the waist.

TRIANGULAR: The shoulder area is wider or more exaggerated than the body beneath. The fashions of the 1980s, with wide (often padded) shoulders narrowing to close-fitting waists, are characteristic. To a lesser degree, the sweaters of the 1940s had this shape: broad cross-shoulder measurements, with full sleeve caps that stand away from the shoulder.

EMPIRE: Fit can be close or loose, but there is a defining line directly below the bust for emphasis. This line can be horizontal, or angled from the center out to each side.

DROPPED WAIST: The defining horizontal line falls below the natural waist, and usually above the widest point of the hip.

BUBBLE: This extreme silhouette is rounder and fuller than a blouson style, with fullness starting in the upper body or as low as below the bust.

The above silhouettes are, for the most part, symmetrical. Less commonly, a garment can be divided

▲ There are many ways a garment can be shaped. Here are just a few:
(1) An "empire" style sweater, with a close fit in the upper body and sleeve areas and a gradually flared lower body.
(2) A "blouson" silhouette in both body and sleeves, where the slightly oversized fabric is drawn in at the bottom by close-fitting edges.
(3) A "tent"-shaped, coat-like sweater has a close fit in the shoulders and flares widely to the lower edge.

vertically or diagonally, for visual interest. The different shapes can occur on either side of the midline or an asymmetrically placed line. For instance, a garment might fit closely on one side of the body, draping to a looser silhouette on the other side. A diagonal line could also divide the left and right sides of the garment.

Varied Silhouette in Sleeves

A sleeve can have a varied silhouette even within its own perimeters. Some of these silhouettes, often exaggerated, are associated with particular decades, yet each continues to find its way into a corner of the fashion world every season.

BELL-SHAPED: Narrow at the top and flared at the lower edge.

PUFFED: Wider at the top and held in by a close-fitting band or lower sleeve. The puffed area can fall just in the cap or extend into the upper sleeve, and can be shaped by gathers, pleats, darts, or other tailored details.

"LEG-O-MUTTON": As young kids, my sister and I had dresses that featured these. The term seemed funny, but it was a carryover from previous eras. This sleeve is sometimes puffed at the cap, then narrowed

either above the elbow or slightly below it, then flared again, to be held in tightly at the wrist. The sections can vary in length.

BLOCKY, UNSHAPED: A kimono-style sleeve that is shapeless can have a variety of silhouettes based on the depth of the armhole: narrow or voluminous.

ELEMENTS THAT CREATE A VARIED SILHOUETTE
Some dressmaker's details can change a silhouette in a part of the garment.
1. Peplums often flare and add additional width to the bottom of a sweater, drawing the eye's attention there.
2. Belts and ties can draw in a garment, making the waist narrow without shaping, and gathering bulk above and below.
3. When parts of a garment are layered, they can have different silhouettes. An outer sweater might have to be larger than the underlayer in order to fit. If a garment features a capelet, this overlayer will need to accommodate the underlayer, even if just in the shoulder area. The coat and overvest on pages 116–118 are an example of two pieces whose shapes must accommodate each other. Pleats are another design detail that features layers and will add bulk to an area of a garment.

▶ Sleeves come in a huge variety of shapes and silhouettes. Here are just a few, from left to right:
(1) A close-fitting, narrow sleeve with little ease.
(2) A "Leg-o-mutton" sleeve, with close fit above and below an oversized section.
(3) A bell-shaped sleeve, flaring from the elbow to the lower edge.
(4) A puffed sleeve is voluminous and gathered into the armhole and often a close-fitting lower band.

ANALYZING A PATTERN
Pleated Peplum Pullover

Project
Pleated Peplum
Pullover
SEE PAGE 130

A lot of thought should go into the choice and manipulation of a sweater pattern, to ensure good fit and to save you time and money—including, of course, consideration of ease and silhouette. I wanted to demonstrate the issues involved in analyzing a pattern by referring to a design of my own that was already made. See how I question myself in the process!

Back in 1986, for the Holiday issue of *Vogue Knitting*, I designed a pleated-peplum sweater, a fun and easy piece to knit. Its skirt-like hem flared in contrast to the close fit above the pleats—a "varied silhouette." The upper body had "negative ease"—the width measurements were close to or a little less than the measurements of the body. The waist was fitted through the insertion of ribbing. And the pleated lower edge was much wider than the body measurement beneath.

When I revisited the design, I analyzed its features with regards to fit. I wanted to reknit it in a fuzzier yarn that would yield the same gauge, but the fabric was going to be thicker because of the surface "halo" of fibers, which makes a garment fit more closely. Would I adjust for this thicker fabric—or simply choose a larger size?

I considered the wide bateau neckline, which created a strong horizontal line across the base of the neck. Was this less flattering for a range of figure types than a V-neckline might have been? A V-neck has a stronger vertical line, and I recalled from my research and from conversations that people of all ages, shapes, and sizes find this neckline the most flattering, especially for a dressy garment. I even pondered placing the lower back neckline at the front.

I decided to rely on my schematic to help visualize the neckline, placing the start of the "V" at about the same point as the start of the armhole shaping, a little above the bust point. I narrowed the neckline slightly, since I wanted a closer-fitting V-neck, not an off-the-shoulder one. I

▶ In my sketches here, I consider ways to alter the close-fitting silhouette of my sweater for a larger figure. In both design ideas, I eliminate the ribbing at the waist and make the pleats longer to lend a more vertical line to the lower body. At right, a raglan instead of a cap sleeve might visually narrow wider-than-average shoulders.

▶ Ribbing is a design detail that can be strategically placed to draw in part of a garment, as here at the sides of the waist.

was able to do this with the narrow type of neckline edge I used: if the trim were wider, enough to "fill in" some of the interior area of the neckline, I would have had to plan a deeper and slightly wider neckline, perhaps as much as the width of the trim. (More about necklines on pages 82–85.)

Next I decided to further vary the silhouette by making the increases for the sleeve fall in the lower arm area, rather than being evenly distributed from the lower edge to the armhole. The sleeve would be the same width at the top, but would become wider earlier in the knitting. Why? This is an easy way to gain fullness without changing a pattern drastically: same number of increases but made earlier. Instead of the sleeve having a gradual angle, the angle would be below the elbow, with a straight, unshaped stretch of sleeve from the elbow to the underarm.

Often, working the increases at a faster rate—say, every 4 rows instead of every 6—can be enough of an adjustment to allow a sleeve to fit a larger upper arm without changing any other numbers in your pattern.

I did not alter the pleats one bit for this version of my sweater! They are multi-layered, but the fabric within each is decreased gradually to avoid extra bulk at the waist.

Look at the measurements of this sweater against your body schematic to see how it compares with your own measurements.

You might consider other possible alterations to this sweater:

1. Choose a larger or smaller size for one section. For instance, if you have narrow hips and a large bust, you might want to use a larger size for the upper body, above the pleats. Or the opposite: if you have a larger hip area and a small bust, knit a smaller size for the upper body.

2. Omit the ribbing at the waist, and work the entire sweater in Stockinette stitch for a more streamlined look, as in my sketch at left.

3. To lengthen the sweater for a more body-skimming look, work the pleats for an inch or two longer before beginning their interior decreases. ∎

Fabric

Individual fiber qualities, yarn characteristics, and fabric weight have a big impact on garment structure and fit. Substituting a different fiber or yarn type must be considered beforehand—even fabrics that share the same gauge are often very different in drape or heft or thickness.

Today we have the choice of so many wonderful fibers and blends, natural and synthetic, along with different yarn structures. When yarn exploits a wide variety of pattern stitches, the fabric possibilities are endless!

When considering any new project, *always* swatch, not just for gauge but also to see how the fiber or yarn will work with the pattern stitch. This will present a fabric to you: Will it work for the garment you have in mind, along with any alteration you may be considering?

Even with all my experience, I always swatch to see in my hands—rather than guess—how a fiber and yarn will combine with a pattern stitch. As a professional designer, I am often asked to knit one of my designs in a yarn I did not plan or choose for the idea. I have to accommodate the yarn, and sometimes it makes the design totally different from my original swatch and my initial conception of the design.

When substituting a different yarn from the one suggested in a pattern, check that your choice will be suitable for the design and contribute to good fit. For instance, picture a garment knitted with a soft, slinky yarn that creates a flowing, body-conscious fabric. Can you imagine that the same silhouette—or the same fit?—would be achieved with a firm, bouncy wool that forms an elastic and dense fabric? That garment would have a much more solid look, and would probably stand away from the body rather than cling to it.

Fiber/Yarn Concerns

We can usually define individual yarns by their primary fiber content. With blends, generally the dominant fiber calls the shots and the yarn and resulting fabric behave with the qualities of that fiber. But there are exceptions: recently I tried a tightly plied yarn that was primarily wool, blended with less than half bamboo. The resulting knitted fabric was more silky and drapey than the wool would have been on its own. Again, you need to swatch to discover what happens!

Remember that the twist or ply of a yarn can lend it a certain quality as well. Multi-plied yarns are more complex in their construction and can form fabrics that are crisper and denser than those knitted from simple, single-ply twisted strands.

▼ I knitted the same textured ribbing and ridged cable patterns in three different yarns, resulting in three very different fabrics.
(1) A mohair yarn knitted to a soft, airy fabric with a lot of surface hair, which will require extra inches in a sweater to cover the body with ease.
(2) This thick, springy, plied wool created a dense and solid fabric, which I imagine would stand away from the body with little drape.
(3) This wool blend was firm and string-like in the strand, and knitted to a very drapey fabric without much elasticity.

Still, we can make some general rules about individual fibers. How do these fibers affect fit? The following characteristics should plant the seed of thoughtfulness about fiber choices for your projects. Always choose a yarn that will support the fit you hope to achieve.

Practical Matters "Wearing" Your Swatch

Some fibers have a disappointing tendency to stretch after the garment is worn, or even while the pieces are being knitted.

How can you determine how much a fabric will stretch or "grow" so this does not affect fit? I tell my students to work a largish swatch, at least 6" to 8" square, then carry it around for a few days. Put it in your purse; transfer it to your pocket; leave it on your desk or table, in the pocket of your bathrobe—all the time handling it whenever you can. It sounds silly, but this casual "wearing" of the swatch gives it a touch of real use! Often the swatch will reveal a much looser gauge after this treatment—which you can use as the real gauge for the knitting. If you find this actual gauge too loose, for your pattern or for your liking, make another swatch with a smaller needle. ▪

FIT TIP

Love and Compatibility

Just because you love a yarn and you love a certain pattern, that does not mean the marriage between them will be a success!

When you love a yarn, make sure you choose a design that suits it. Likewise, when you find a pattern that seems perfect, use a yarn that best enhances its features.

Always swatch in the major pattern stitch of a design and take a long, hard look at the results, considering everything we're discussing in this book. No disappointing relationships in future projects!

NATURAL ANIMAL FIBERS

WOOL is bouncy when twisted and exhibits even more springiness when plied. There are many kinds of wool from a wide variety of sheep, and some, like merino, are more soft and elastic than others. Wool has a more solid quality when knitted than other fibers.

ALPACA, a member of the camel family, tends to be shinier and with a slicker feel than most sheep wool. Alpaca can hang with gravity heavily when it is the only fiber in a yarn, but it has a luxurious drape in knitted fabric. Mixed with a more elastic yarn, it is springier and has less chance to drape or stretch.

BABY ALPACA tends to be much lighter than pure adult alpaca, and can be softer and more drapey.

MOHAIR, from the slightly wiry hair of the Angora goat, often makes a fabric that has a fuzzy surface on both sides. Because of this, it stands away from the body, and more ease may be needed than for a smoother fiber/yarn. Mohair is not as springy as wool but makes up for that in its fullness and lightness.

CASHMERE at its best is weightless and very soft. Cashmere does not have the spring associated with wool, so it is not always a good substitute when elasticity is important. For instance, if a pattern relies on an area of very elastic ribbing, cashmere may not have the spring to create that same quality. So use it for drapey garments where softness and lightweight luxury are a plus. It's expensive, but cashmere is often a great choice for oversized pieces—it keeps a large garment lightweight.

SILK is a fiber that can be shiny and luxe, or nubby and more rustic. Silk alone has a tendency to stretch, despite its strength, and you should always work a large swatch and test it. See the sidebar at left about testing your swatch for stretch.

VEGETABLE FIBERS

COTTON is soft and tends to have weight and bulk in a thicker yarn. Pima cotton is shinier and lighter and usually bouncier and less bulky.

LINEN, unblended, tends to be stiffer than cotton but has a gorgeous drape and falls with gravity, with little bounce.

BAMBOO has a light yet drapey quality that feels almost slippery in some yarns.

All vegetable fibers, unblended, tend to be less elastic than wool when used in ribbed patterns.

SYNTHETICS AND OTHERS

RAYON is one of those lovely, often lustrous, fibers that have a tendency to "grow" in the final sweater. It has a slippery, drapey quality. When blended with more elastic fibers, it contributes drape and not bulk.

ACRYLICS come in a wide variety of forms, and are often blended with other fibers. Acrylic can mimic the elasticity of wool, especially in multi-plied yarns and when it is a large proportion of the components of a yarn.

METAL yarns have a stiffness that does not bear much relation to animal or vegetable fibers. Since they are so unforgiving in stretch, show off their unique quality in the simplest of garments that do not cling to the body.

Yarn Qualities

Consider how yarn texture can contribute to fit, with ease and silhouette in mind:

Smooth yarns add the least bulk to a silhouette and often fall more gracefully in a larger garment.

Tweedy or "wooly" yarns that are rougher or more "rustic" can work well for larger silhouettes. In finer gauges, they are suitable for closer-fitting garments.

Nubbed or deeply textured yarns will add bulk to a silhouette and might create fabrics that require extra ease in order to accommodate thickness.

Hairy yarns can add a halo above the fabric that adds extra dimension to the body—a visual effect. In addition, they can add a small layer of bulk inside the garment, often requiring extra ease.

Combining Ease, Silhouette, and Fabric

Now that we have reviewed these three issues, how do we consider the ways they interact together? Let's look at the different starting points for making a knitted garment: it can be the desire to make a certain kind of garment, to use a pattern we've found, or to knit with a specific yarn.

Asking yourself a series of questions, as I always do when starting a project, will help define your needs and lead you to consider fit issues. The basic questions that follow do not cover every situation, but they should start you on an inner dialogue regarding the elements of ease, silhouette, and fabric that can help you avert problems with fit.

Starting with a Garment Type

You might search out, or fall in love with, a certain kind of garment based on shape, silhouette, or style—and we'll discuss these garment types in the next chapter.

How much ease is appropriate for this kind of garment for your figure type? For instance, if you want to make a ribbed garment, are you comfortable with a tight fit or a slightly looser close fit? What yarn or fiber would work best for the ribbed fabric? For a straight falling cardigan, would you choose a classic fit or are you more comfortable with a slightly oversized fit? Once that's settled, would you choose a yarn/fiber that has graceful drape or woolier bulk?

How would details you'd like to add affect the sweater? If you'd love to incorporate a pleat, where would the upper edge of it best begin for your body type? Would a crisp yarn work better than a soft one for your vision of the pleated sweater? If you were to add length, would your choice of yarn add undesirable weight?

Starting with a Pattern

When looking at a pattern, can you compare your measurements with those presented and choose a size that suits your body? If you are full-figured, does the upper size range offer enough ease to accommodate the kind of fabric the sweater will be made from? If you have doubts about any of the measurements— given that now you know your own!—is there a schematic drawing that can help you see any large differences you might need to accommodate?

If you choose to alter a pattern

for better fit, have you considered what areas are essential for change? Will this alter the silhouette of the sweater and change the design so that you are not so keen on it after all? At the same time, are there any details that you think might be changed to be more flattering for your body type?

How will the yarn and fiber affect the amount of ease you will need in various areas? Will the yarn change the shape or drape of the garment?

Starting with Yarn

When you love a specific yarn, you want to choose the best design for its use. When substituting a yarn, ask yourself if it will suit the design: Will the resulting fabric enhance the design and retain the silhouette, or will you need to add or subtract ease to accommodate its qualities? Is the yarn stiffer or softer than the yarn suggested—how will this alter the silhouette of the sweater, and could that affect the fit? Think about your figure type and your personal needs; will any parts of the garment have to be altered for a better fit because of your yarn choice? For instance, what if you have to add ease both for yarn qualities and to accommodate measurement differences?

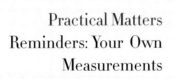

Practical Matters
Reminders: Your Own
Measurements

Here are useful tips to remember when choosing pattern measurements or thinking about making changes to accommodate your figure, with the topic of this chapter in mind.

IMPORTANT EQUATION: **Body measurement + ease = size of garment part**. Adding ease to your body measurements creates the shape and size of the individual parts of a garment.

A MEMO TO YOU PERSONALLY: You may need to adjust one or two measurements every time you start a sweater project.

DIFFERENCES IN THE SAME GARMENT: Some garments have a varied silhouette—areas that have a different ease within the same garment. A garment with a close fit in the torso might not have the same in the sleeves, or vice versa. When you choose a pattern, notice whether you need to add extra ease, or less, in the various parts to accommodate your needs.

GET SOME HELP! Before beginning a project or pattern, refer to a similar garment that fits you well. See if they have characteristics in common. Decide if any of the pattern measurements could benefit from being made closer to this garment's measurements. ▪

Looking Back and Looking Forward

At this point in your fit-awareness journey, you have acquainted yourself with the important basic issues that contribute to good fit. All of the ideas I have presented so far should be considered in every garment project you will encounter. Keep them as keystones for your successful exploration of fit, and as you move into the chapters ahead.

When you read my experiences with sweater ideas, think about your own needs. I found it difficult to choose sample projects for this book, because I could never represent every aspect of fit for a wide range of body types in a limited number of garments. *But I hope to show how my process is exploratory—and inspire you to use my examples to develop a process that works for you and your needs.*

Think back on some projects you might have made in the past, whose fit was a disappointment: Can you identify what might have been lacking in the choices you made? Can you imagine how the fit might have been better?

What about sweaters you are planning for the near future? How can this information shine a light on your project?

Can you envision yourself as more than a knitter? By adding new information to your own skills and interests, can you expand your vision of yourself to "garment-maker"—one who needs to explore the project at hand before jumping in? It is a whole new world . . .

VARIATIONS ON A THEME
Ribbed Yoke Cardigan • Short-Sleeved Cardigan • Collared Cardigan • Peplum Cardigan

To design four sweaters that might fit a wide range of figure types, I chose to create three new variations on a favorite design of mine that appeared a few years ago in *Vogue Knitting*. I wanted to achieve a range of silhouettes and kinds of fit, in different sizes. My goal was to use the elements of *line*, *pattern*, and *silhouette* in interesting ways.

The pattern stitches of my original sweater were just simple knit 2, purl 2 ribbing and a gorgeous allover lace pattern. For two of the sweaters, to get away from the strong fitted lines the ribbing caused,

I added one more pattern—a simple flat garter rib on a field of Stockinette stitch.

I worked all four sweaters in a soft wool/synthetic/cashmere blend that had a lot of elasticity and drape, suited to both the lace and ribbed patterns. These variations show how patterns can be aligned in different ways for different effects. I hope my process might inspire you to plan and knit a variation on your own favorite sweater, to create an altogether different result.

Ribbed Yoke Cardigan

My original cardigan is ribbed in both upper body and upper sleeves. The lower body and sleeves flare into the allover lace pattern. This sweater was very popular with knitters, and I believe the proportions were flattering and easy to wear for a wide range of figure types.

The close-fitting silhouette in the upper body is created with a smooth rib that ends below the bust in empire style. The deep neckline is flattering, especially for a larger figure, since it opens up a wider field of fabric: the soft curve of the neckline frames the face.

The lower body looks good on both narrow and fuller figures. The beautiful lace pattern is the focus, rather than the body underneath. This fabric falls in a soft way: in a stiffer yarn the lace would stand away from the body more.

The ¾-length, bell-shaped sleeve seems to keep the focus on the upper body. In a longer length, this flared sleeve might seem heavy.

Project
Ribbed Yoke
Cardigan
SEE PAGE 132

Project
Short-Sleeved
Cardigan

SEE PAGE 134

Short-Sleeved Cardigan

For this variation, I was inspired by a classic fitted "poor boy" silhouette in the sleeves, neckline, and shoulder areas. I arranged a single repeat of the lace panels to align next to the front opening, creating a longer, leaner line. The ribbed sides give this sweater an allover close fit. I retained the same neckline as in my original sweater.

This kind of silhouette, ribbed at the sides only, can be slimming to many figure types. The fit is closer at the sides, but the garment does not cling in the center front and back.

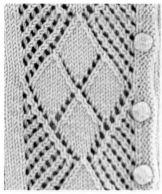

**Project
Collared Cardigan**

SEE PAGE 136

Collared Cardigan

Even though this variation is the largest sweater of the group, it has the longest visual lines and would be flattering to all figure types. With just one elongating panel at the front edge, the sweater has a lean line despite its flared shape. The ribbing at the upper body and sleeves gives a close fit in this area, and the rest of the jacket is slightly wider, accommodating larger hips and waist, but designed to flatter a narrow frame as well.

The lace at the lower sleeve lends detail, and the wide, spreading collar, set into a shallow V-neckline, frames the face.

Peplum Cardigan

In my final variation, I combined the flared lower edge of the original sweater with the elongated panels of the second cardigan. Ribbing a little below the natural waist creates a closer fit at the high hip area, not right at the waist, making it wearable by those of us without an hourglass figure. I wanted a flared sleeve, but a bit narrower than in the original sweater, since they were three-quarter length.

Since I wanted the lower sleeves to be less fitted, I used the flat Stockinette stitch ribbed with lines of garter stitch. This also inserted another element of visual texture into my new design. ∎

Project
Peplum Cardigan
SEE PAGE 139

CHAPTER 4

All About
Garment Types

This is where the fun begins!

The heart of garment-making—and good fit—
     lies in understanding garment shapes and types.
I am in love with the exploration of these types
     and how they differ from one another. This
knowledge—combined with up-front planning,
     recording of measurements, and considerations of
ease, silhouette, and fabric characteristics—is
     how we learn to adapt patterns for better fit.

Garment Structure and Shape

When you make garments professionally, as I do, an apprenticeship occurs over years. I've had the opportunity to encounter, design, and understand many kinds of garments and their variations. Some have been created with a conservative edge, others with a more high-fashion attitude—I love them all.

I have designed, knitted, and finished sweaters of all shapes and sizes—including necklines, sleeve types, and lengths. Always trying new (and challenging!) things helps my understanding to grow. I tell my students that my work has been one long, interesting course of study that never gets old: I can always find a new variation to try.

I also love to fiddle with numbers—making alterations to a pattern is like solving a puzzle, and I try to keep that element of fun in mind as I work. The time is well spent: a good investment! As I've said, when you do all the planning up front, the knitting proceeds with pleasure—and with a minimum of doubt.

We come to this with the appropriate focus on fit, but at the same time you will become well versed in the structure and shape of knitted garments. This takes practice: one project at a time. Try new shapes and make sweaters that you find challenging, all with an eye to learning. As you figure out how to adapt them for good fit, you will start to see similarities and make comparisons. When you become confident with one kind of garment shape, you will see that it shares characteristics with another, even in small ways—these shapes form families of sweaters. Your fluency in the language of fit will expand, and you will approach new projects with confidence.

Understanding Garment Shapes

When I started designing sweaters and trying to understand the various types of garments, I often wanted to create a new shape or make something I had no experience with. I had to experiment with measurements, ease, and fit. Today I still push myself to go to new places, try new shapes, as a way of expanding my vocabulary of techniques and my knowledge of garment shapes.

A simple garment is not better or worse than a complex one, just different. Knitted garments can be ultra simple and still extremely effective—even rectangular body pieces without neckline shaping or intricate body consciousness. The simplest sweater in a wonderful yarn and pattern stitch—*or even basic Stockinette stitch*—made with the perfect amount of ease for the weight of the fabric and the wearer's measurements, knitted to a size and shape that flatters, is a thing of beauty.

Or a sweater can be more detailed in proportion: perhaps a fitted shape that conforms to the body, sporting a more complicated type of armhole. Or a garment might have a varied silhouette, combining fitted and loose-fitting areas in the same shape. Other shapes use modular, geometric, or circular pieces arranged to conform to the body, or flare away from it. *But complexity is not necessarily better than simplicity.* Also, no matter how beautiful and

intricate the design, it will not work as a sweater if it does not fit.

Here I'll present the various types of garments, with an eye toward understanding their characteristics. Then you'll learn how to alter them for a variety of your own reasons, which will help you understand them in relation to your own measurements.

Each garment type has its own quirks and characteristics, and each has a "best way" of being reshaped and altered to change the fit. The more you learn about different shapes, the easier it will be to alter them, keeping in mind all we have explored so far.

The following information applies to a wide variety of garments: sweaters, coats, dresses, tank tops, capes, and ponchos—anything knitted with yarn and needles. That is what's wonderful about understanding structure: the knowledge keeps working, over and over, in each project you encounter.

Sweaters Defined by Sleeve Types

Since the way a garment fits is greatly determined by the type of armhole, I naturally tend to see sweaters in this way. When I am designing and I want a certain fit, I often think about the armhole first, even though it might not be the focus of the design.

In most cases, except (as you will see) for the simple T-shaped dropped shoulder style, a sweater's structure is defined by the very top of the sleeve, which joins to the upper body in the "cap." This sleeve cap can be shaped in a variety of ways: curved at the top, deeply angled along the sides, or with an extension that becomes part of the shoulder area.

There are several basic types of what I call "sleeve-determined sweaters," and for me they form the most exciting aspect of design and good fit. The possible variations are infinite: in any fashion season, one can see numerous ways each type can be altered to look a little bit different. Many of the sweater patterns you will encounter as a knitter will be based on one of these types, so it is useful to understand how they are constructed, and how they can differ within the same type.

Each of these shapes fits the body in a specific way, and knowing these qualities helps you understand how to alter them. I will define the characteristics of each, so you can see how they differ or are related, and show schematics for each, as I might have drawn them when planning a project.

Dropped Shoulder

The dropped shoulder garment is the simplest sweater shape: a basic "T" that has little or no shaping at the neckline and at the armhole. It is an iconic shape, found in the earliest "folk" sweaters from the British Isles and Scandinavia. A tube-like, unshaped body meets simple sleeves, usually straight or slightly angled at the top.

Because there is no shaping at the armhole, several things occur:

1. The cross-shoulder area is the same width as the lower body width, below the armhole.

2. On the body, the shoulder seam falls across the upper arm.

3. A lot of extra fabric is present in the underarm area, which can create bulk.

This shape works best when the silhouette is oversized, with extra ease.

If your upper body is bulky or you are large busted, this shape is often not flattering because the extra fabric in the underarm adds bulk. Adapt instead to the slightly shaped "modified dropped shoulder sleeve cap" version, shown on the next page.

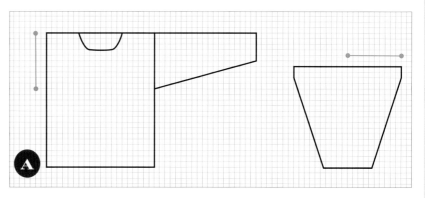

The simplest dropped shoulder has a sleeve that meets the body in a straight line, with no cap at the upper sleeve.

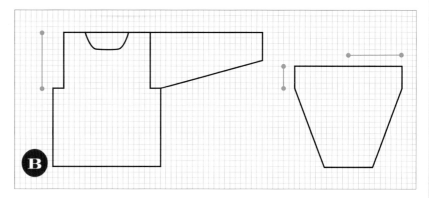

(b) The "indented armhole" is a slightly more fitted version of a dropped shoulder: the sleeve insets into the body slightly, so the upper sleeve seam relates more to the cross-shoulder measurement of the body.

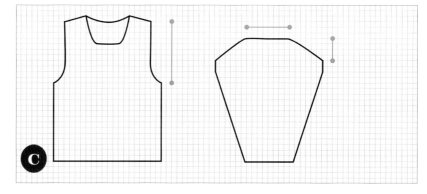

(c) The wide-top shallow sleeve cap creates a little more shaping: consider altering a dropped shoulder pattern in this way to eliminate bulk in the underarm area.

◀ This more "modern" version of a dropped shoulder sweater, with shaping at the sides of the body, has a closer fit than traditional versions (seen on the previous page). The shape actually resembles a dolman sleeve, which can have a very deep armhole.

The benefits of this sweater shape are several:
• It's often the perfect canvas for complex patterning. The simple shape allows you, as a knitter, to concentrate on the qualities of the fabric rather than on shaping.
• In an oversized silhouette, this shape is dramatic and falls beautifully in a drapey yarn.
• When knitting a traditional sweater, like a Gansey, Aran, Shetland, or Scandinavian classic, I feel connected to my handknitting ancestors by working the garment shapes that they did. It is a rite of passage to make a traditional sweater with this type of sleeve/body connection.

Dropped Shoulder Variations

There are two basic alterations of the dropped shoulder type of sweater that help eliminate bulk from the underarm area and make this style easier to wear. Try these options to refine a dropped shoulder shape for a better fit.

INDENTED ARMHOLE

1. If the area where the upper sleeve attaches to the sweater is indented, and the top of the sleeve is set into this indentation, then the line where the sleeve meets the body falls closer to the shoulder, rather than at the upper arm. This does not change the basic shape of the sweater or the armhole, but the illusion it gives of a narrower cross front is often more flattering.

To achieve this slightly different look, bind off at the armhole depth (half the sleeve width) as much as 1–2" on each side. Make your sleeve longer by this same amount.

MODIFIED DROPPED SHOULDER SLEEVE CAP

2. In this more refined version of the indented armhole, both the armhole and upper sleeve are shaped slightly. This is the simplest version of a sleeve cap. Note that the way this sleeve attaches to the body is still the same as with the dropped shoulder: the top of the sleeve is wide and largely flat. However, even the small amount of curved shaping allows the armhole to conform more to the curves of the body, carving out some of the bulk inherent in the dropped shoulder shape.

For this shape, bind off at the armhole depth (half the sleeve width) as much as 1" on each side, then gradually decrease stitches over another 1–1½" to curve the armhole. Shorten the sleeve length, from the top, by 3–4", depending on size, and begin to shape the cap in the same way as the armhole over 3–4" so that the bind-off is wide: at least one-third of the sleeve width.

Practical Matters
Modifying a
Dropped Shoulder

The modified version of a dropped shoulder sweater, with a little shaping at the armhole and a shallow cap, eliminates some of the extra fabric in the armhole.

This modification allows you to wear a silhouette that is simple, yet narrower across the shoulder than the lace dropped shoulder sweater shown at right, and therefore have a good fit in the armhole and shoulder area. With less structure than the full sleeve cap in the four sweaters on pages 60–65 or the pleated peplum sweater on page 55, the look is casual and sporty.

You can easily alter a dropped shoulder pattern in this way for a better fit:
1. Make sure the body is not close-fitting but slightly oversized—about 4–8" wider than the body itself.
2. Plot your changes on a schematic drawing first, to create an instruction to follow as you knit.
3. Plan to bind off gradually where the armhole would begin, over just an inch or two, carving out an area that will leave the cross-shoulder fairly wide.
4. Shape the top of your sleeve over 2–3", binding off gradually to achieve a wide section at the top.
5. Be sure to slope the shoulders gradually over 6 or 8 rows.
6. Since this is a simple alteration, take some time to try it out. Hold the sleeve, with the shaped cap, up to your body: looking at it in relation to the armhole, you can refine the fit for yourself. For example, making the cap deeper or wider at the very top is easy. Ripping out and reknitting a small cap like this takes no time at all.
7. Be sure to capture the altered shape and the dimensions on your schematic drawing for future reference.

THE SIMPLEST SWEATER SHAPE
Dropped Shoulder Lace Pullover

Project
Dropped
Shoulder Lace
Pullover
SEE PAGE 141

A simple dropped shoulder sweater can be shaped in a few ways, as seen in my drawings on page 69. Variations are aimed at reducing bulk in the armhole area, but still retaining the easy-to-knit sleeve that is flat across the top, with no cap-like shaping.

The key to success with a dropped shoulder is to avoid a narrow body and sleeves. If the body is narrow, with no shaping to define an armhole, excess fabric bunches at the underarm—very uncomfortable!

For me, the most graceful way for any-one to wear this garment shape is with a very oversized, drapey body and narrow sleeves. The close-fitting sleeves anchor the expansive fabric of the body. Shaping at the shoulders and neckline is also im-portant to create a similar relationship to the sloping and rounded body beneath.

This garment is perfect for highlight-ing both yarn and pattern: a canvas for an arrangement of complex stitches that might be lost or awkwardly placed in a smaller silhouette. And since shaping happens only in the shoulder area and the sleeves, bold patterning takes center stage.

For the best sleeve length, take the measurement from mid-back to wrist and subtract half the width of the body of your sweater. If your sweater's shoulders have a long slope, as in this one, I sug-gest subtracting an additional inch. If you like, as I do, the long, over-the-hand look for a drapey sweater, then add an inch. (I will not be working while wearing this!)

Do not be afraid of width with a sweater like this! It is better for a boxy sweater without a sleeve cap to drape, rather than cling. As long as the sleeves are a length that works for you, this is a chance to have a large, cozy shape that is easy to knit: a backdrop for beautiful yarn and patterning. Look at this sweater as a template, and use lace patterns of your own choice. ■

Several sweaters we've seen in Chapters 1–3 feature a cap-sleeve style, including the four cardigans shown on pages 60–65. Also note that the cabled sweater on page 82 is an example of a modified dropped shoulder style.

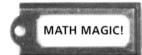

MATH MAGIC! CALCULATING SLEEVE LENGTH FOR A DROPPED SHOULDER SWEATER

Mid Back to Wrist (taken at 45° angle) - half of Sweater Cross Front = Sleeve Length

If your fabric is heavy, or very stretchy, I suggest shortening the resulting number by 1" to 1½" to compensate for these fabric qualities.

The above equation takes into account one side of the body. It can also be written this way, to consider both arms!

(Mid Back to Wrist) X 2 - Cross Front = Sleeve Length

HELPFUL MATH HOMEWORK:
Try working these equations with your measurements, and compare them with a sweater that fits you well.

Practical Matters
Adjusting
Sleeve Caps

It can be difficult to get a perfect fit in a smooth-fitting cap-sleeve style. Either the cap is too large and puckers, or it lacks enough fabric to fit the armhole.

This is not necessarily an error of the pattern: it usually reflects personal differences in row gauge. If your row gauge differs from the pattern, you may find your cap is either too high (looser gauge) or too short (tighter gauge). The good news: this is easily adjusted.

First, always sew in a sleeve cap from underarm up to mid-armhole, on both sides. Leave the top 3–4" of the cap open and unsewn. From this point you can easily see if the cap has the right amount of fabric to "fill" the armhole and fit perfectly. If *not*:

1. If the cap is too large, unravel the bind-off row, rip down, and bind off again (gradually if necessary, over 4 rows) to the cap height that gives the best fit.

2. If the cap is too small, unravel the bind-off row, rip down, and work a few more rows until the cap height fits well. If it is necessary to rip down below your seaming to do this, rip out a few rows of seaming.

Note: even a cap designed to fit without gathers or pleats needs a little bit of ease, or else the armhole of the body will seem larger than the cap, and the cap will retreat *into* the armhole.

MATH MAGIC! UPPER-BODY WIDTH IN A CAP OR RAGLAN SWEATER

This equation will reveal whether a sweater pattern has enough width to encompass your upper body. This assumes you are comfortable with the body and sleeve widths—if not, adjust those areas first!

Cross-Shoulder Sweater Front + Cross-Shoulder Sweater Back + (Cap Width at Midpoint) X 2 = Your Upper Body Width, Including EASE

If the above measurement is too small, you need to either add width to your upper front and back, or make the sleeve caps wider by decreasing at a slower rate.

If the sum of the equation seems too large, you can decrease width in the pieces. Compare the individual body measurements with the sweater pieces to determine where to add or subtract width. A minor change to all pieces sometimes distributes the width in a more even way.

Fitted Cap-Sleeve Type

A "cap-sleeve" type sweater is one in which the cap—the top of the tube of the sleeve—is more complexly rounded and shaped. This type of sleeve/armhole combination is a further refinement of the indented armhole sweater. In addition to the top of the sleeve being shaped, the armhole and upper front of the body are carved out to more closely approach the actual cross-shoulder body measurement, allowing the sweater to conform more closely to the body.

I learned a basic rule in my early days of creating garments: there are many ways to shape a cap sleeve, and each fits differently based on the height of the cap. For instance:

• The higher the cap, the closer it will conform to the body.

• Conversely, the shallow cap of the modified dropped shoulder (see page 70) does not conform to the body, but assumes something like a "T" shape.

• The narrower the cap, the wider the cross front and back must be to accommodate the bulk of the upper body (this relates to the equation above that calculates the upper body width or circumference).

A few notes about fit and the cap-sleeve style:

1. The fitted cap sleeve conforms most closely to the body of any sleeve/body connection.

2. Shaping eliminates extra fabric at the underarm.

3. For the most body-conscious look, the cross front (and cross back) of the sweater should be as wide as the body itself at the armhole. If they are wider, a 1940s "Joan Crawford" effect will result, where the shoulders extend beyond the body and the extra fabric, if not padded, will collapse.

4. If you do want a wide-shouldered look, the cross front (and cross back) should be wider than the body beneath, and the cap can be narrower. A shoulder pad can also be used to help fill the space.

5. For a puffed or gathered sleeve, extra fabric width is seamed evenly into the armhole.

Benefits of using this shape in a garment:

• A refined and body-conscious fit for all body types.

• Works well with a close-fitting to classic fit in the upper body, less effectively in oversized garments.

• Works for every body type, if the proportions are correct.

Concerns:

• For good fit, the width of both caps added to the combined width of the cross front and the cross back should be *slightly* larger than the body measurement called "Around shoulders, arms down" on our chart (pages 20–21), based on ease.

• Extra ease is needed for a thick fabric.

• If the upper sleeve is very narrow, the shaping for

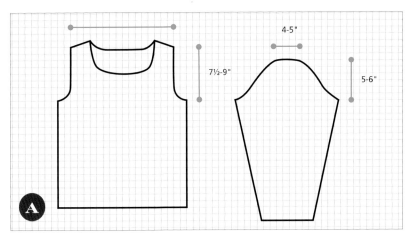

(a) A sleeve cap helps the top of a sleeve fit closely into the armhole, replicating the body itself, with ease added. To better fit your own measurements, the armhole depth can be varied, as can the upper sleeve width and sleeve cap height.

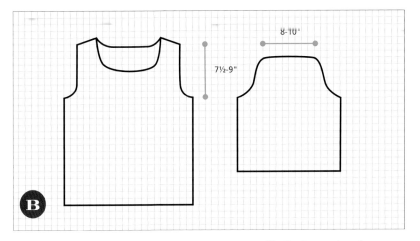

(b) A wider and/or deeper cap can create a "puffed" sleeve that is gathered into the armhole. If the fabric is thick, the armhole should be slightly deeper than average to accommodate the extra bulk.

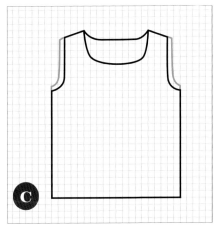

(c) For sleeveless garments, the finished armhole should be about 1" less deep than one that has a sleeve in it.

▶ Note: raglans usually have the same number of rows in the body and the sleeve at armhole and cap, even if they are shaped differently.

a) The simplest raglan, with the least sophisticated fit, has the front and back shaped the same, with a flat, unshaped sleeve top.

b) For a better fit, the back of a raglan can be higher than the front by 1–2". So the sleeve cap will correspond, the top of the sleeve is slanted. The shorter front edge of the raglan cap is the same height as the armhole of the front body.

c) For the most sophisticated, smooth shape, the neckline edges at front and back can be slightly curved. Note that this neckline is wider than (b), making the raglan line more vertical and suitable for a large bust.

d) A saddle shoulder sweater has a band that emerges from the top of the cap to become part of the shoulder, contributing to the armhole depth and the neckline edge. In a sophisticated version like this, the top of the band can be shaped to form a graceful neckline edge.

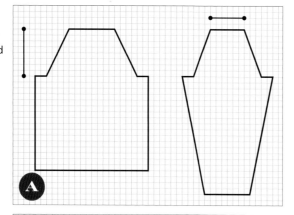

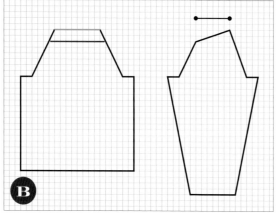

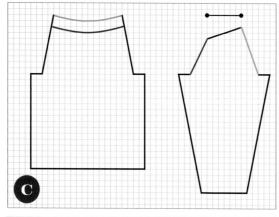

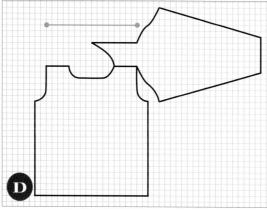

the cap may be more gradual to keep the necessary width and get the height to fill the armhole.
• If the upper sleeve is wide, the cap will have to be decreased more quickly to achieve the height needed to fill the armhole.
• For a fitted cap, the top should measure between 4" and 5" wide, depending on the armhole depth and the size of the wearer.

Raglan Sleeve Type

A raglan sweater is characterized by a diagonal line where the sleeve cap meets the body. This line can be steeply angled, almost vertical, or gracefully curved—all determined by the rate of decreasing in the armhole area on both sleeve and body.

The top of the raglan sleeve cap usually forms part of the neckline edge: this area can be as small as a few stitches, or very wide. *In addition to being part of the neckline edge, and contributing width there, this area of the cap is also part of the armhole depth: an important aspect to consider for good fit!*

Often the shaping in a raglan sleeve cap is the same as the shaping on the front and back body. *However, the shaping does not need to match: the rate of decrease in the sleeve can be totally different from the rate in the body pieces.* In a very refined raglan, the rate of decrease on one side of the cap can even be different from the other side. In fact, this is one way to alter a raglan for fit.

Unlike the cap-style sleeve, where extra ease can be adjusted in the seaming at the top of the armhole (see page 72), *the sleeve cap and body in raglan seams must share the same number of rows along their diagonal lines to fit together.*

Benefits of using this shape in a garment:
• Works for a wide range of garments: close-fitting to oversized.
• Flatters a variety of body types (see next section).

THE RAGLAN CRINGE FACTOR

I see two mistakes all the time in raglan armholes in otherwise successful designs.

First, in many raglan sweaters the armhole is too short, and the underarm clutches at the body in an unattractive way. Often these garments have a poor fit in the neckline as well. This looks so uncomfortable it makes me cringe! It is curious: the body of the sweater fits, and the lower sleeve looks fine, but the armhole and neckline are a disaster.

What causes this? I think it is the common belief that raglan armhole decreases need to be worked on every right-side row, or that the shaping in the front and back armhole must match the shaping on the cap. But there may not be enough width in the upper sleeve to do this *and* achieve the correct armhole depth. In addition to a too-short armhole, the raglan cap comes to a severe point, rather than a flat top that contributes to the necessary neckline edge measurement.

Likewise, shaping on every right-side row in the body can narrow the front too much, causing poor fit in the neckline area.

Always figure out how much depth is needed for a comfortable armhole. If you won't have enough rows (more about this in the alteration section on pages TK–TK), vary your rate of decrease: instead of every right-side row, work them less frequently, and perhaps at different rates in body and sleeve.

Saddle-Shoulder Sleeve Type

A saddle-shoulder type sweater is characterized by the piece of fabric that extends from the top of a sleeve cap across the shoulder area to the neck edge. This shoulder strap both contributes to the armhole depth and forms part of the neckline edge. The cap section, below the strap, is unique in that it can be shaped as either dropped shoulder, raglan, or fitted cap style: the fit of the upper body depends on the choice of shaping.

This style draws attention to the shoulder and face and thus is not ideal for the already wide-shouldered person. It works best for those with an average to narrow upper body.

The saddle shoulder style has a wide range: it can be worked in a close-fitting (cap or raglan-style shaping) to very oversized silhouette (dropped shoulder or variations).

Dolman Sleeve Type

I cannot rightly include the dolman among the "cap" sleeve styles, because it has no cap! A dolman sleeve sweater is best described by saying the sleeve is knitted as part of—and at the same time as—the body. The dolman style can be knitted either from the lower edge toward the neckline, or from cuff to cuff. A dolman fits better if it has a deep armhole, with tapered shaping above and below. Although always deeper than most armholes, the armhole depth of a dolman can vary greatly: from starting at the waist for a deep, "wing-like" effect, to a shallow armhole with a close fit. This is often wrongly called a kimono: a true kimono has no shaping in sleeve or armhole and is more of a T-shaped dropped shoulder type.

Different dolman arrangements have seams in different places:

• Working from lower edge to shoulder, when the bottom of the desired armhole is reached, the stitches for the sleeve can be gradually cast on until the full sleeve length is reached. If you need a longer sleeve, cast on extra stitches at the armhole edge. When the sleeve edge (at wrist) is the desired depth, stitches can be bound off at the shoulder. To avoid a shoulder seam, you can continue the knitting over the shoulder, without binding off.

• For a more refined fit, when the sleeve edge (at wrist) is the desired depth, stitches can be bound off gradually to reach the shoulder for the desired armhole depth. To avoid a seam, instead of binding off, you can work the upper sleeve in short rows and then the opposite side of the body can be worked downward.

• A dolman can be worked side to side, from one cuff to the other. The first sleeve is gradually widened, then stitches for the body cast on, and then, after the body is worked, the second sleeve is worked with reverse shaping. In this case there is only an underarm seam. For a side-to-side dolman, be sure to plan any changes in sweater width before you reach the midline of the body.

In lightweight fabric, a dolman sleeve can be worked in a close-fitting to oversized silhouette. With heavy fabric, this shape works well when the silhouette is slightly oversized to very oversized.

This sweater type works for most body shapes, but less well for the large-busted, as it tends to add bulk in the upper body. A small frame can be dwarfed by a dolman if its scale is too large, with a deep armhole.

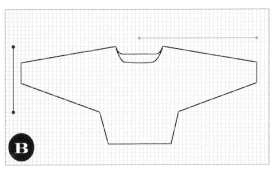

◄ **(a)** This boxy dolman shape has a lot of fabric in the armhole area for an oversized fit, well suited for soft and drapey fabrics.

(b) This dolman variation has the same armhole depth as (a), but the shaping at shoulders and sides eliminates bulk.

RAGLAN RULES!
Textured Raglan Pullover

**Project
Textured
Raglan
Pullover**

SEE PAGE 144

Unlike the sweaters we've looked at so far, which have front and back meeting at the shoulders, a raglan is a more complex garment shape. When you understand the three major parts of a raglan, you will more easily understand how to adjust for fit.

The schematic drawings at on page 74 show various ways a raglan can be shaped, but the basic concept and issues are the same:

1. The width of the upper body along the upper arm, cross front, and cross back (all along the same line) should relate to the width of the raglan front and back—and the cap of the raglan sleeve—in the same place. These pieces need to add up to a measurement that corresponds to the body itself at this point. With lightweight fabrics, they can measure the same or a little less (for negative ease); with heavier fabrics, your pieces need to measure *more* than the body for enough ease.

2. The combined width of the *tops* of *all* the raglan pieces forms the neckline, and must measure a little larger than the neckline you desire: trim or edging will draw it in. So—any width added to your pieces needs to be decreased to achieve this neckline width. I suggest a generous number of stitches for the final neckline width for a raglan: it should fit well in the shoulder area, with ease, to avoid the neckline being tight or strained.

3. The diagonal lines of the raglan shaping do *not* need to be the same for sleeve and body. And decreases do not need to be worked on every right-side row or every other row, a feature of many poorly designed raglans. For example, if you need to widen a sleeve to accommodate the arm, the cap decreases might differ from the adjacent decreases on the body.

4. When planning your raglan sweater armhole depth to fit your measurements, calculate how deep the armhole is in the body piece (usually the back), then add approximately half of the width of the top of the raglan cap. Will this armhole depth be enough for you? If not, add rows to the armhole and cap, or add width to the top of the cap.

Many large-busted women complain that they cannot wear a raglan style—that the diagonal line where sleeve meets body looks awkward. To adjust:

1. Have enough fabric across the front of your sweater, below the armhole, even if the front is wider than the back.

2. Plan the body armhole decreases to form a less angular raglan line, one that is more vertical than a 45-degree angle. Try to shape the line of the raglan more toward the outer clavicle than toward the midline of the front. Note: if this widens the front of your sweater, you might need to narrow the sleeve cap to keep the same "around the upper body" measurement.

3. Incorporate darts (see pages 99–103) if it helps to adjust for the necessary length you need in the front to accommodate your bust.

My Design

A flattering raglan feature is represented by the design I have made here. The seam line from lower armhole to neckline edge is not a sharp angle, but a gently sloped one that does not approach the bust point. This allows the cross front to be wider and more accommodating for someone with a large bust.

This raglan is also a flattering style for a person with a smaller frame and smaller bust, though they can easily wear a raglan with a narrower front and wider sleeve cap.

As a designer, I've always felt it is an omission not to accent the raglan somehow: here I used patterning on both sides of the seam line.

Note that my ribbed neckline edging also narrows along the raglan line. This continuation of the shaping in the trim helps to avoid gaping at the neckline, a refined feature that you might want to employ in any raglan. It allows you to add detail to the neckline and also keep the line of the raglan as a detail. I like a full, unstrained trim at a raglan neck edge: be sure to pick up a generous number of stitches for any edging, decreasing if necessary as you progress. it is a crime if a raglan fits well in the body but the neckline trim is skimpy and strained.

Raglan Suggestions

Here are some ideas for other alterations to a raglan style. These apply to both seamed sweaters and those worked in the round. Note that the rate of decreasing for a raglan does not have to be the same for sleeve and body, nor for back and front!

1. If you have a larger-than-average upper arm, you can add width to your sleeve below the armhole. To

keep the same width at the top of the sleeve, simply decrease along the raglan at a faster rate to eliminate the extra stitches over the same number of rows.

2. Conversely, if you want to narrow the sleeve, lessen the number of stitches in the upper sleeve below the cap. Then, to keep the same width at the top of the sleeve, decrease along the raglan less frequently, over the same number of rows.

3. For a deeper armhole for any given size, add rows: the sleeve and body should always have the same number of rows along the raglan seam where they meet.

4. For a larger bust, make the front wider than the back. As in number 1 above, you can decrease the extra stitches at a faster rate in the front to eliminate the extra stitches over the same number of rows. ▪

▲ I accented the raglan line with patterning, plotting my decreases inside the patterning on both the sleeve and the body pieces.

Test Garments

Struggling with an oversized yarn stash? Assign certain yarns to become "test garments" for exploring good fit.

People who sew often make a "muslin" first, so they know their pattern fits before making the actual garment. A sweater that is an experiment can free your mind and help you look at projects in a new way. If you want to knit a sweater with complex patterning, try a simple, unadorned version first, to check the fit! Your test garment can be adapted in progress, and when you make the final, more complex version, your valuable alterations can be incorporated. This might seem like a lot of work, but it is the way industry professionals do things. Why not approach your own work with this kind of attention, especially in the early stages of exploring ideas? Think again about adopting the "garment-maker's mindset" I described in Chapter 1. Ask yourself, as I do, how you can plan for each project to be the most beautiful and well-fitting garment you are capable of making. By taking these preparatory issues seriously, you will be preparing for success!

MATH MAGIC!   SLEEVE ISSUES

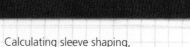

Calculating sleeve shaping, when sleeve widens from wrist to upper arm:

(Sts for Upper Sleeve – Sts for Lower Sleeve) ÷ 2 =
Number of Incs Needed for Shaping Each Side

Plotting increases over a certain length:
Number of Rows for Sleeve ÷ Number of Incs Each Side =
Rate of Increase (every _th row)
If increases are to be worked on odd-number rows—for example, every 7 rows—the same effect can be had by working every 6th and 8th row alternately. Both methods yield 2 increases every 14 rows.

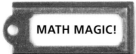

MATH MAGIC!   UPPER BODY WIDTH IN A CIRCULAR YOKE SWEATER

Your Upper Body Width + EASE =
Circumference of Sweater at Mid-Yoke
Settle this essential equation for circular yokes after the body and sleeve widths.

The measurements' placement should correspond from sweater to body. To find the correct point on the sweater, refer to the schematic, or read the pattern to find the number of stitches at the mid-yoke point and divide by gauge to yield the measurement.

If you feel the measurement is too small, look at the next size: even if it's a little large, that is easier to accommodate than too small! If the measurement is too large, likewise check the next smaller size. To enlarge without going up a whole size, plan to add a few carefully placed stitches between motifs or patterns: more about this in Chapter 5.

The Circular Yoke Style

The circular yoke sweater has a cap—but it is invisible! I like to imagine the parts of the upper body melding together to make this swathe of fabric that encircles the shoulders and upper arms, so we can envision the factors we need to consider to achieve an ideal fit.

Since the yoke is often worked in the round, let's consider the rest of this garment style that way, too. Picture the yoke sweater shape as comprised of three types of tubes, with invisible perimeters where the tubes meet.
• The sleeves are one kind of tube.
• The second tube covers the lower torso, below the yoke area.
• The third type, the upper tube, encircles the shoulder and upper arm area, and is shaped to narrow toward the neckline.
• Sleeves and body tubes are shaped simply at the underarm area, and the remaining stitches contribute to the circular yoke.

This construction is seen almost exclusively in knitwear, because it works well only when a fabric is stretchy. A classic example is the traditional Icelandic sweater worked in stranded colorwork.

More modern adaptations feature a band of fabric—often textured or patterned—that accentuates the circular nature. This kind of yoke can be made from any knitted fabric at all, but the patterning has to allow shaping so that a certain narrower neckline width can be achieved: often the patterning is worked in bands to more easily facilitate this.

This shape works best when the silhouette is classic to slightly oversized.

Care must be taken to accommodate the shoulder area without pulling. Be sure of two things:
• Refer to the measurement on the chart on pages 20–21 called "Around shoulders, arms at 45 degrees": make sure you add ease to this based on fabric weight.
• The circular yoke style needs width to accommodate the shoulder area. If the shaping that narrows the sweater to the neckline happens too soon, the upper body can resemble a cone: the sweater will pull across the shoulders and the neckline will pull widthwise.
• This style needs enough armhole depth to avoid strain at the underarm and neck edge when you lift your arms. Luckily, a circular yoke sweater is easy to try on in progress: if you have doubts about the armhole depth, slip your stitches onto a stitch holder and try the sweater on. Adjust the fit by adding or subtracting rows if necessary.

<table>
</table>

FIT LAB

CIRCLE OF MOTIFS
Lace Yoke Pullover

Project
Lace Yoke
Pullover
SEE PAGE 146

Although the most well-known is the traditional Icelandic patterned version, you might see any kind of patterning in a circular yoke sweater.

Any sweater that encircles the shoulders needs to fit that area in the same way a raglan does: the circumference of the yoke needs to measure *at least* as much as the body itself in this area. Ease is added to accommodate the thickness or weight of the fabric.

Even though this is one of the least challenging styles to alter, I still see many ill-fitting circular yoke sweaters. Why? First, the body must fit below the yoke, and then the yoke itself must fit: these two units are not always in sync.

What issues do you need to be aware of in this kind of sweater?

1. A crucial point: the line between the body and the yoke patterning should not fall at or below the bust point, unless the sweater is deliberately oversized. This line looks best when it is 1–2" above the base of the armhole shaping.

2. Because there is no "neckline shaping," just the opening at the top of the yoke, the back of the sweater needs to be longer than the front, so the neckline dips slightly to accommodate the front neck. Read your pattern carefully to see if this detail is accommodated. If not, work extra rows (if your sweater is in pieces) or short rows (if your sweater is knitted in the round) on the back piece just before the yoke is begun.

3. Since the extra rows described in #2 don't always work with the yoke patterning, it is easier to get this out of the way before approaching the yoke. In either case, add at least 1–2" of extra length for better fit in the neckline. This length can also be worked in the last rows of the neckline, to add height at the back neck.

4. Note the number of stitches in the yoke at the midpoint: Does this number, divided by stitches per inch (gauge), yield a measurement that is close to *your* body at this

point, giving thought to ease and fabric weight? If not, you may want to change the number of stitches to accommodate your needs. The lower body may fit fine, but the yoke, if you are larger or smaller than average, may need to be adjusted.

Another common feature of a yoke knit in the round is motifs or patterns that reduce in size gradually toward the neckline. You might have to consider adding (or removing) pattern repeats, rather than just a certain number of stitches. Sometimes motifs stack on top of one another, as in this sweater design. To narrow or widen, it might work to simply add or subtract a unit of patterning: a smaller size might do this for you.

In other designs, the yoke is formed of horizontal bands that might not stack or align: the patterning changes as the width of the yoke diminishes. In either case, if you need to change the width for a better fit, you might add or subtract stitches or individual motifs in each band of the yoke.

My sweater here features a yoke with lace patterning, and the pattern units stack on top of one another: the larger repeats are at the bottom of the yoke, followed by others that diminish in size as they approach the neckline. I allowed a generous amount of ease in the lace-patterned yoke: I personally like some drape, rather than to see it stretched to the limit. Yokes often look too small—there is a fight between the lower and upper body, and the armhole is the victim, with strain that looks and feels uncomfortable.

Within this category, there is also the sweater with a horizontal, shoulder-circling detail such as a cable or patterned band. Be sure to check that the length given for your size of the cabled band that encircles the shoulders equals the measurement of your body, given ease and fabric weight considerations. ■

▲ The bands of patterning that form this yoke have "stacked" motifs that diminish in size toward the neckline.

◀ Another classic circular yoke design is the traditional Icelandic "lopapeysa" sweater. The yoke is worked with snowflake motifs, which diminish in size to draw in the yoke toward the neckline. To enlarge a yoke in a pattern like this, you might not need to go up a whole size— instead plan to add one or two stitches between motifs in selected areas.

BATEAU   CREW NECK   WIDE SCOOPED   NARROW SCOOPED   V-NECK

Necklines

Once again, with an eye toward fit, you can borrow measurements from a garment that fits you well in the neckline. Be sure it shares a similar weight with your swatch fabric.

And, as mentioned in the section about dress forms on page 46, a useful way to determine the size and shape of a neckline is to arrange a loop of un-stretchy yarn or string in a shape and then re-create this on your schematic. You can use this technique for a round, square, or V neckline. If necessary, use pins to hold the string in place as you measure.

If your sweater's sleeve type contributes width and/or depth to your neckline, as in a raglan or saddle shoulder, remember to consider that when making alterations.

Also remember that an edging, added in finishing, will narrow your measurements. In fact, if you find a neckline to be too wide, you can work an edging to fill some of the space.

Boat or Bateau Neckline

This is the simplest neckline there is. It must be wide enough to pass over the head, and can be as wide as the body pieces, for a slouchy, off-the-shoulder look. Choose which end of the spectrum works best for you. This neckline can have a trim or not.

Scooped Neckline Variations

For good fit, the wider your neckline, the less deep it must be. If both the neck depth and the neck width are extreme, the garment will have an off-the-shoulder look.
• Crew neckline
• Wide scooped
• Narrow scooped

V-Neck

A V-neckline is one of the most flattering styles for all body types. It is visually elongating and thus works well for those who have a short neck. A V-neck can come to a sharp point at its base—flattering for a large-busted or wide frame—or have a broad horizontal base with edgings that meet or overlap, a bulkier version more well suited to smaller figures. A shallow V-neck that is wide can be similar to—but more flattering than—a bateau neckline.

MATH MAGIC! V-NECKLINE

Plotting decreases over a certain length:
Number of Rows for Neckline ÷ Number of Decs Each Side = Rate of Decrease (every _th row)
If decreases are to be worked on odd-number rows—for example, every 5 rows—the same effect can be had by working a decrease every 4th and 6th row alternately. Both methods yield 2 decreases every 10 rows.

I often use a length of string to help envision the shape and placement of a neckline. Capturing both depth and width measurements on a schematic drawing will help you plan a new or revised neckline for your pattern.

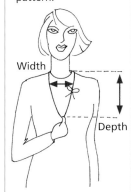

Width

Depth

FIT LAB EXPLORING NECKLINES
Center Cable Pullover

This pullover appeared in *Knit Simple* and inspired me to explore alternate necklines. The modified dropped shoulder sleeve cap style, with a wide cross-shoulder measurement, allows space to consider a wide variety of necklines, as a similar sweater might for you.

The original neckline is wide and fairly shallow, edged with a wide ribbing. Note that any trim around an edge fills in space within the original neckline: if my ribbing were narrower, the neckline would appear wider and deeper. If a neckline seems too wide, just work a little more trim, decreasing if necessary, to narrow and fill in the space.

Here I have given general measurements, for a size Small sample, to give you an idea of what they look like in a finished piece. For the same effect in larger sizes, the neckline measurements should grow

in increments of about ½" per size. If you make changes in a neckline, be sure to plot the width and depth on your schematic.

All necklines that are set into cap-sleeve types should be considered along with shoulder shaping: this depth contributes to neckline fit. If your pattern does not have shoulder shaping, it is wise to add it. Shoulders should slant over a depth of ¾–1" for fine to medium-weight fabrics, and over 1½–2" for heavy fabrics. If a garment has a cross-shoulder width close to that of the body, this can be done over 6–8 rows.

These necklines should be shaped at least a little along the back neck edge, to conform to rather than stretch straight across your shoulders.

Take into account that yarn weight and neckline edgings do, to some degree, "fill in" the area. No matter what style of neckline, allow enough room for your own body measurements. In a close-fitting neckline, this trim may actually stand up along the back of the neck and lie flat along the front neck edge.

For a close-fitting neckline that follows the line of the base of the neck itself, be sure to add ease and extra depth, depending on the yarn: if the yarn is fine, the neckline need only be a little larger for a good fit. But if the yarn is heavy and you are concerned that the opening might be too tight, then add width and/or depth, based on your body and garment schematics.

Unless you want an off-the-shoulder look, deep necklines fit best when they are narrow, with the neck width close to the body's back neck width—and wide necklines fit better if they are not too deep.

▲ Turn the page to see how I had fun playing with neckline types in "swatch" form—another way to explore shaping—with the help of my dress form!

FIT TIP

Incremental Stages

Do you know that most necklines, in average-weight yarns, have width increments of ¹/₂" between sizes? Do you know that most armholes, in average-weight yarns, also have a depth increment of ¹/₂" between sizes?

So, if you want a slightly larger neckline, follow the numbers for a larger size when planning the shape of the neckline. Same holds true for the armhole: if you want a slightly larger armhole, make the next larger size—and be sure to also knit the sleeve cap that corresponds to it.

Project
Center Cable
Pullover
SEE PAGE 149

NECKLINE GALLERY
Getting creative with necklines

I experimented with some alternate necklines for the sweater on page 82. It was fun to work with the large "swatches" and test a variety of embellishments!

Here's what I did—a process you can borrow when you would like to make changes to a neckline in a pattern:

1. I plotted the shape of each new neckline on a schematic, deciding width and depth, considering any edging or trim I might add.

2. Referring to gauge and the width of the cable panel, I figured out how many stitches and rows were needed to obtain the width and depth of each neckline.

3. I rewrote the instructions for the necklines. I could have also just noted these numbers on my schematics for a "visual pattern."

4. I knitted the "base" pieces for each neckline, following my revised instructions.

5. I trimmed each of the first three necklines in a way that pleased me: fun and spontaneous. However, for the last, I planned my edgings ahead of time and plotted them on the schematic in the planning stages.

Consider the measureme nts I have given here for my neckline widths and depths as general guidelines for making changes of your own.

Four Variations

a) This variation has a moderately deep "V" of about 10" depth, and a fairly wide back neckline measurement of 9", for a Small sample size. The neckline has a wide base—the width of the cable panel at center front. The soft, deep k4, p3 rib features bobbles near the pick-up row and is long enough for the bound-off edges to meet.

(b) This "portrait" neckline has a flattering curve, and the depth is the same as the mock turtleneck but with a width of 11". I trimmed the edge with a decorative seed stitch band that draws attention to the neckline.

(c) This mock turtleneck, with rib that changes pattern at the halfway point, sits in a neckline that falls close to the measurement of the body, with some ease added for this mid-weight fabric. The back neck was planned to be 8" wide, and the depth is 3".

(d) I create a ridged "tuxedo" effect. The original neckline was deeply curved: 10" deep and 10" wide. I added trim to the edges of the ridged pieces, as well as around the completed neckline edge. For a more flattering and relaxed opening, I used only one button, allowing the front to fall slightly open. ■

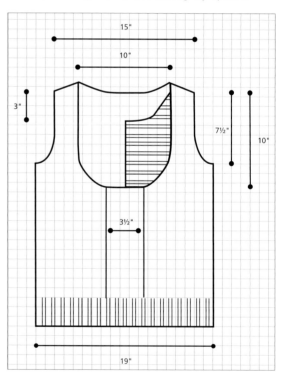

▲ This was my schematic for the "tuxedo"-front variation in the fourth photo. The pieces I inserted to make the ridged front were knitted separately and sewn in: I planned their lower edges to be the same shape as the neckline.

Sleeveless Garments

Armhole depth for garments without sleeves is crucial, and should be closer to the actual armhole depth of our own body. Vests are less tricky because they are often worn with other layers underneath, so armhole depth can conform to the body itself or be very deep. Sleeveless tops or dresses worn without layering need to be closer to the body measurement, especially if the armhole edging is narrow.

Each of us prefers our sleeveless garments to fit in a certain way—often related to the cross-shoulder width. Here are a few suggestions for pattern alterations:

1. For the most coverage, eliminate all or some of the armhole shaping, and plan to add a wide edging. If a large number of stitches are bound off at the under-arm, make the bind-offs more gradual.

2. For a cutaway effect at the armhole, halter-style, plan a narrower cross-shoulder width and decrease your stitches at an angle toward the neckline.

3. For vests or other garments to be worn over layers, make sure to add the necessary ease to the armhole depth to accommodate the bulk.

Practical Matters
Sleeveless Sweater
Suggestions

Here are some sleeveless designs of mine that have appeared in *Vogue Knitting*. Each had different concerns, based on shape, style, and fabric.

This heavy-gauge vest has a very deep armhole, almost like a dolman armhole, providing great ease of movement: it has a sporty, relaxed look for wearing over other clothing. To alter this silhouette for a closer fit, the armhole depth could be shortened by as much as 4–6" and indented to conform to the curve of the body. In this case, darts could easily be added to a plain vest like this to accommodate a large bust (see pages 99–103).

This close-fitting, dressy intarsia top has armholes very similar to the actual armhole depth of the body, along with narrow trim that does not add width.

This simply shaped pullover has no armhole shaping. The deep ribbing at the armhole acts as a kind of dropped shoulder sleeve, falling at the upper arm. This needs a deeper armhole than the close-fitting tank, because it has no shaping to correspond to the body.

The Shoulder–Armhole–Neckline Connection

Three elements in the upper body have a strong and crucial relationship: cross-shoulder measurement, armhole depth, and neckline width. When you plan a sweater, these should always be considered together.

Because an infinite number of combinations exist, depending on sleeve type, silhouette, and fabric weight, here I give some guidelines to help you focus on these elements in the crucial planning stage of a sweater. For top-down projects, determining these measurements is especially important, since the upper body is knitted first.

1. If any *one* of these three elements—cross shoulder, armhole depth, or neckline width—is too loose or too tight, the fit in the upper body will be off and the other elements strained. If *two* elements are not correct, the upper body will not fit well at all. So they must *all* be considered together.

2. When planning the upper body of a sweater with a cap-type sleeve, I almost always decide the width of the cross shoulder first, based on the body beneath. Why? It is the largest of the three elements, and has a direct relationship to the bust. Think about it: space is carved out of the lower body to accommodate the bust, thus creating a shape that must accommodate the cross shoulder.

After the cross shoulder, I move to the armhole depth. Be sure the armhole of your pattern is deeper than your own armhole, plus ease.

3. Sleeve width can come into play here, too. If you are widening or narrowing the upper sleeve, you may need to reshape the armhole to accommodate this change. Also, give attention to the sleeve cap itself. For a cap-sleeve sweater, the width of the cap adds to the cross shoulder measurement.

4. Once the cross shoulder and armhole depth seem right, with ease for fabric weight added, then the neckline can be settled. If you have any doubts, refer to an existing sweater neckline that fits you well.

5. For a raglan sweater, the measurement around your upper body must be met, with ease for fabric weight added: see the "Math Magic!" equation on page 72. The width of the cap plus the widths of the cross front and back pieces, all measured at mid cap depth (3–4" below the shoulder), must equal *you* in this same place. If you are large busted, you will want a steeper raglan line, so the cross front of the sweater is wider and the sleeve cap narrower (for other large-bust issues, see the discussion of darts on page 99).

All the pieces of a raglan need to narrow to form an appropriately wide neckline edge—not too tight!

Always plot the changes you are considering on your schematic: don't just think you will figure it out when you get there in the knitting. Plan ahead!

After you have accommodated the upper body width and plotted the pieces on a schematic, do not be alarmed if the neckline—formed from the tops of the front, back, and sleeves—seems large. A hint from my experience: necklines in raglans and circular yoke sweaters are best planned to be larger than you think they need to be. Create good fit in the armhole and cross-shoulder area, and allow for ease at the neckline. The easy solution for extra width: pick up a ribbing or trim along the edge to draw it in.

FIT TIP

Adding Stitches

In Chapter 5 I will explain more complex ways of shaping in pattern, but here are a few easy ways to add width that can work with simple garments:
- *Add a few plain Stockinette stitches or other basic textured stitches.*
- *Add a pattern repeat (divide by the gauge to see how much this will widen your piece).*
- *Take note of how these extra stitches will affect other parts of your sweater: Will stitches added below the armhole have to be bound off or decreased at the armhole to achieve the desired cross shoulder width? Will stitches added to a sleeve affect the cap shaping?*

Practical Matters
Sleeve / Armhole
Concerns

We need to acknowledge from the start that the armhole area is very complex. For good fit, the following elements must work together, so keep them in mind for the various types of sleeve-determined garments:

- The armhole depth of a sweater must be longer than the armhole depth measurement of the body to a comfortable degree. The heavier the fabric, the deeper the armhole should be.
- The cross-shoulder measurements, front and back, must combine with the widths of the very tops of the sleeves to fit the upper torso measurement with ease.

I have a pet peeve: in many patterns for close-fitting sweaters, the armhole is very tight. This reveals a misconception about ease and fit. Often these garments have an armhole depth that is equal to the armhole depth of the body itself, without any ease. A garment can be close- or even tight-fitting, and the armhole can still look sleek and body-conscious without clutching at the underarm. A sweater lasts longer and is more comfortable when there is ease in the armhole area! ■

MY SIDE-BY-SIDE SWEATERS
Long Dolman Cardi • Short Sleeveless Cardi

As a designer, I like to explore new ways of working a classic shape. I have many times explored dolman shapes that look like the schematics on page 75. For a change, I wanted to try a style that had parts that were worked in different directions. Here I designed two related sweaters, one sleeveless and one with an elbow-length sleeve.

The lower sections of both of these sweaters are knit side-to-side, instead of in the more common directions: from lower edge to neckline or "top down." The yoke sections are worked from the bottom of the yoke to the shoulder and include neckline shaping. Since the sleeves are knit-in extensions of the body, this can be considered a kind of dolman style.

What are the fit concerns for a sweater made in this way? A schematic drawing is useful to plan changes. Also have your body schematic handy for comparisons.

These sweaters were planned to have a slightly oversized fit. To avoid a completely boxy look, I added shoulder shaping and a gently shaped back neckline, ensuring a more subtle fit. If you knit straight to the neckline without shoulder shaping, the dolman-like cardigan would hang like a kimono: a much less complex design, but one that might appeal to you. (See the schematic on page 152.)

You can analyze the schematic of this type of sweater for ways to eliminate bulk or bring it closer to your own measurements.

Both Sweaters
Even though this dolman style has a more complex structure, considerations for fit are still the same. This style has more inherent ease than other, more body-conscious styles, so alterations tend to be not so complicated. We need to accommodate our basic body width measurements and consider the neckline. Since there is no sleeve cap, and no sleeve seam around the armhole, the neckline can be considered on its own. Here are a few suggestions.

For a closer fit:
• Choosing a smaller size might work, but

Project
Long Dolman Cardi
SEE PAGE 151

make the armhole a little deeper so the sleeve doesn't strain: this can be done by adding length to the yoke alone.

For a looser fit:

• Compare the measurements for a size up from the one you usually choose, allowing for more ease.

• For a large bust, adding depth in the armhole area, rather than widening the lower body below the sleeve, is one approach.

• Conversely, for larger hips, if the dolman offers enough bulk in the upper body you might widen this style only below the sleeve.

Also for a larger bust:

• Adjust the yoke depth *in the front only,* adding an inch or two; AND/OR:

• Make the front wider, but not the back.

Pick up the same number of yoke stitches along the fronts and work the yoke section the same as for the back.

To lengthen sweaters with horizontal panels of patterns:

• For longer allover length, add additional panels. OR:

• For deeper armholes and a slight increase in length, keep the lower panels the same but work the yoke 1–2" more before beginning the shoulder shaping and neckline.

If you have a large upper arm, you may want to deepen the armhole another 1–2".

Sleeveless Cardi

The boxy sleeveless cardigan has unshaped armholes, so they need to be deeper than for a sleeveless garment that has a shaped armhole. ▪

Project
Short
Sleeveless
Cardi

SEE PAGE 151

CHAPTER 5

All About Alterations

Depending on its silhouette, a project may require different kinds of alterations to suit your size and shape.

In this chapter we will look at choosing the correct size for a pattern and identifying areas to alter. I'll show you a way to commit the changes to paper, using your own body schematic to revise the pattern for your needs.

The Alteration Landscape: One Area at a Time

In addition to alterations for fit, you might want to make actual design changes to a sweater pattern: tweaking the silhouette for your own taste, not for sizing! I hope some of the material that follows inspires you to try new things when you are in that frame of mind.

Alteration is so much about developing an eye for what might be done, pondering what is possible—it's fun to be creative with the myriad ways to change a pattern. I'll show you how to look at pattern stitches and knitted fabric with an eye for alteration. And the projects in this chapter illustrate different ways of shaping, which you'll learn to apply yourself. Your choices can help you grow as a knitter and look at fabrics in a new way.

Step 1: Pattern Chosen!

At this point, let's say you have fallen in love with a pattern that has a range of sizes from which to choose. I have already mentioned that pattern sizing will not always be well suited for you, and that you may have to modify one size—or the look of a sweater—for your needs.

1. When choosing a size from a pattern, compare the measurements of the pattern with your own, considering ease, and then assess how to accommodate the pattern to your needs. This means generally choosing a size that accommodates your bust, with ease.

I feel it's easiest to choose a size that reflects good fit in your upper body, because that area includes shaping for armhole and neckline, too. When the bust—plus ease, of course—is correct, then you can make plans to alter other areas.

Some patterns indicate size by referring to the body's bust measurement. Some say merely "Small/Medium/Large," etcetera. Some refer to both the bust of the wearer and the bust of the garment. The most important thing is to consider your needs and your fabric when choosing a size.

Is your size missing? If the smallest size in the pattern is still too large for your petite figure, you should make alterations based on that smallest size. Likewise, if you are larger than the largest size in the pattern, use that size as a jumping-off point for adding necessary inches.

Once the size is chosen, it's time to look at the issues about how that size might fit you and to plan for alterations, if necessary.

Working Swatches

You should have, at this point, knitted a swatch—a fabric sample both for gauge purposes and to see the thickness and drape of the fabric, to consider the necessary ease. Working the actual pattern stitches will allow you to think about how you might increase or decrease in pattern. Also, if there are any vertical panels or horizontal areas of patterning, you can be aware of their qualities—and widths—to determine how they might change in alteration.

Keep Fit Concepts in Mind

After you choose your size, there is a logical progression to studying the aspects of fit. Keep in mind the concepts presented in the previous chapters, and be prepared with the following:

1. Have your measurement chart and completed body schematic: see Chapter 1, pages 20–28.

2. Keep in mind—maybe you've made a list!—the areas of fit that can be problematic for you.

3. If you are not using the yarn suggested in the pattern, will the weight/thickness of your new choice necessitate additional ease? For instance, if a sweater pattern were designed in a smooth alpaca that drapes over the body, what would need to change if you substituted a bulkier yarn with a hairy surface, which might form a fabric that stands away from the body?

Hard Copy!

Compare the measurements of your body with the pattern, to ensure that changes will be adequate.

1. Pencil in the schematic for your chosen size of the pattern over your body schematic.

2. If your choice of pattern does not have a schematic, or does not have one for your size, create one by reading the pattern carefully and draw it over your body schematic. Refer to the information in Chapter 1 about making a schematic (pages 26–28).

Analysis!

Looking at the garment schematic drawn around your body schematic, can you see where the lines that represent your body intersect the lines of the pattern? Are there areas they might be very close—or too loose and oversized? Mark any definite places where the pattern needs to be larger or smaller.

Even if the fit looks good in the body, what about the details? Are you happy with the neckline of the pattern? If you would like to change it, draw it in now. Are the lengths to your liking? For example, have you checked the lengths that determine the sleeve—both below the armhole and in any cap?

Making Changes

After you have committed the alteration lines to paper, and compared your body with the size and shape of the pattern schematic, you will be ready to:
1. Calculate new stitch counts.
2. Consider alterations to the pattern stitches and motifs to create better fit.

3. Rewrite the pattern to include new stitch counts and shaping elements.

Don't worry! The above steps may seem daunting at first, but with experience, the process will get easier. Even after one or two sweaters created in this deliberately planned manner, you will be learning what works best for you, and adding new skills to your repertoire. In time you will know what has to be done to alter any pattern to suit your measurements.

<table>
<tr><td>FIT LAB</td><td># FIT WITH PATTERNING IN MIND
Textured Ribbed Cardigan • Eyelet Ribbed Cardigan</td></tr>
</table>

How might you change the patterning of a knitted fabric—not just the shape or size—to alter the fit? Asking this question can inspire you to look at a sweater in a new way.

Some patterns are interchangeable: for example, one lace pattern often has the same flat texture and depth as another lace pattern. Ribbing seems to have more variations, with different degrees of elasticity. One ribbing cannot always substitute for another! Although often confined to the edges of a sweater, ribbing can be used as an allover fabric, as in these projects; in combination with other patterns (see the four sweaters on pages 60–65); or to shape areas of a garment, as with the peplum sweater on pages 55–56.

I wanted to see how differently a sweater could fit based only on the elasticity of the ribbing. So I was inspired to do something unprecedented in my years of designing: I made two different sweaters, both with approximately *the same number of stitches in the body sections*, each in a different ribbed pattern.

The first sweater, a pumpkin-colored zipped cardigan, is knitted in a very elastic ribbing, alternating narrow 4-stitch textured panels with 2 purl stitches. Made in a small size, the sweater will follow the lines of the body with a close-fitting silhouette: lying flat, it is much smaller than the body it will cover: a case of negative ease. The sleeves were shaped for a close fit as well, and the neckline is close along the back neck, with a narrow fit in the cross shoulder. I knitted with a soft, twisted wool and alpaca blend yarn without a lot of elasticity—the ribbing provided that.

For a totally different effect, I made the brown buttoned cardigan with an eyelet rib pattern: each eyelet panel is 5 stitches wide, alternating with 2 purl stitches. I used a soft, plied alpaca blend and the

Project
**Textured Ribbed
Cardigan**
SEE PAGE 154

fabric is drapey and refined, rather than clingy and body-conscious. You can see the contrasting silhouettes, despite the fact that the body pieces of the two sweaters differ by only 1 stitch and were knitted using the same size needle!

So what does this tell you about ribbed fabrics?

1. Ribbing can be used for a close fit, or a looser fit.

2. You might successfully exchange one type of ribbing for another in a pattern, to achieve different effects: swatch carefully and compare schematics.

3. Ribbing can be affected by yarn choice: experiment with needle sizes for your desired effect, to see how the fabric will conform—or not—to the body.

Since the bodies of these two sweaters have almost the same stitch counts, I can imagine making yet a third variation that features both ribbed fabrics, one with a fitted body and unfitted sleeves! ∎

The ribbing and cable in **(a)** at right were firm and elastic, qualities I observed in my swatch. In **(b)**, you can see the softer and fuller lace cable that complements the much less elastic eyelet ribbing.

B

A

Project
Eyelet Ribbed
Cardigan
SEE PAGE 154

Kinds of Alterations

As I've mentioned, scrutinizing the measurements offered by a pattern and its schematic is an important first step in your process. Since we come in all shapes, often not reflected in the "ideal" sizing of a pattern, we can expect to make alterations.

If you have drawn a sweater schematic over your own body schematic, you can see right away what alterations need to be made! For good fit, often more than one area of a pattern needs tweaking. And don't think you will be altering every sweater in the same way: if garment shapes are different, so are the methods of changing them to suit you.

I list the following areas as reminders: you will not necessarily need to address each one in every project. Every project you encounter will be a little different. Again, keep these elements in mind, along with your knowledge of your own body needs and measurements, as you read more about the specifics of garment shaping.

Torso

• Make sure sweater widths will allow enough ease in bust, waist, and hip. If not, extra width will need to be added to those areas.
• Accommodate differences in your body between front and back. Is your front width/length much larger than your back? If so, each piece should be considered separately, perhaps with darts added (see pages 99–103).

Armhole, Neckline, and Cross Shoulder

• Be sure, as I mentioned in Chapter 4, that your own cross shoulder is accommodated on both front and back pieces.
• Armhole depth should be deeper than your body's.
• If you are widening the sleeve, consider the corresponding cap and where they connect. Will shaping require you to widen or narrow the sleeve cap? (This can be done in the knitting stage.)
• If you want to change the neckline, does the width of the pattern's neckline provide a good basis for your changes? If not, draw in a new neckline width and adjust stitch counts for shoulder and neckline.

Sleeves

• Consider the tips I've given about sleeve length in chapters 3 and 4, and adjust your schematic to reflect any changes.
• Make sure the sleeve is large enough to accommodate your arm's circumference measurements.

Body Lengths

• Consider whether the total sweater length is flattering to you. If not, decide where it would be best to shorten or add length: from shoulder to waist, or from waist to lower edge?
• For an "empire" style, look at the length from shoulder to below the bust: If you are long- or short-waisted, will the line below the bust be in the right place?
• Where does your own bust point fall on the pattern schematic? If it intersects with pattern stitches in an odd way, will you want to adjust those patterns for a better look?
• Consider lengths when planning skirts, shorts, or pants. Also, you might need to plan the shaping from waist to hip, or hip to waist, depending on the direction of your knitting.

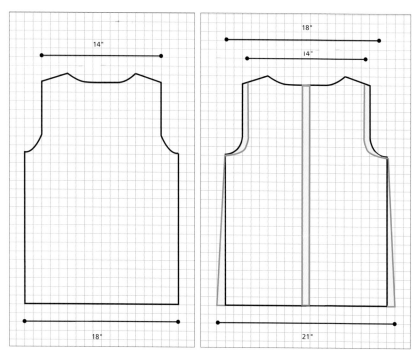

▲ I often "cut and paste" a schematic drawing on grid paper to make alterations: this is how a dressmaker works to alter a paper sewing pattern. To widen, I can cut my schematic along the midline, then spread it out over another piece of grid paper and tape it down to my desired width. This also works for adding length: I might choose to split the pattern at a point that relates to certain patterning, instead of just adding length to the bottom. I re-mark the widths and lengths on the new, altered drawing.

At left is my original schematic. At right, note how I altered this schematic by expanding the width at the center and at the armhole to add 2" across the shoulders. I then added width at the sides (gradually narrowed toward the bust) to accommodate wider hips. To make the shoulders wider than my center adjustment allowed, I also added a little width at the armhole.

DESIGNING WITH DARTS
Button-Back Sweater with Pockets
Button-Back Sweater with Darts

Project
**Button-Back
Sweater with
Pockets**
SEE PAGE 158

This button-back sweater was adapted for look and fit from a sweater I designed for *Vogue Knitting* Early Fall 2014.

I designed the original *Vogue Knitting* sweater with whimsy in mind: I considered the details of a curved lower edge, the decidedly different approach of putting the button opening in back, and the idea of using patch pockets in an unusual way. I wanted it to have an easy, comfortable fit, with a modified dropped shoulder and a shallow cap for the sleeve. How to juggle all these concerns easily? Of course, I sat down to plan it all in schematic form! I drew a basic boxy outline and then refined it with these changes in mind.

I wanted the sides of the curved lower edges of the sweater, including the garter stitch trim, to fall lower than the waistline. So I plotted the shape on graph paper first, as exactly as I could, by referring to the average neck-to-waist measurement. I also drew in the depth of the trim I hoped to add after the sweater pieces were complete.

I love working out designs on paper first— it is so reassuring! I wanted the pockets to be well positioned above the curved edges of the sweater, on either side of the center lace panel. My carefully drawn schematic also allowed me to plot the best placement for the pockets, and their unique shape. For whimsy's sake, I plotted the pockets a little high, giving them a cute feel.

Last, I used my schematic drawing to help me divide the back, which was to be the same width as the front, with no lace panel.

The second button-back sweater, the sunny yellow version shown on page 102, was adapted for look and fit from this same sweater. In this new version, I considered still other subtle (and not-so-subtle) alterations to adapt the sweater even more, creating a very different design from either of the other two.

Sometimes an area of a sweater requires more fabric due to your unique shape. For example:

1. Large-busted women need extra length—not necessarily width—in the front of a sweater.

You can adapt this instruction to your needs, adding or subtracting stitches for more or less dart width, or adding rows (working to fewer stitches each time) to create more depth. Always work your dart in a swatch first to see how it looks with your pattern stitch. This instruction is for a single dart.

RS row: Work to last 8 sts of row, yf, sl 1, yb, sl st back to LH needle, turn; work to last 8 sts of WS row.

On WS, yarn forward (if not there already) sl 1, yb, sl st back to LH needle and turn.

RS row: Work to last 16 sts of row, yf, sl 1, yb, sl st back to LH needle, turn; work to last 16 sts of WS row.

On WS, yarn forward (if not there already), sl 1, yb, sl st back to LH needle and turn.

RS row: Work to last 24 sts of row, yf, sl 1, yb, sl st back to LH needle, turn; work to last 24 sts of WS row.

On WS, yarn forward (if not there already), sl 1, yb, sl st back to LH needle and turn.

Work back over the entire row, working each wrapped st with the strand that surrounds it; turn and continue in pattern. ■

Placing buttons in the back is playful and leaves room for other design elements in the front.

2. Someone with a curved upper back might need to add extra rows in this area, both for good fit and so the length of the finished sweater is the same in front and back.

3. You might want to narrow a sweater that has straight lines, preferring to place a shaping element in the interior space rather than at the sides.

4. I can envision using extra fabric at elbows or knees, for what is known as an "articulated" look.

One way fabric can be added or eliminated, length added or subtracted, is with the dressmaker detail known as a *dart*. A horizontal dart is most often placed at the side of a sweater, next to the bust point: short rows are worked to insert a pie-shaped wedge. This gives more length to the area over the bust without lengthening the piece at the sides. Short rows added across the interior of a piece to add length, as in item #2 above, are another kind of dart.

Vertical darts—taking wedges out by decreasing and then increasing—can narrow an area in the interior of a piece, rather than at the sides.

Sweater with Darts

This second new button-back sweater was even further altered from the *Vogue Knitting* original. In the new version, I made three significant changes for both fit and visual effect. By pondering the details and making small changes in a pattern as I did here, *you* can transform a sweater into something that fits and flatters you in a better way.

First, I decided to add darts adjacent to the bust points. I was pleasantly surprised that the darts integrated into the knit/purl patterning without much disruption of the texture—they are almost invisible. I worked a 24-stitch dart (about 4½" wide) over 6 rows.

Second, to elongate the silhouette without changing the sweater otherwise, I removed the pockets. The lines of the front panel give this slightly oversized sweater a longer, leaner look than the original.

Last, I shortened the three-quarter sleeve to a flattering elbow length that works for all figure types. ■

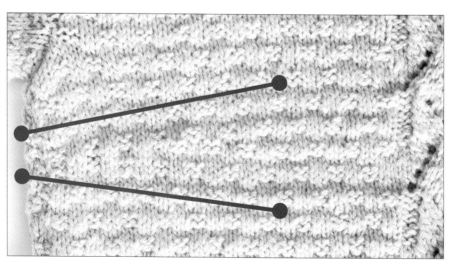

◀ This detail of the dart worked in the sweater on page 102 shows how a dart can be added even in a detailed, textured fabric without being unsightly. Work a swatch when planning your dart to see how it will affect the appearance of your knitted fabric.

Project
Button-Back
Sweater with Darts
SEE PAGE 158

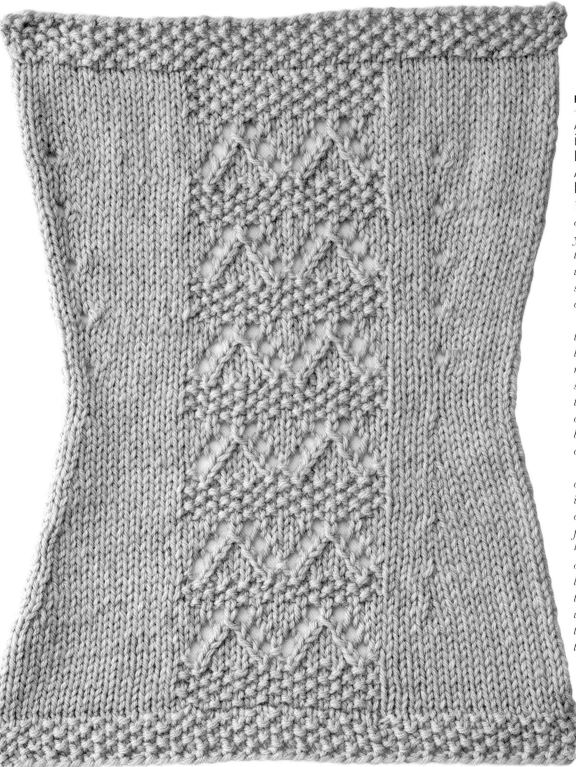

FIT TIP

Adding Length in Front for a Large Bust—an Alternative to Darts

When working darts to accommodate a large bust, you are adding length to the front of your sweater while keeping the front side seams the same length as the back side seams.

While browsing stores to examine sweaters in larger sizes, I noticed that many had a front length slightly longer (1–2") than the back. This was a way of accommodating a larger bust without working darts!

If you don't want to work darts in a garment worked in pieces, you can work an extra ¹/₂" length at each front side and also add ¹/₂" to the armhole depth on the front. This extra length, distributed over the two areas, can be eased in when seaming front to back and sewing in the sleeves.

▲ Choice of shaping methods is important not only for function but for visual effect. In this swatch, side shaping is juxtaposed with a vertical dart worked in the interior fabric. At the left side, the decreases (bottom half) and decorative eyelet increases (top half) are worked a few stitches in from the edge, for easy seaming. The vertical dart on the right side of the swatch, also formed by decreases and eyelet increases, mirrors the shape of the left side but is more decorative.

103

Knitting from the Top and/or in the Round

If you are a knitter who enjoys top-down projects, or working in the round, all of the information in this section—and throughout the book—applies to you, too.

If you make garments that have a seamless construction, you still need to consider all the elements of fit as they apply to your measurements and concerns. Examine all aspects of your pattern. *Even though you are not working your garment in pieces, still consider it as if you were.* Why? Because the potential for good fit resides in analyzing individual sections. If you are knitting from the top, adjustments for the neckline cannot be put off, since you will be working on that area right out of the gate! And since skirts and pants are best knitted from the top, and in the round, their measurements should be considered carefully too.

Read your pattern from beginning to end and see if you can discern how many stitches correspond to each section. Can you isolate the number of stitches allocated for the sleeves, front(s), and back? Based on these numbers, you can construct a schematic.

Front and back are the same width in most symmetrically designed patterns, and that can help you define the width of the garment below the armhole. If you need to adjust the stitch counts for a different proportion from front to back, you will need to make those changes before you begin to knit, in any case.

One advantage of knitting from the top is that you are often able to try on pieces as you go. Make this a test of your ability to plan ahead for good fit, not a chance to rip out more easily!

FIT LAB

PANELED PATTERNING
Leaf-Embossed Skirt

Because this skirt is worked in panels, from the waist down, there are a few ways it could be altered for fit, as well as for yarn and silhouette issues. Consider it an exercise in deciding how to alter a pattern, and moving further toward the mindset of examining projects with fit as a priority.

Here are my thoughts: maybe they will inspire further insights in you as well!

1. For a different silhouette, with greater volume than your size requires, try adding a unit. The waistband, worked last after the skirt is complete, could be knitted in a smaller size to draw in the volume.

2. To lengthen the skirt, extra rows could be worked after the fullest part of the hip.

3. To widen the waist but retain the width of the hips and lower edge, you can add stitches to each unit at the outset (the waist) and then all shaping worked to reach the fullest part of the hip, the point indicated in the pattern.

4. To widen the waist to hip width, the full number of stitches called for at the hip could be cast on at the waist, making a straight shape to the hip, with no waist-to-hip increases.

5. To flare the lower edge even more, for a wider silhouette, work one or more extra increases in the purl sections.

When you think this way, even about a garment you don't plan to make, you start to see how individual elements and whole sweaters might be altered. ▪

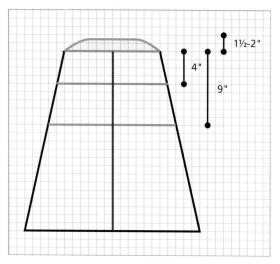

▲ A well-fitting skirt needs to accommodate the waist, the high hip, and the full hip measurements, with ease added for fabric weight and desired silhouette. If your body measurements are different front to back, the back can be made both wider and longer from waist to hip by short rowing. Pants also need to accommodate the waist, the high hip, and the full hip, as well as crotch depth, with ease added for fabric weight and silhouette.

Project
Leaf-Embossed
Skirt

SEE PAGE 162

PANTS IN PROPORTION
Rib & Twist Shorts

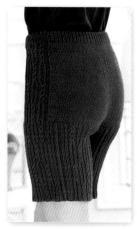

I allowed for plenty of give in the back area.

These pants were designed to coordinate with a trenchcoat-inspired belted cardigan that appeared in *Vogue Knitting* Early Fall 2012.

I have aspirations to make myself the softest, most comfortable pair of stretchy knitted pants (or, in this case, shorts). How will I do it?

1. Choose a very soft yet strong yarn, and swatch to get a stretchy but not stiff gauge. No baggy knees for me!

2. Find my most comfortable pair of yoga pants—slightly loose—and make a schematic, as I did for my store-bought sweater on page 37.

3. Compare my crotch depth measurements, and decide if I want the pants to be deeper in the back and/or front. Adjust my schematic drawing.

4. Consider ease to accommodate my fabric—which I plan to be thicker and cozier than the machine-knit cotton blend of my template pants.

5. Figure out the numbers, based on lengths and widths, taking into account issues of ease.

6. Knit the pants in the round, incorporating a soft, elastic waistband (see page 108).

7. Wear around the house forever in bliss.

Someday, in my busy life, I will find time for this. If you, too, lack the time to make pants in the method I described, then you might want to knit them from a pattern. What can you do to assure they will fit?

Pants or shorts are much like skirts, in that you need to consider waist, high hip, and full hip measurements. You'll also need the front crotch depth and back crotch depth (taken from your measurement chart on pages 20–21).

Depending on the style, including the length and width, upper thigh and other leg circumferences may prove essential, along with the inseam.

Pants are best knitted in the round in one piece, but it is easier to look at the front and back as pieces for planning and alterations. They need to fit width-wise as well as depth-wise. And since our fronts and backs are not shaped the same, we need to consider whether the back of our pants needs to be not only wider but also deeper than the front.

Since I designed the shorts shown here with a waif-like model in mind, I planned the front and back to be roughly the same width. They were knitted in the round, but patterning at the sides divides front from back. It would be easy to add an inch or two in the Stockinette stitch area at the back of the shorts, and to add a few more short rows at the top of the back to make the back crotch depth slightly deeper.

The slightly ribbed patterning at the sides is an easy way to get a close fit without actually shaping the sides of the shorts.

The schematic at left shows one-half of a pair of pants (upper section, not legs) in a side view, and is a good way to depict your own version: you can see the front and back at the same time. Note how the back is higher than the front.

Here are some hints:

• If you want to make close-fitting pants, the legs must be shaped to accommodate the various widths from thigh to ankle.

• Boot-cut pants fit closely down to the knee and then flare slightly: 2–4", or much wider for vintage-inspired bell-bottoms. Real sailor pants, which resemble bell-bottoms, are the same width from crotch to lower edge.

• With knitted pants, expect some stretching—make the inseam an inch or so less than your desired length. Use yarns that have body and hold; avoid fibers that tend to droop or sag. ■

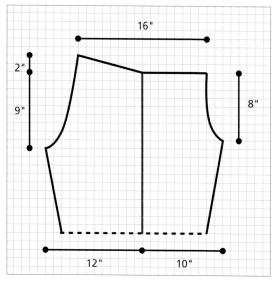

◀ This schematic represents half of the upper part of pants or shorts for someone who is larger in back than in front. The width of one side of the back is 2" wider than for the front, and the depth of the crotch is 3" more in back than at front.

Project
Rib & Twist
Shorts
SEE PAGE 164

Changing Size with Panels

Just as I chose to work an entire skirt based on a single panel (page 105), repeated around to make my desired circumference, a single panel can also be used in isolation, as with the side seam insert I created for my raglan sweater, seen on page 76.

I began this panel with a lace pattern that I love from Barbara Walker's *Charted Knitting Patterns*. The diamond motif was originally set into Stockinette stitch, but I worked the lower edge as a triangle and then worked a long, narrow piece above it, narrowing to my desired width. Of course, I plotted the shape in schematic form first! This panel can be adjusted to fit any sweater length if you plan.

▲ A panel like this is a pretty detail that's also functional, if you insert it for better fit.

Practical Matters
Skirts and
Waistbands

The best way to knit a skirt is from the top down. That way you can be sure it fits in the most crucial place: from waist to hip; or from high hip to full hip, if you prefer to wear your skirts lower than the waist.

A waistband corresponds to the measurement of the waist—or stretches to fit the waist—not the fabric directly below it, which should have a bit of ease even in a close-fitting skirt. Since the waistband often contrasts with the skirt fabric, it is a decision I almost always save for last.

Since knitted fabrics, even strong, stretchy ribbings, are not usually elastic enough to hold the weight of a skirt securely, a waistband must either fit very closely or include a facing or casing that holds a piece of commercially made elastic. My favorite width of elastic is ¾", but you could use narrower (½") for a small, lightweight skirt, or 1" or wider for a heavier skirt.

I pick up my waistband stitches along the cast-on edge of the skirt (assuming the skirt is knitted from the top down).

When using a ¾" elastic, I always knit a 2" waistband: this allows the band to fold over at the halfway point and be large enough for the elastic to pass through.

If the yarn is very springy and stretchy, I very loosely bind off when I finish knitting the waistband; then I sew this bound-off edge to the ridge formed by the picked-up stitches.

If the yarn is less elastic, rather than bind off, I sew the band down to the inside stitch by stitch.

With thick yarns, as in the green leaf motif skirt on pages 104–105, I like to make a smooth Stockinette waistband. With thin, less elastic yarns, I work a knit 1, purl 1 ribbed band, with many more stitches than in the skirt below—20% more is good. Since I am a stickler for detail—and good fit!—I often do a small swatch in the ribbed pattern to get a gauge for my waistband before I pick up the stitches. ■

Fabric Fun: Changes in Pattern Stitches

Making changes to a sweater pattern will alter the knitted fabric. Sometimes, with easy-to-knit pattern stitches, it is simple to add increases or decreases and no initial preparation is necessary. In other situations, where a pattern is unique and more complicated, you may want to work a swatch to plan how the fabric can be altered for a successful visual result.

We've seen how we can change our schematic to reflect changes that make pieces larger or smaller. That can also be done within the patterning itself, keeping the integrity and contributing to the beauty of the fabric.

This kind of "fabric fun" can give alterations a more "knitterly" foundation and make the process more interesting than just adding or subtracting stitches. As a designer, I like to have an eye open to what a pattern stitch can tell me about how a garment can be shaped. Since making alterations is really about "re-designing"—and being a planner par excellence!—you should always consider fabric an inspiration for whatever you have to do to make a sweater fit better. Even if there is no special way to alter a pattern stitch, this kind of analysis is fun and leads to a new kind of thinking about garments and their shapes.

Here's a useful comparison: a dressmaker/tailor/seamstress makes changes to a garment by pinning on the body to fit, and then re-sewing to make the changes revealed by the fitting. But since as knitters we create pieces to a predetermined shape when following a pattern, we must think about how to alter the fabric before we start a project!

We are faced with a huge array of knitting pattern stitches. So it helps to have a process in mind for different types, to see how they might be shaped for the best look. I am a stickler for detail, and attention to the details in knitted fabric makes all the difference in the beauty of a garment. By working swatches, I can envision shaping elements before I write the pattern for a sweater, and see how any changes will affect the look of the fabric.

Look at my swatches in this section as examples of shaping options for different pattern stitches. When you're planning, think about the best way to enlarge your sweater, or diminish its size, within the confines of the pattern stitch or the arrangement of pattern stitches. This might not always work, but when it does, it is both fun to do and helpful for fit.

Some patterns are easy to alter: simple knit/purl arrangements. Others, such as cables, can have complex crosses that can't easily be altered. Also, you might find patterns that require a certain multiple of stitches for a repeat, like some allover lace patterns, harder to alter.

Add Width the Simple Way

Sometimes, if you need just a little extra width, you can add a few stitches worked gradually over a few rows. For example, perhaps you want to widen the lower edge of a sweater, and narrow toward the bust. You can:

• Add stitches in the same pattern.

• Add stitches in a new, coordinating pattern of your choice.

• Add a panel within the sweater or at the sides. This panel can be shaped, like the side-seam insert shown on page 108 or the cable at the back of the coat on page 117.

Narrow to Eliminate Width

Likewise, to narrow areas in a simple way, you can decrease in pattern by simply working fewer stitches in the pattern itself. When adding increases or decreases at the sides of a piece, work them within your edge stitches, to make seaming easier. ■

FIT TIP

When a Finished Sweater Doesn't Fit

I devoted a section of my book Finishing School *to how to make adjustments in the finishing stage to a sweater that does not fit. So here I will say only that the most important thing when beginning an alteration on an ill-fitting sweater is to be absolutely sure what size you want it to measure! There is no point in making even more errors.*

Take time to alter your original schematic, or make a new one, to reflect the revised, corrected measurements. Additions such as panels or gussets at the underarm can add ease and even contribute to the design if well considered. See Chapter 6 of Finishing School *for more detailed instructions.*

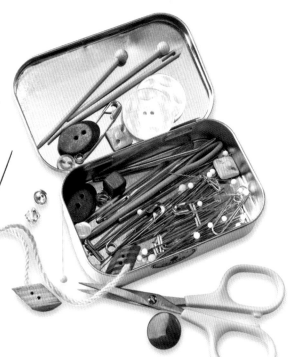

Shaping in Easy and Complex Patterns

Planning ahead is important if you want to alter a garment with complicated pattern stitches. If you intend to work increases and decreases to change the shape, don't wait until you encounter the pattern in progress.

I love to work out problematic issues in swatch form first. Then the actual knitting can proceed easily—all the problems have been solved!

Here are some general guidelines for different kinds of pattern stitches.

Knit/Purl Patterns

These simple textured patterns are generally easy to work, with no complicated knitting techniques. Still, it is easier to increase or decrease when you employ a few plain Stockinette stitches at the edges of your pieces, or a panel of one or two plain Stockinette stitches between rounds if you are working circularly. The edge stitches form a boundary for the adjacent knit/purl pattern.

Increases or decreases can be worked right next to these stitches: the effect is clean and the shaping is outlined in the garment—a design detail. (See my swatch at right.)

Note, however, that while adding or subtracting stitches at the sides of pieces can be an easy solution, if it's a large number of stitches, this can affect how the knitted garment will fall. It is often better to spread the increases or decreases out over an area of fabric, if possible.

Ribbed Knit/Purl Patterns

Knit ribs that have purl stitches between them can be shaped in a couple of ways. For the most invisible look, place increases or decreases within the purl ribs.

You can also shape at the sides of pieces, using edge stitches as described above.

Cabled and Twisted Patterns

In an allover fabric that includes cable crosses or twists, it is best to work as much of a pattern repeat as possible as you change its size in order for the pattern to retain an unbroken appearance. For example, instead of crossing 3 stitches over 3 stitches, after decreasing you can cross even just 1 stitch over 3 stitches. Likewise, when increasing, you can add stitches in other areas, as in the purl sections that divide cable panels.

Shaping elements can also be worked within an individual cable, to widen or narrow it, as I did in the purple swatch on page 112, which was my test for the cable on the back of the coat on page 117. I have used this technique many times with great success.

To widen a cable, simply increase in one or more of the cable "strands" a row or two before the cross row. The shaping elements will be invisible, hidden by the depth of the subsequent cable cross.

Enlarging or Reducing Pattern Elements

This technique is very effective when working with a pattern stitch that has individual elements.

With a panel element, like the lace panel repeated around the skirt on page 115, increases or decreases can be used to widen or narrow, while keeping the basic pattern stitch intact. Working the skirt from the top down, I increased a stitch on certain rows in each lace panel to widen them slightly until the lower edge was much wider overall. You could do this to change the width of a sweater, as well. Add the shaping in each panel, or in only a few.

Often shaping within a panel applies to regularly repeating chevron patterns, or undulating "Old Shale"–type lace motifs. At the desired point in the row repeats, increase or decrease evenly in each unit—or in just a few—to widen or diminish the fabric. Keep in pattern with the new number of stitches. This may sound complicated—but just try a swatch of my skirt pattern and you'll see how easy it is!

When you have a block pattern that's like a checkerboard, you can increase or decrease within each unit, as I did in the green swatch on page 112.

Lace Patterns

Even the most expert lace knitters find shaping in lace challenging. Knitted lace encompasses a huge family of patterns, and it is hard to address every possibility. Swatching is helpful, as always, to familiarize yourself with the elements of a specific lace and better understand its structure before you begin your larger project.

Here are a few simple guidelines and approaches that might help when shaping in lace patterns.
1. If you are trying to stay in pattern as you increase or decrease, remember that for *most* lace patterns, to keep the stitch count correct, you need to have a *pair of elements*: a yarn over element paired with a compensating single decrease formed of two stitches (either k2tog or ssk). Or, alternately, two yarn overs can be paired with a double decrease, such as [sl 1, k2tog, psso]. So, if you eliminate *one* stitch, you must

These swatches, in the process of being seamed, depict decreasing in knit/purl fabrics. Both are edged where they meet with 2 Stockinette stitches. At right, shaping in the knit/purl chevron pattern is done by knitting together the last stitch of the pattern with the first edge stitch: this creates a smooth, easy-to-seam edge. The shaping for the ribbing at left is worked away from the edge, for more graceful patterning. The two pieces are decreased at different rates, something you might do when you need a front and back that are shaped differently.

I worked this swatch to figure out how to widen and flare the cable that I wanted to insert in the back of the coat on page 117. I started the swatch at the narrow end and then, after an interval, increased each strand by one stitch to widen it. I repeated the strand increases one more time.

When you have a distinct, stand-alone motif or pattern element, you can often change its size to shape your fabric. I worked the blocks of this checkerboard-type pattern in two full-size bands at the lower edge of this swatch. Then, to shape the swatch, as I might shape a garment, I decreased 1 stitch in each pattern block over the next two bands.

work that single "lone" stitch by itself until another stitch is decreased in order to resume the yarn over–and–decrease combination. Do not pair a yarn over with a single stitch (instead of a decrease), or a new stitch will be added!

2. If you are concerned about the look of your lace as the piece is shaped, why not isolate it and work your shaping elements in a simpler pattern at the sides? You can use simple Stockinette stitch, reverse Stockinette, or some other easy-to-work texture pattern. This kind of contrast flanking a central lace area can visually enhance it—a positive thing!

3. A lace "motif" can sometimes be reduced or enlarged by eliminating or adding stitches, while maintaining the pattern's rhythm. The lace pattern on page 79 and the swatch at left are examples of "stacking" lace motifs of diminishing sizes on top of each other to narrow the yoke.

Shaping in Colorwork

There are so many approaches to colorwork, from stranded Fair Isle to slipped stitch patterns. Since slipped stitch patterns tend to have dense row gauges, it is difficult to pair them with other patterns. However, decreases or increases are less problematic, since, unlike lace, a slipped stitch pattern is easy to maintain despite being manipulated.

Decreasing in stranded colorwork is often an opportunity to do something interesting, like working the new stitches into a new pattern, or adding a section of a contrasting pattern that can absorb the shaping, as with the side panels I inserted in my coat on page 117.

To add stitches within patterning, not at the sides of a piece, try adding space between motifs.

Colorwork motifs can be reduced in size while keeping their basic shapes, as with the snowflakes on the Icelandic pullover shown on page 80. It is fun to play around on grid paper with a pattern like this and see how you can reduce or enlarge it.

Imagine this swatch as a miniature version of a sweater yet to be made. By working lace patterns of varying sizes and arrangements, a garment could be shaped to flare or to conform to the body. Increases or decreases can be worked as patterns change to accommodate the width of pattern repeats.

To widen this colorwork swatch, I increased between the angular snowflakes.
To fill the space in a decorative way, I filled in with small motifs.

SHAPING IN PATTERN STITCHES
"Marbelized Paper" Skirt

Project
"Marbelized
Paper" Skirt
SEE PAGE 165

As long as you plan well for good fit in the waist and hip areas, there are endless ways to add detail to a skirt. By making a schematic, you will actually be making a template for a pattern you can use for many skirts to come.

Inspired by the wonderful knits of the Italian Missoni family, I wanted to make a gently flared skirt, knitted from the top down. I had seen many evenly striped chevron patterns used for skirts, but that seemed too predictable to me. In some cases they looked like afghans! I wanted a skirt with some subtlety.

Looking for something a little more off-kilter, I experimented with a wavy lace panel. In my swatches, I found that if I used stripes of different widths, they would have a less regular, more uneven appearance. Also, if I gradually increased the width of the lace panel toward the bottom to flare the skirt, the stripes would wave in an almost unpredictable way, lending a painterly look to the fabric.

After I was done, a friend told me it looked like marbleized paper: I could not have been more pleased!

Beginning with a narrow lace panel of 9 stitches, I also charted the pattern in 3 gradually wider variations: panels of 10, 11, and 12 stitches. Each successive variation was also longer, row-wise. By using these panels in multiple repeats, in succession from narrow to wide, I was able to widen the skirt gradually from waist to hip, and then a little more to flare the lower edge, all the time working stripes of different colors.

Of course, I had to check the measurement and gauge for each panel to plan the measurements of the areas of the skirt that had to fit: waist, high hip, and full hip. The widest lace panel allowed for the skirt to flare to a gentle A-line shape.

To plan for good fit in a skirt like this, compare your measurements with the schematic for your size. If your hips are larger than the pattern, transition to a wider lace panel sooner, or choose a larger size and make the final waistband smaller. Since this fabric is thin, the jump in size would not create a lot of extra bulk.

For a fuller version, simply work a larger size, and then work the waistband last for your smaller size. ◼

115

Shaping by Design

When does alteration transcend the ever-important need for good fit and become a design tool? Ponder that question within your own knitting world.

As a designer, my process evolves from knitting a satisfying swatch, which leads me to a sketch to solidify my ideas. Then I move on to the final stage of capturing the measurements of my project in schematic grid form. Sometimes when my schematic seems "etched in stone" and I am sure I'm ready to start the knitting process, I will look at my swatch again, or ponder my schematic one more time . . .

I believe in taking a little time between the planning stage of a project and the actual knitting—letting the pot boil for a while often makes for a more flavorful stew. And the same is true of unconscious thought: give your idea a chance to brew, and sometimes a better one—or a supportive detail!—emerges. We knitters can be so excited to start a new project that we fail to create an empty space of contemplation first and linger there. I love to knit, and I want to get started as soon as possible (especially if I have a deadline!)—but pausing before jumping in has made me a more thoughtful and effective knitter and designer.

PAST AND PRESENT
Recipe for a Coat of Many Colors

I knew I wanted to design a coat—something that would be slightly oversized and would use a yarn and color range that I love. I started with a vague notion and ended in a new place, all due to altering my plans as I went along.

An aside: I love coats. I love knitted coats, woven coats, and raincoats. One of my favorites is a vintage velvety-black corduroy coat from the 1950s whose tag reveals that it came from Paris. Another, from the 1960s, is edged in leather and has a pleat at the back that disappears when the coat is not in movement! One of my favorite books is *Coats! Max Mara, 55 Years of Italian Fashion*, an inspirational volume of some of the greatest iconic overcoats of the twentieth century. I adore coats from all periods—I am always looking for new shapes and details.

A coat is a functional garment but can also be whimsical. Coats have weight, which makes a visual impression. And though they serve a very utilitarian purpose, they can be detailed in so many ways.

For This Book . . .

I wanted a coat made from a knitted fabric with a "woven" look. I chose a color scheme as part of my yarn selection, lingering first in beautiful, natural "sheepy" shades, but finally settling on a palette that merged denim-y tones with brights. I made swatches of several plaid or checked patterns, and

◀ I thought it would be fun to add an "overvest" for extra warmth and further contrast in patterning.

Project
Houndstooth Coat
and Overvest
SEE PAGE 168

▲ I used a smaller version of a houndstooth pattern to form the shaped "wedge" at each side, and for the overvest.

▶ I used my long, 32" original swatch to make the hood for the overvest!

tried a slipped stitch pattern—none pleased me. Then I recalled a large houndstooth pattern I'd seen, and when I tried it, I enjoyed the play of colors so much that I knitted a 32"-long swatch—my biggest ever!

A schematic was essential, not only for capturing the shape on paper, but to envision the color placement. Since I wanted to work the colors in an asymmetrical way, planning on paper would be useful.

At first I planned on a boxy-looking coat, with the flavor of those designed by Bonnie Cashin in the 1960s. Her coats were boldly patterned and often had big pockets and other large details. But then I started playing with shape on my schematic and wondered what it would be like to insert a triangle shape into each side, to give it flare! Soon I had knitted a second swatch, in a smaller-scale version of my large houndstooth pattern. Why not highlight my shaping? The knitted wedges at the sides in a smaller, contrasting pattern altered the shape of my coat to a more dramatic one. The bust measurement did not change—only the silhouette of the lower body.

Since I didn't want to sew the wedge into side seams, I decided to do something new to me: make a garment in two halves, to be joined by a panel at the back. A bold cable sewn in at the center back—and shaped to flare the coat further—was a nod to the fact that this was not a woven fabric coat, but a knitted *sweater*, a bit of whimsy that pleased me.

I hated to not use my large swatch—I thought of making it a scarf, but instead it formed the hood for the overvest, which was somewhat inspired by the notion of a deerstalker's cape. The vest was shaped to show you that anything worn *over* something else, especially something thick, has to be much larger and share the same silhouette. You can see in the measurements how much larger the vest is than the coat.

In keeping with the theme of the coat's details, I added some little cables at the side of the vest. Consider using additions like these in your own sweaters, to add shaping as well as detail. The vest, by the way, can also be worn separately—it has an oversized silhouette without the coat underneath to support it.

Alterations to my schematic, and using a smaller variation of my houndstooth pattern, helped me transform a nice, unshaped coat into one with a dramatic silhouette and interesting side detail.

In my work, alteration is often a way into a design, a process that can take me from the acceptable (yet mundane!) into a new area to explore. Often by making an alteration to what I thought was a firm idea, I find a way to tweak the design on paper—or in the knitted fabric—that makes it extra-special. ■

FIT LIST   TOP-TEN CHECKLIST

I have distilled the information in this book to reveal my "Top-Ten Checklist" of must-do elements. Keep these areas in mind as you begin to explore the issues of better fit.

If your personal goal is to make good fit a part of your knitting life, start a self-directed course of study now with this essential list as your condensed guide!

1. Develop a garment-maker's mindset.

2. Know your own measurements and always refer to them before considering new projects.

3. Be familiar with sweaters that fit you well: their measurements and shapes.

4. Learn to make and rely on schematic drawings of sweaters, using them for current and future reference.

5. Consider carefully the important issues of ease, silhouette, and fabric before any project.

6. Rely on your swatch, not only to obtain the crucial correct gauge but to understand your fabric's weight and drape as well.

7. Examine the characteristics of your knitted fabric in the planning stages to plan creative alterations.

8. Explore various garment types and their characteristics.

9. Try new and unfamiliar sweater shapes to expand your knowledge of fit.

10. Develop the patience to make alterations to a pattern before you begin to knit.

IDEAS

Knit Tips & Projects

Take time to save time. Always check your gauge!

KNITTING NEEDLES

U.S.	METRIC
0	2MM
1	2.25MM
2	2.75MM
3	3.25MM
4	3.5MM
5	3.75MM
6	4MM
7	4.5MM
8	5MM
9	5.5MM
10	6MM
10 ½	6.5MM
11	8MM
13	9MM
15	10MM
17	12.75MM
19	15MM
35	19MM

GAUGE

Make a test swatch at least 4"/10cm square. If the number of stitches and rows does not correspond to the gauge given, you must change the needle size. An easy rule to follow is: To get fewer stitches to the inch/cm, use a larger needle; to get more stitches to the inch/cm, use a smaller needle. Continue to try different needle sizes until you get the same number of stitches in the gauge.

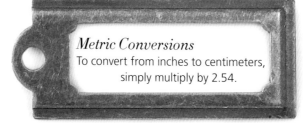

Metric Conversions
To convert from inches to centimeters, simply multiply by 2.54.

Abbreviations

approx	approximately
beg	begin(ning)
CC	contrasting color
ch	chain
cm	centimeter(s)
cn	cable needle
cont	continu(e)(ing)
dec	decreas(e)(ing)
dpn(s)	double-pointed needle(s)
foll	follow(s)(ing)
g	gram(s)
inc	increas(e)(ing)
k	knit
kfb	knit into the front and back of a stitch—one stitch has been increased
k2tog	knit 2 stitches together—one stitch has been decreased
LH	left-hand
lp(s)	loop(s)
m	meter(s)
mm	millimeter(s)
MC	main color
M1 or M1L	make one or make one left (see glossary)
M1 p-st	make one purl stitch (see glossary)
M1R	make one right (see glossary)

oz	ounce(s)
p	purl
pfb	purl into front and back of a stitch—one stitch has been increased
pat(s)	pattern(s)
pm	place marker
psso over	pass slip stitch(es)
p2tog	purl two stitches together—one stitch has been decreased
rem	remain(s)(ing)
rep	repeat
RH	right-hand
RS	right side(s)
rnd(s)	round(s)
SKP	slip 1, knit 1, pass slip stitch over—one stitch has been decreased
SK2P	slip 1, knit 2 together, pass slip stitch over the k2tog—two stitches decreased
S2KP	slip 2 stitches together, knit 1, pass 2 slip stitches over knit 1
sc	single crochet
sl	slip

sl st	slip stitch
spp	slip, purl, pass sl st over
ssk (ssp)	slip 2 sts knitwise one at a time, insert LH needle through fronts of sts and knit (purl) together
sssk	slip 3 sts one at a time knitwise, insert LH needle through fronts of sts and knit together
st(s)	stitch(es)
St st	stockinette stitch
tbl	through back loop(s)
tog	together
WS	wrong side(s)
wyib	with yarn in back
wyif	with yarn in front
yd(s)	yd(s)
yo	yarn over needle
*****	repeat directions following * as indicated
[ ]	repeat directions inside brackets as indicated

Glossary

bind off Used to finish an edge or segment. Lift the first stitch over the second, the second over the third, etc. (U.K.: cast off)

bind off in rib or pat Work in rib or pat as you bind off. (Knit the knit stitches, purl the purl stitches.)

cast on Place a foundation row of stitches upon the needle in order to begin knitting.

decrease Reduce the stitches in a row (for example, knit two together).

increase Add stitches in a row (for example, knit in front and back of stitch).

knitwise Insert the needle into the stitch as if you were going to knit it.

make one or make one left Insert left-hand needle from front to back under the strand between last st worked and next st on left-hand needle. Knit into the back loop to twist the stitch.

make one p-st Insert needle from front to back under the strand between the last stitch worked and the next stitch on the left-hand needle. Purl into the back loop to twist the stitch.

make one right Insert left-hand needle from back to front under the strand between the last stitch worked and the next stitch on left-hand needle. Knit into the front loop to twist the stitch.

no stitch On some charts, "no stitch" is indicated with shaded spaces where stitches have been decreased or not yet made. In such cases, work the stitches of the chart, skipping over the "no stitch" spaces.

place marker Place or attach a loop of contrast yarn or purchased stitch marker as indicated.

pick up and knit (purl) Knit (or purl) into the loops along an edge.

purlwise Insert the needle into the stitch as if you were going to purl it.

selvage stitch Edge stitch that helps make seaming easier.

slip, slip, knit Slip next two stitches knitwise, one at a time, to right-hand needle. Insert tip of left-hand needle into fronts of these stitches, from left to right. Knit them together. One stitch has been decreased.

slip, slip, slip, knit Slip next three stitches knitwise, one at a time, to right-hand needle. Insert tip of left-hand needle into fronts of these stitches, from left to right. Knit them together. Two stitches have been decreased.

slip stitch An unworked stitch made by passing a stitch from the left-hand to the right-hand needle as if to purl.

work even Continue in pattern without increasing or decreasing. (U.K.: work straight)

yarn over Make a new stitch by wrapping the yarn over the right-hand needle. (U.K.: yfwd, yon, yrn)

121

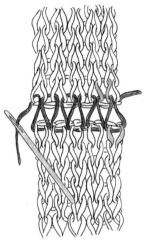

Seaming Tips

I always seam with the right side of the fabric facing so I can see how the seam looks as I sew it. Here the shoulder seam is partially sewn. This method allows me to match the ribs where they meet at the shoulder. I prefer a firm shoulder seam over a loose grafted one.

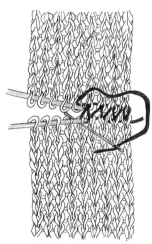

Grafting

Grafting is easiest if done directly off the knitting needles. I prefer to first weave in the ends of the fabric pieces to the back to make the pieces very neat. Then I use a new strand to graft the pieces together.

Standard Yarn Weight System

CATAGORIES OF YARN, GAUGE RANGES, AND RECOMMENDED NEEDLE AND HOOK SIZES

Yarn Weight Symbol & Category	0 Lace	1 Super Fine	2 Fine	3 Light	4 Medium	5 Bulky	6 Super Bulky	7 Jumbo
Type of Yarns in Category	Fingering 10-count crochet thread	Sock, Fingering, Baby	Sport, Baby	DK, Light Worsted	Worsted, Afghan, Aran	Chunky, Craft, Rug	Super Bulky, Roving	Jumbo, Roving
Knit Gauge Range* in Stockinette Stitch to 4 inches	33–40** sts	27–32 sts	23–26 sts	21–24 sts	16–20 sts	12–15 sts	7–11 sts	6 sts and fewer
Recommended Needle in Metric Size Range	1.5–2.25 mm	2.25—3.25 mm	3.25—3.75 mm	3.75—4.5 mm	4.5—5.5 mm	5.5—8 mm	8—12.75 mm	12.75 mm and larger
Recommended Needle U.S. Size Range	000–1	1 to 3	3 to 5	5 to 7	7 to 9	9 to 11	11 to 17	17 and larger
Crochet Gauge* Ranges in Single Crochet to 4 inch	32–42 double crochets**	21–32 sts	16–20 sts	12–17 sts	11–14 sts	8–11 sts	6–9 sts	5 sts and fewer
Recommended Hook in Metric Size Range	Steel*** 1.6–1.4 mm	2.25—3.5 mm	3.5—4.5 mm	4.5—5.5 mm	5.5—6.5 mm	6.5—9 mm	9—16 mm	16 mm and larger
Recommended Hook U.S. Size Range	Steel*** 6, 7, 8 Regular hook B–1	B–1 to E–4	E–4 to 7	7 to I–9	I–9 to K–10 1/2	K–10 1/2 to M–13	M–13 to Q	Q and larger

* Guidelines only: The above reflect the most commonly used gauges and needle or hook sizes for specific yarn categories.
** Lace weight yarns are usually knitted or crocheted on larger needles and hooks to create lacy, openwork patterns. Accordingly, a gauge range is difficult to determine. Always follow the gauge stated in your pattern.
*** Steel crochet hooks are sized differently from regular hooks—the higher the number, the smaller the hook, which is the reverse of regular hook sizing.

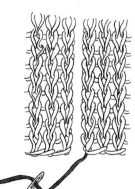

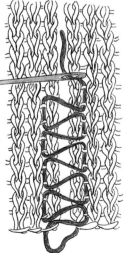

Sewing a Vertical Seam

When joining two pieces vertically, I always use the "tail" or strand at the cast-on edge to avoid an extra end to weave in.

As you seam up the length of the pieces, scoop the needle around two bars on each side for a faster seam and to add elasticity.

Long-Tail Cast-On

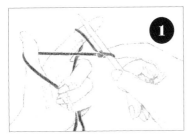

1 Make a slip knot on the right needle, leaving a long tail. Wind the tail end around your left thumb, front to back. Wrap the yarn from the ball over your left index finger and secure the ends in your palm.

2 Insert the needle upward in the loop on your thumb. Then with the needle, draw the yarn from the ball through the loop to form a stitch.

3 Take your thumb out of the loop and tighten the loop on the needle. Continue in this way until all the stitches are cast on.

Backward-Loop Cast-On

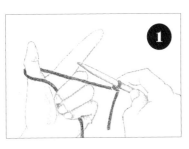

1 Make a slip knot on the right needle, leaving a short tail. Wrap the yarn from the ball around your left thumb from front to back and secure it in your palm with your other fingers.

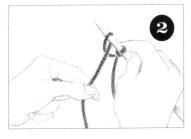

2 Insert the needle upward through the strand on your thumb.

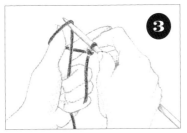

3 Slip this loop from your thumb onto the needle, pulling the yarn from the ball to tighten it. Continue in this way until all the stitches are cast on.

Cable Cast-On

1 Make a slip knot on the left needle. Insert the right needle knitwise into the stitch on the left needle. Wrap the yarn around the right needle as if to knit.

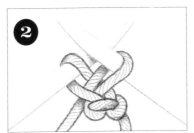

2 Draw the yarn through the first stitch to make a new stitch, but do not drop the stitch from the left needle.

3 Slip the new stitch to the left needle as shown.

4 *Insert the right needle between the two stitches on the left needle.

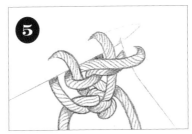

5 Wrap the yarn around the right needle as if to knit and pull the yarn through to make a new stitch.

6 Place the new stitch on the left needle as shown. Repeat from the *, always inserting the right needle in between the last two stitches on the left needle.

Oversized Wrap

page 29

SIZE
Instructions are written for one size.

MEASUREMENTS
Approx 21" x 72"/53cm x 183cm

MATERIALS
• 9 50g/1¾oz hanks (each 154yd/139m) of Plymouth Yarn Company *Royal Cashmere* in #102Z Green (4)
(NOTE: This yarn has been discontinued. I suggest substituting Plymouth's *Cashmere*, which is the same weight and fiber content.)
• One pair each sizes 7 and 8 (4.5 and 5mm) needles *or size to obtain gauge*
• Stitch markers

GAUGE
20 sts and 26 rows to 4"/10cm over wavy lace pat using size 8 (5mm) needles.
Take time to save time—check your gauge.

WAVY LACE PATTERN
(multiple of 11 sts plus 1)
Row 1 and all WS rows K1, *p10, k1; rep from * to end.

Rows 2 and 4 P1, *k10, p1; rep from * to end.
Rows 6, 10, and 14 P1, *k1, [yo, k1] 3 times, ssk 3 times, p1; rep from * to end.
Rows 8 and 12 P1, *k1, [k1, yo] 3 times, ssk 3 times, p1; rep from * to end.
Rows 16 and 18 Rep rows 2 and 4.
Rows 20, 24, and 28 P1, *[k2tog] 3 times, [k1, yo] 3 times, k1, p1; rep from * to end.
Rows 22 and 26 P1, *[k2tog] 3 times, [yo, k1] 3 times, k1, p1; rep from * to end.
Rep rows 1–28 for wavy lace pat.

LACE BORDER PATTERN
(multiple of 10 sts plus 4)
Row 1 (WS) Purl.
Row 2 K2, *yo, ssk, k8; rep from *, end k2.
Row 3 K2, *yo, p2tog, p5, p2tog tbl, yo, p1; rep from *, end k2.
Row 4 K4, *yo, ssk, k3, k2tog, yo, k3; rep from * to end.
Row 5 K2, p2, *yo, p2tog, p1, p2tog tbl, yo, p5; rep from *, end last rep p3, k2.
Row 6 K6, *yo, SKP, yo, k7; rep from *, end last rep k5.
Row 7 K2, *p3, p2tog tbl, yo; rep from *, end k2.
Row 8 K3, *yo, ssk, k3; rep from *, end k1.
Row 9 K2, p1, *p2tog tbl, yo, p3; rep from *, end last rep p2, k2.
Row 10 K5, *yo, ssk, k3; rep from *, end last rep k2.
Row 11 K1, *p2tog tbl, yo, p3; rep from *, end p1, k2.
Row 12 K2, *yo, ssk, k3; rep from *, end k2.
Rows 13, 14, 15, and 16 Rep rows 3, 4, 5, and 6.
Row 17 K2, p1, *p3, yo, p2tog; rep from *, end k1.
Row 18 K5, *k2tog, yo, k3; rep from *, end last rep k2.
Row 19 K2, p1, *yo, p2tog, p3; rep from *, end last rep p2, k2.
Row 20 K3, *k2tog, yo, k3; rep from *, end k1.
Row 21 K2, *p3, yo, p2tog; rep from *, end k2.
Row 22 K1, *k2tog, yo, k3; rep from *, end k3.
Rows 23, 24, 25, and 26 Rep rows 3, 4, 5, and 6.
Row 27 Purl.
Work rows 1–27 for lace border pat.

WRAP
With size 8 (5mm) needles, cast on 104 sts.
Set-up row (RS) K2 (edge sts), p1, *k10,

p1; rep from * to last 2 sts, k2 (edge sts).
Next row (WS) P2 (edge sts), work row 1 of wavy lace pat over 100 sts, end p2 (edge sts). Cont in wavy lace pat, keeping first and last 2 sts in St st, until piece measures 64"/162.5cm, end with a row 5 or 19. Bind off loosely.

BORDERS
With RS facing, pick up and k 100 sts evenly along bound-off edge.
Row 1 (WS) P2, k1 (edge sts), k to last 3 sts, k1, p2 (edge sts).
Row 2 K2, p1 (edge sts), k to last 3 sts, p1, k2 (edge sts). Rep last 2 rows once more.
Next row (WS) P2, k1, work row 1 of lace border pat over 94 sts, k1, p2. Cont as established, working first and last 3 sts as edge sts, until 27 rows of lace border pat are complete.
Next row (RS) K2, p1 (edge sts), k to last 3 sts, p1, k2 (edge sts).
Next row P2, k1 (edge sts), k to last 3 sts, k1, p2 (edge sts). Rep last 2 rows once more. Bind off loosely.
Rep border along cast-on edge.

FINISHING
Steam lightly. Weave in ends. ■

Poncho Pullover

page 31

SIZES
To fit sizes Small/Medium (Large/X-Large).
Shown in size Small/Medium.

MEASUREMENTS
Length from shoulder to lower edge
of cuff, along fold:
approx 27"/68.5cm
Length from lower V-neck to point:
approx 28 (30)"/71 (76)cm
Sleeve width at lower arm: 9¼ (11½)"/
23.5 (29)cm

MATERIALS
• 6 (7) 100g/3½oz hanks (each
215yd/198m) of Berroco *Ultra Alpaca*
(alpaca/wool) in #62180 Grove Mix
• One pair each sizes 7 and 8 (4.5 and
5mm) needles *or size to obtain gauge*
• Stitch markers

GAUGE
20 sts and 26 rows to 4"/10cm over wavy
lace pat using size 8 (5mm) needles.
Take time to save time—check your gauge.

WAVY LACE PATTERN
(multiple of 11 sts plus 1)
Row 1 and all WS rows K1, *p10, k1;
rep from * to end.
Rows 2 and 4 P1, *k10, p1; rep from *
to end.
Rows 6, 10, and 14 P1, *k1, [yo, k1] 3
times, ssk 3 times, p1; rep from * to end.
Rows 8 and 12 P1, *k1, [k1, yo] 3 times, ssk

3 times, p1; rep from * to end.
Rows 16 and 18 Rep rows 2 and 4.
Rows 20, 24, and 28 P1, *[k2tog] 3 times,
[k1, yo] 3 times, k1, p1; rep from * to end.
Rows 22 and 26 P1, *[k2tog] 3 times, [yo,
k1] 3 times, k1, p1; rep from * to end.
Rep rows 1–28 for wavy lace pat.

LACE BORDER PATTERN
(multiple of 10 sts plus 4)
Row 1 (WS) Purl.
Row 2 K2, *yo, ssk, k8; rep from *, end k2.
Row 3 K2, *yo, p2tog, p5, p2tog tbl, yo,
p1; rep from *, end k2.
Row 4 K4, *yo, ssk, k3, k2tog, yo, k3;
rep from * to end.
Row 5 K2, p2, *yo, p2tog, p1, p2tog tbl,
yo, p5; rep from *, end last rep p3, k2.
Row 6 K6, *yo, SKP, yo, k7; rep from *,
end last rep k5.
Row 7 K2, *p3, p2tog tbl, yo; rep from *,
end k2.
Row 8 K3, *yo, ssk, k3; rep from *, end k1.
Row 9 K2, p1, *p2tog tbl, yo, p3;
rep from *, end last rep p2, k2.
Row 10 K5, *yo, ssk, k3; rep from *,
end last rep k2.
Row 11 K1, *p2tog tbl, yo, p3; rep from *,
end p1, k2.
Row 12 K2, *yo, ssk, k3; rep from *, end
k2.
Rows 13, 14, 15, and 16 Rep rows 3, 4, 5,
and 6.
Row 17 K2, p1, *p3, yo, p2tog; rep from *,
end k1.
Row 18 K5, *k2tog, yo, k3; rep from *, end

last rep k2.
Row 19 K2, p1, *yo, p2tog, p3; rep from *,
end last rep p2, k2.
Row 20 K3, *k2tog, yo, k3; rep from *,
end k1.
Row 21 K2, *p3, yo, p2tog; rep from *,
end k2.
Row 22 K1, *k2tog, yo, k3; rep from *,
end k3.
Rows 23, 24, 25, and 26 Rep rows 3, 4, 5,
and 6.
Row 27 Purl.
Work rows 1–27 for lace border pat.

PONCHO PULLOVER
Note: Measurements are based on st count
before edge sts, since these sts roll to the
inside.

SWATCHES/SLEEVES (MAKE 2)
Note: You can check your gauge with the
first swatch. If you need to use another
size, just keep the first swatch for the first
sleeve; a slight variation in gauge will be
fine for this small piece.

With size 8 (5mm) needles, cast on 38 sts.
Set-up row (RS) K2 (edge sts), p1, *k10,
p1; rep from * to last 2 sts, k2 (edge sts).
Next row (WS) P2 (edge sts), work row 1
of wavy lace pat over 34 sts, end p2 (edge
sts). Cont in wavy lace pat, keeping first
and last 2 sts in St st, for 60 (74) rows total.
Bind off.

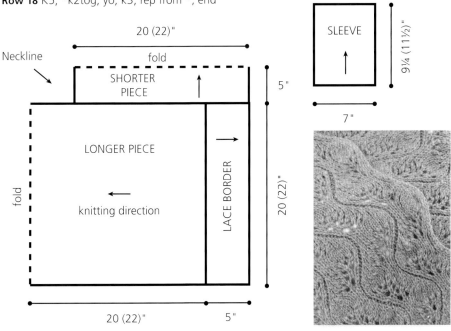

Longer BODY piece

With size 8 (5mm) needles, cast on 104 (115) sts.

Set-up row (RS) K2 (edge sts), p1, *k10, p1; rep from * to last 2 sts, k2 (edge sts).
Next row (WS) P2 (edge sts), work row 1 of wavy lace pat over 100 (111) sts, end p2 (edge sts).
Cont in wavy lace pat, keeping first and last 2 sts in St st, until piece measures approx 40 (44)"/101.5 (111.5)cm, end with a row 5 or 19. Bind off loosely.

LACE BORDER

With RS of bound-off edge facing and size 7 (4.5mm) needles, pick up 100 (110) sts evenly.

Row 1 (WS) P2, k1 (edge sts), k to last 3 sts, k1, p2 (edge sts).
Row 2 K2, p1 (edge sts), k to last 3 sts, p1, k2 (edge sts).
Rep last 2 rows once more.
Next row (WS) P2, k1, work row 1 of lace border pat over 94 (104) sts, k1, p2. Cont as established, working first and last 3 sts as established for edge sts, until 27 rows of lace border pat are complete.
Next row (RS) K2, p1 (edge sts), k to last 3 sts, p1, k2 (edge sts).
Next row P2, k1 (edge sts), k to last 3 sts, k1, p2 (edge sts).
Rep last 2 rows once more. Bind off.
Rep lace border along cast-on edge.

Shorter BODY piece

Work same as for longer piece, without borders, until piece measures 10"/25.5cm.

FINISHING

Steam pieces lightly.
On longer piece, on one side only, place marker 20"/51cm up from each bound-off edge.
Pin the cast-on edge of the shorter piece underneath the scalloped edge of the longer piece between one bound-off edge and the marker next to it: allow the scallops to extend over the piece underneath so that the edge of the shorter piece is covered. With RS facing, beginning at the marker, sew through both layers. Rep on other end of the two pieces.
Fold the layers so the border edges of the larger piece are aligned: the "fold" on either side, at sides of neckline opening, will be the "shoulder." Place marker at outer edge of each fold, along scalloped edge.

SLEEVES

Mark the center of each sleeve/swatch, along a scalloped edge, and match to the marker on the main pieces, each side. With RS facing, sew edge of swatches to main pieces, matching 2 rows for 2 rows between edge sts so that the scallops match. Sew cast-on edge to bound-off edge to complete sleeve.
Weave in all ends. ▨

Detachable Cowl Pullover ■■☐☐

page 37

SIZES

To fit sizes Small (Medium, Large, X-Large, XX-Large). Shown in size Large. Cowl: One size.

MEASUREMENTS

Bust at underarm: approx 36 (40, 44, 48, 52)"/91.5 (101.5, 11.6, 122, 132)cm

Length from outer shoulder: 30 (30½, 31, 31½, 32)"/76 (77.5, 78.5, 80, 81)cm
Sleeve width at upper arm: 12 (13, 13½, 14½, 16)"/30.5 (33, 34.5, 37, 40.5)cm
Cowl—neckline edge: approx 28"/71cm
Cowl—upper edge: 32"/81cm

MATERIALS

- Pullover: 4 (5, 5, 6, 6) 4oz/114g hanks (each 395yd/359m) of Imperial Yarn *Tracie Two* (wool) in #302 Rain (A) **❷**
- Cowl: 2 4oz/114g hanks (each 225yd/205m) of Imperial Yarn *Erin* (wool) in #302 Rain (B) **❹**
- One pair size 6 (4mm) needles
or size to obtain gauge
- One each sizes 5 and 9 (3.75 and 5.5mm) circular needles, 24"/60cm long

GAUGES

- 25 sts and 33 rows to 4"/10cm over textured pat using size 6 (4mm) needles and A.
- 26 sts and 33 rows to 4"/10cm over lace rib using size 6 (4mm) needles and A.
- Lace panel over 27 sts measures approx 4"/10cm wide using A.
- 21 sts and 24 rows to 4"/10cm over textured pat using size 9 (5.5mm) needles and B.
Take time to save time—check your gauges.

STOCKINETTE STITCH (ST ST)

(over any number of sts)
Knit RS rows, purl WS rows.

REVERSE STOCKINETTE STITCH (REV ST ST)

(over any number of sts)
Purl RS rows, knit WS rows.

LACE RIB (IN ROWS)

(multiple of 8 sts plus 3)
Row 1 (RS) P3, *yo, ssk, k3, p3; rep from *.
Row 2 and all even-numbered rows K3, * p5, k3; rep from *.
Row 3 P3, *yo, k1, ssk, k2, p3; rep from *.
Row 5 P3, *yo, k2, ssk, k1, p3; rep from *.
Row 7 P3, *yo, k3, ssk, p3; rep from *.
Row 9 P3, *k3, k2tog, yo, p3; rep from *.
Row 11 P3, *k2, k2tog, k1, yo, p3; rep from *.
Row 13 P3, *k1, k2tog, k2, yo, p3; rep from *.
Row 15 P3, *k2tog, k3, yo, p3; rep from *.
Row 16 K3, *p5, k3; rep from *.
Rep rows 1–16 for lace rib worked in rows.

LACE RIB (IN THE ROUND)

(multiple of 8 sts)
Rnd 1 (RS) *Yo, ssk, k3, p3; rep from *.

3 (3¼, 3½, 4, 4½)"

9½ (9¾, 10, 10, 10)"

5½ (6, 6½, 6½, 6½)"

30 (30½, 31, 31½, 32)"

7½ (8, 8½, 9, 9½)"

22½"

BACK & FRONT

18 (20, 22, 24, 26)"

22 (24, 26, 28, 30)"

Rnd 2 and all even-numbered rnds
*K5, p3; rep from *.
Rnd 3 *Yo, k1, ssk, k2, p3; rep from *.
Rnd 5 *Yo, k2, ssk, k1, p3; rep from *.
Rnd 7 *Yo, k3, ssk, p3; rep from *.
Rnd 9 *K3, k2tog, yo, p3; rep from *.
Rnd 11 *K2, k2tog, k1, yo, p3; rep from *.
Rnd 13 *K1, k2tog, k2, yo, p3; rep from *.
Rnd 15 *K2tog, k3, yo, p3; rep from *.
Rnd 16 *K5, p3; rep from *.
Rep rnds 1–16 for lace rib in the rnd.

TEXTURED PATTERN
(multiple of 6 sts plus 2)
Rows 1, 3, and 5 (RS) P2, *k4, p2;
rep from *.
Rows 2 and 4 K2, *p4, k2; rep from *.
Rows 6 and 8 (WS) P3, k2, *p4, k2;
rep from *, end p3.
Rows 7 and 9 K3, p2, *k4, p2; rep from *,
end k3.
Row 10 Same as row 6.
Rep rows 1–10 for textured pat.

BACK
With size 6 (4mm) needles and A, cast on
127 (143, 159, 175, 175) sts.
Next row (RS) K2 (St st edge sts), work in
lace rib over center 123 (139, 155, 171,

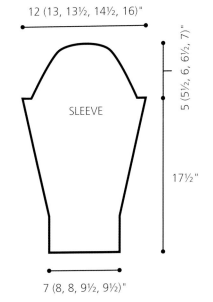

12 (13, 13½, 14½, 16)"

5 (5½, 6, 6½, 7)"

SLEEVE

17½"

7 (8, 8, 9½, 9½)"

171) sts, end k2 (St st edge sts).
Work even for 47 rows, ending with RS
row 15 of pat.
Mark center 27 sts (this represents center 3
lace ribs with 3 sts each side) and 50
(58, 66, 74, 74) sts to either side.
Next (inc) row (WS) P2 (edge sts), work
row 16 of lace rib to marker; AT THE SAME

TIME, inc 8 (6, 4, 2, 8) sts evenly spaced, sl
marker, work center 27 sts in pat, sl marker,
cont row 16 of lace rib to the last 2 sts;
AT THE SAME TIME, inc 8 (6, 4, 2, 8) sts
evenly spaced, end p2 (edge sts)—143
(155, 167, 179, 191) sts.
Next row (RS) K2 (St st edge sts), work in
textured pat over 56 (62, 68, 74, 80) sts,
cont lace rib over center 27 sts, work in
textured pat over 56 (62, 68, 74, 80) sts,
end k2 (St st edge sts). Work even for
5 more rows, end with a WS row.
Next (dec) row (RS) K1, ssk, work as established to last 3 sts, k2tog, k1.
Rep dec row every 6th row 9 times more—
123 (135, 147, 159, 171) sts.
Work even until piece measures
22½"/57cm, end with a WS row.

ARMHOLE SHAPING
Bind off 3 sts at beg of next 2 rows, then 0
(0, 0, 2, 2) sts at beg of next 2 rows.
Next (dec) row (RS) K1, ssk, work to last
3 sts, end k2tog, k1
Next row (WS) Work as established,
keeping first and last 2 sts in St st.
Rep last 2 rows 8 (11, 15, 16, 20) times
more—99 (105, 109, 115, 119) sts.
Work even until armhole measures 7½
(8, 8½, 9, 9½)"/19 (20.5, 21.5, 23, 24)cm,
end with a WS row.

SHOULDER AND NECK SHAPING
Mark center 21 (23, 25, 25 25) sts.
Bind off 7 (7, 7, 9, 9) shoulder sts, work
to center 21 (23, 25, 25, 25) sts and join a
second ball of yarn, bind off center 21
(23, 25, 25, 25) sts and work to end.
Working both sides at the same time with
separate balls of yarn, bind off 7 (7, 7, 9, 9)
sts at beg of next 1 (5, 3, 1, 5) rows, then
6 (0, 8, 8, 0) sts at beg of next 4 (0, 2, 4, 0)
rows; AT THE SAME TIME, bind off 10 sts
from each neck edge twice.

FRONT
Work same as for back until armhole depth
measures 2 (2, 2, 2½, 3)"/5 (5, 5, 6.5,
7.5)cm, end with a WS row.

NECK SHAPING
Mark center 23 (25, 27, 27, 27) sts.
Next row (RS) Cont armhole shaping, work
to center marked sts, join a second ball of
yarn and bind off center marked 23 (25,
27, 27 27) sts, work as established to end.
Cont armhole shaping and, working both
sides at the same time with separate

balls of yarn, bind off 2 sts from each neck edge once.

Next (dec) row (RS) Work to last 3 sts of first side, k2tog, k1, on second section, k1, ssk, work as established to end.

Next row (WS) Work as established, keeping 2 sts at neckline edges in St st. Rep last 2 rows 16 times more—19 (21, 22, 25, 27) sts rem each side. Working both sides at the same time with separate balls of yarn, work even until arm-hole measures same as back to shoulder.

SHOULDER SHAPING
Bind off 7 (7, 7, 9, 9) sts from each shoulder 1 (3, 2, 1, 3) times, then 6 (0, 8, 8, 0) sts 2 (0, 1, 2, 0) times.

SLEEVES
With size 6 (4mm) needles and A, cast on 47 (55, 55, 63, 63) sts.

Next row (RS) K2 (St st edge sts), work in lace rib over center 43 (51, 51, 59, 59) sts, end k2 (St st edge sts).

Work even for 32 rows, inc (dec, dec, dec, dec) 1 (1, 1, 3, 3) st on last WS row—48 (54, 54, 60, 60) sts.

Next row (RS) K2 (St st edge sts), work in textured pat over center 44 (50, 50, 56, 56) sts, end k2 (St st edge sts). Work even for

5 rows, ending with a WS row.

Next (inc) row (RS) K2, M1, work to last 2 sts, M1, end k2.

Working incs into textured pat, rep inc row every 8th (8th, 8th, 8th, 6th) row 13 (13, 14, 14, 19) times more—76 (82, 84, 90, 100) sts.

Work even until sleeve measures 17½"/44.5cm, end with a WS row.

CAP SHAPING
Bind off 3 sts at beg of next 2 rows, then 0 (0, 0, 2, 2) sts at beg of next 2 rows.

Next (dec) row (RS) K1, ssk, work to last 3 sts, end k2tog, k1.

Keeping first and last 2 sts of every row in St st, rep dec row every 4th row 3 (2, 3, 4, 2) times, then every RS row 9 (13, 13, 13, 18) times.

Bind off 2 sts at beg of next 6 (6, 6, 6, 8) rows—32 sts. Bind off rem sts.

FINISHING
Sew front to back at shoulders. Sew side and sleeve seams. Sew sleeve caps into armholes.

NECKLINE TRIM
With RS facing and size 5 (3.75mm) circular needle, starting at right shoulder seam,

pick up 52 (54, 56, 56, 56) sts evenly across back neck, then 90 (92, 94, 94, 94) sts around front neck edge—142 (146, 150, 105, 105, 150) sts. Place marker (pm) and join to work in the rnd. Purl 1 rnd, [knit 1 rnd, purl 1 rnd] 5 times. Bind off with larger needle. Weave in ends.

COWL
Note Cowl is worked from the top down. With size 9 (5.5mm) circular needle and B, cast on 168 sts. Pm and join to work in the rnd, being careful not to twist sts. Work in rnds of lace rib until piece measures 7"/18cm.

Next rnd Work as established, p2tog in each p3 rib, 21 sts decreased—147 sts. Cont in pat as established, working p2 instead of p3, until cowl measures 14"/35.5cm, end with row 8 or row 16. Bind off in pat.

FINISHING
With RS of cast-on edge facing, pick up 146 sts evenly spaced. Pm and join to work in the rnd. Purl 2 rnds. Bind off purlwise. With RS of bound-off edge facing, pick up 126 sts evenly spaced. Pm and join to work in the rnd. Purl 2 rnds. Bind off purlwise. ■

Striped Blocks Pullover

page 43

SIZES
To fit sizes Small (Medium, Large, X-Large, XX-Large). Shown in size Small.

MEASUREMENTS
Bust at underarm:
38 (42, 46, 52, 56)"/96.5 (106.5, 116.5, 132, 142)cm
Length from shoulder:
23 (23½, 24, 24½, 25)"/58.5 (59.5, 61, 62, 63.5)cm
Sleeve width at upper arm:
12½ (13½, 14½, 15½, 16½)"/31.5 (34.5, 37, 39.5, 42)cm

MATERIALS
• 1 (1, 1, 2, 2) 8¾oz/250g skeins (each 491yd/449m) of Plymouth Yarn Company *Mushishi* (wool/silk) in #0015 Creams (A) (**4**)
• 4 (5, 5, 6, 6) .35oz/10g balls (each 49yd/45m) of Plymouth Yarn Company *Angora Glitz* (angora/metallic/nylon) in #709 Cream (B) (**4**)
• 4 (5, 5, 6, 6) 1¾oz/50g skeins (each 130yd/119m) of Plymouth

Yarn Company *DK Merino Superwash* (superwash merino wool) in #1117 Lt Grey (C) (**3**)
• One pair size 7 (4.5mm) needles *or size to obtain gauge*
• Stitch markers
• Tapestry needle

GAUGE
20 sts and 29 rows to 4"/10cm over stripe pat using larger needles.
Take time to save time—check your gauge.

STOCKINETTE STITCH (ST ST)
(over any number of sts)
Knit RS rows, purl WS rows.

GARTER STITCH
(over any number of sts)
Knit every row.

STRIPE PATTERN
(multiple of 4 sts plus 1)
Odd-numbered rows are RS rows.
Rows 1–4 With A, work in St st.
Rows 5–6 With B, work in St st.

Rows 7–8 With C, work in St st.
Rows 9–10 With B, work in St st.
Row 11 With C, knit.
Row 12 With C, p1, *k2, p2: rep from *.
Row 13 With C, knit.
Row 14 With C, p1, *k2, p2; rep from *.
Rep rows 1–14 for stripe pat.

NOTES

1) Trims at lower edges are worked after pieces are complete.
2) Carry yarns up the side of pieces as you knit, to avoid weaving in ends.

BACK

With size 7 (4.5mm) needles and A, cast on 97 (105, 117, 133, 141) sts. Work in stripe pat until piece measures 14½"/37cm, end with a WS row.

ARMHOLE SHAPING

Bind off 5 (5, 6, 6, 6) sts at beg of next 2 rows—87 (95, 105, 121, 129) sts.
Next (dec) row (RS) K1, ssk, work to last 3 sts, k2tog, k1.
Work WS row as established.
Rep last 2 rows 4 (6, 9, 12, 13) times more—77 (81, 85, 95, 101) sts.
Work even until armhole measures 7½ (8, 8½, 9, 9½)"/19 (20.5, 21.5, 23, 24)cm, end with a WS row.

NECK AND SHOULDER SHAPING

Mark center 29 (29, 29, 31, 31) sts.
Bind off 4 (6, 6, 8, 9) sts, work to center marked sts, join a 2nd ball of yarn and bind off center 29 (29, 29, 31, 31) sts, work to end. Working both sides at once, bind off 4 (6, 6, 8, 9) sts at beg of next WS row, then bind off 5 (5, 6, 7, 8) sts from each shoulder edge 2 times more; AT THE SAME TIME, bind off 5 sts from each neck edge twice.

LEFT FRONT

With size 7 (4.5mm) needles and A, cast on 57 (61, 65, 73, 77) sts. Work in stripe pat until piece measures 14½"/37cm, end with a WS row.

ARMHOLE SHAPING

Next row Bind off 5 (5, 6, 6, 6) sts at beg of row—52 (56, 59, 67, 71) sts.
Next (dec) row (RS) K1, ssk, work as established to end.
Work WS row as established.
Rep last 2 rows 4 (6, 9, 12, 13) times more—47 (49, 49, 54, 57) sts.

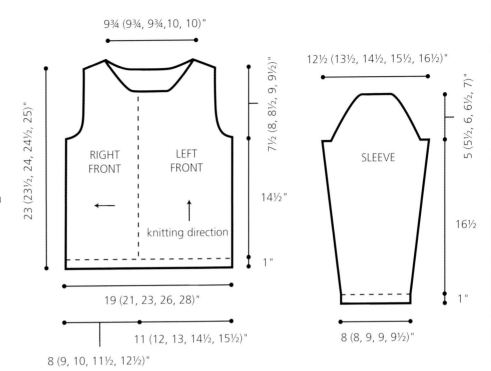

9¾ (9¾, 9¾, 10, 10)"

7½ (8, 8½, 9, 9½)"

23 (23½, 24, 24½, 25)"

RIGHT FRONT | LEFT FRONT

← knitting direction ↑

14½"

1"

19 (21, 23, 26, 28)"

11 (12, 13, 14½, 15½)"

8 (9, 10, 11½, 12½)"

12½ (13½, 14½, 15½, 16½)"

5 (5½, 6, 6½, 7)"

SLEEVE

16½

1"

8 (8, 9, 9, 9½)"

Work as established until armhole measures 5½ (6, 6½, 7, 7½)"/14 (15, 16.5, 18, 19)cm, end with a RS row.

FRONT NECK SHAPING

Bind off 19 (19, 19, 20, 20) sts, work to end—28 (30, 30, 34, 37) sts.
Work RS row as established.
Bind off 2 sts at beg of next 7 (7, 6, 6, 6) WS rows; AT THE SAME TIME, when armhole measures same as back to shoulder, bind off at shoulder edge 4 (6, 6, 8, 9) sts 1 (1, 3, 1, 1) times, then 5 (5, 0, 7, 8) sts 2 times.

RIGHT FRONT

With RS facing, size 7 (4.5mm) needles and A, pick up 99 (101, 105, 107, 109) sts evenly spaced from neck edge to bottom. Work row 2 of stripe pat. Cont in pat for 6 more rows.

FRONT NECK SHAPING

Keeping in pat, cast on 2 sts at beg of next 8 RS rows—115 (117, 121, 123, 125) sts. Work WS row as established. Place marker at beg of next row.

SHOULDER SHAPING

Next row K1, ssk, work as established to end.
Work even for 3 (5, 5, 3, 3) rows.
Rep dec row once, then every 4th (4th, 4th, 6th, 6th) row 2 (2, 2, 3, 3) times more—

111 (113, 117, 118, 120) sts.
Work as established until piece measures 6 (6½, 6¾, 7¾, 8½)"/15 (16.5, 17, 18, 21.5)cm from pick-up row, ending with a WS row.

ARMHOLE SHAPING

Bind off 29 (28, 29, 30, 29) sts at beg of next row—82 (85, 88, 88, 91) sts.
Bind off 3 sts at beg of next 3 (4, 5, 5, 6) RS rows—73 sts.
Work even until piece measures 8 (9, 10, 11½, 12½)"/20.5 (23, 25.5, 29, 31.5)cm from pick-up row. Bind off rem 73 sts.

SLEEVES

With size 7 (4.5mm) needles and A, cast on 41 (41, 45, 45, 49) sts. Beg stripe pat and work for 4 rows.
Next (inc) row (RS) K2, M1, work to last 2 sts, M1, k2.
Cont in pat, work even for 9 (7, 7, 5, 5) rows more.
Rep inc row on next row, then every 10th (8th, 8th, 6th, 6th) row 9 (12, 12, 15, 15) times more—63 (69, 73, 79, 83) sts.
Work even until sleeve measures 16½"/42cm, end with a WS row.

CAP SHAPING

Bind off 5 (5, 6, 6, 6) sts at beg of next 2 rows—53 (59, 61, 67, 71) sts.
Next (dec) row (RS) K1, ssk, work to last 3 sts, k2tog, k1.

Next row P2, work to last 2 sts, p2.
Rep last 2 rows 17 (20, 21, 23, 25) times
more—17 (17, 17, 19, 19) sts. Bind off.

SLEEVE TRIM
With RS facing, size 7 (4.5mm) needles and
C, pick up 36 (36, 40, 40, 44) sts evenly
spaced. Knit 7 rows. Bind off on RS.

FINISHING
Sew front to back at right shoulder.

NECKLINE TRIM
With RS facing, size 7 (4.5mm) needles and
C, pick up 56 (56, 56, 58, 58) sts evenly

along front neckline, then 52 (52, 52, 54,
54) sts along back neckline—108
(108, 108, 112, 112) sts.
Knit 7 rows. Bind off on RS.
Sew left shoulder seam, including trim.
Sew front to back at right side.

LOWER EDGE TRIM
With RS facing, size 7 (4.5mm) needles and
C, pick up 172 (188, 210, 226, 240) sts
evenly spaced along lower edge.
Knit 7 rows. Bind off on RS.
Sew sleeve seams and remaining side seam.
Sew sleeve caps into armholes. Weave in
ends. Steam lightly if necessary. ■

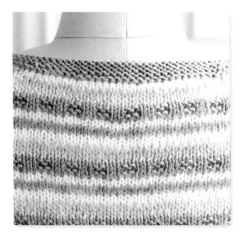

Pleated Peplum Pullover ◼◼◼◻

page 55

SIZES
To fit sizes Small (Medium, Large, X-Large,
XX-Large). Shown in size Small.

MEASUREMENTS
Bust at underarm: 34 (36, 38, 40, 42)"/43
(91.5, 96.5, 101.5, 106.5)cm
Length from back outer shoulder: 22 (23,
24, 25, 26)"/56 (58.5, 61, 63.5, 66)cm
Sleeve width at upper arm: 14 (14½, 15,
15½, 16)"/35.5 (37, 38, 39.5, 40.5)cm

MATERIALS
• 7 (7, 8, 8, 9) 1¾oz/50g balls (each
153yd/167m) of Rowan *Kid Classic*
(wool/kid mohair/polyamide) in
#888 Pumice ④
• One pair sizes 5 and 6 (3.75 and 4mm)
needles *or size to obtain gauge*
• Size 5 (3.75mm) circular needle,
24"/61cm long
• Stitch markers
• Stitch holder
• Approx 1½yd/1.4m of slate gray satin
ribbon, 1½"/4cm wide
• Approx 18"/45.5cm of gray velvet ribbon,
⅝"/1.5cm wide
• Sewing thread and needle

GAUGE
20 sts and 28 rows to 4"/10cm over
St st using size 6 (4mm) needles.
Take time to save time—check your gauge.

STOCKINETTE STITCH (ST ST)
(over any number of sts)
Knit RS rows, purl WS rows.

PLEAT
(panel of 32 sts, dec to 2 sts)
Note Slip always as if to purl.
Row 1 (RS) Sl 1 wyib, k7, p1, k14, p1,
k7, sl 1 wyib.
Row 2 and all even-numbered (WS) rows
Purl, slipping p sts of previous row wyib.
Rows 3 and 5 Rep row 1.
Row 7 Sl 1 wyib, k4, k2tog, place marker
(pm), k1, p1, k1, ssk, k8, k2tog, k1, p1, k1,
pm, ssk, k4, sl 1 wyib.
Rows 9 and 11 Sl 1 wyib, k6, p1, k12,
p1, k6, sl 1 wyib.
Row 13 Sl 1 wyib, k to 2 sts before marker,
k2tog, sl marker, k1, p1, k1, k to 2 sts

before next marker, k2tog, sl marker, k1,
p1, k1, ssk, k to last st, sl 1 wyib.
Cont in this way, as described, to dec
1 st each side of markers every 6th
row until there are 12 sts, end with a
RS row.
Next row (WS) Sl 1, k2tog, p1, ssk, k2tog,
p1, ssk, sl 1—8 sts.
Work 4 rows even.
Next row (RS) K1, bind off center
6 sts—2 sts rem.

BACK
With size 6 (4mm) needles, cast on 118
(122, 128, 132, 136) sts. If long-tail
method was used, purl 1 row.

BEGIN PLEAT
Next row (RS) K1 (edge st), k42 (44, 47,
49, 51), pm, work pleat over next
32 sts, pm, k42 (44, 47, 49, 51), end
k1 (edge st).
Cont to work St st at sides, outside of
markers, and pleat inside markers for 12
(12, 10, 10, 10) rows.
Next (dec) row (RS) K1, ssk, work as
established to last 3 sts, end k2tog, k1.
Rep dec row every 12th (12th, 10th, 10th,
10th) row 2 (2, 3, 3, 3) times more.
After all pleat rows are complete, purl WS
row over all 82 (86, 90, 94, 98) sts.
Note Hole formed by 6 bound-off sts at top
of pleat will be sewn closed after piece is
complete.

WAIST RIBBING
Next row (RS) K1, (k1, p1) 16 (17, 18, 19,
20) times, pm, k16, pm, (k1, p1) 16
(17, 18, 19, 20) times; end k1.
Next row (WS) Knit the k sts and purl the p
sts as they face you.

Rep last 2 rows 2 more times.

Next (inc) row (RS) K1, work in rib as established to first marker, sl marker, k2, M1, k12, M1, k2, sl marker, work as established to end. Working incs into St st, rep inc row every 4th row 1 (2, 2, 3, 3) times more—86 (92, 96, 102, 106) sts. Work WS row as established.

Next row (RS) Work to last p st in first rib section, k1, knit to first p st in next rib section, k1, work in rib as established to end. Cont in this way to work 1 less p st in rib in each rib section every RS row (working rib st in St st) until all sts are worked in St st. Cont in St st until piece measures 8 (8½, 9, 9½, 10)"/20.5 (21.5, 23, 24, 25.5)cm from beg of waist rib, end with a WS row.

ARMHOLE SHAPING
Bind off 5 sts at beg of next 2 rows.
Next row (RS) K1, ssk, work to last 3 sts, k2tog, k1.
Rep dec row every RS row 4 (5, 6, 7, 8) times more—66 (70, 72, 76, 78) sts. Work even until armhole measures 7 (7½, 8, 8½, 9)"/18 (19, 20.5, 21.5, 23)cm, end with a WS row.

NECKLINE AND SHOULDER SHAPING
Mark center 22 (22, 24, 24, 26) sts.
Next row (RS) Work to center marked sts, join a second ball of yarn, bind off center 22 (22, 24, 24, 26) sts, work to end. Working both sides at the same time with separate balls of yarn, bind off from each neck edge 5 sts 2 times; AT THE SAME TIME, when armhole measures 8 (8½, 9, 9½, 10)"/20.5, 21.5, 23, 24, 25.5)cm, bind off from each shoulder edge 4 (4, 4, 6, 6) sts 3 (1, 1, 1, 1) times, then 0 (5, 5, 5, 5) sts twice.

FRONT
With size 6 (4mm) needles, cast on 148 (152, 158, 162, 166) sts. If long-tail method was used, purl 1 row.

BEGIN PLEAT
Next row (RS) K1 (edge st), k19 (20, 21, 22, 23), pm, work pleat over next 32 sts, pm, k44 (46, 50, 52, 54), pm, work pleat over next 32 sts, k19 (20, 21, 22, 23), end k1 (edge st).
Cont to work St st at sides and center, and pleat inside markers; AT THE SAME TIME, work dec's at sides as for back until all pleat rows have been worked—82

(86, 90, 94, 98) sts. Purl 1 row.
Work same as for back to armhole, including waist rib (with inc sts), end with a WS row—86 (92, 96, 102, 106) sts.

ARMHOLE AND V-NECKLINE SHAPING
Mark center space.
Work armhole shaping as for back; AT THE SAME TIME, work V-neck shaping as foll:
Next row (RS) Knit to 2 sts before center space, k2tog, join a second ball of yarn and ssk in first 2 sts after center space, knit to end.
Next row Working both sides at once, purl. Rep last 2 rows 20 (20, 21, 21, 22) times more; AT THE SAME TIME, when armhole measures same as back to shoulder, work same shoulder shaping as for back.

SLEEVES
With size 6 (4mm) needles, cast on 19 (19, 20, 21, 21) sts, with 2nd ball of yarn, cast on 19 (19, 20, 21, 21) sts—38 (38, 40, 42, 42) total sts. Work both pieces at the same time, with separate balls, as foll:
Purl next (WS) row if long-tail method was used to cast on.
Work 4 rows in St st.
Next row (RS) K2 (edge sts), M1, k to end of first section, drop yarn and work with second strand to last 2 sts, M1, k2 (edge sts).
Next row Purl.

JOIN PIECES
Knit to end of first section, then with same strand cast on 2 sts, and with same strand knit to end of second piece (cut strand for second section)—42 (42, 44, 46, 46) total sts. Work in St st for 3 more rows.
Next (inc) row (RS) K2, M1, k to last 2 sts, M1, k2.

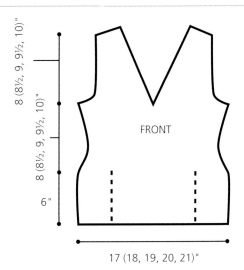

FRONT

8 (8½, 9, 9½, 10)"

8 (8½, 9, 9½, 10)"

6"

17 (18, 19, 20, 21)"

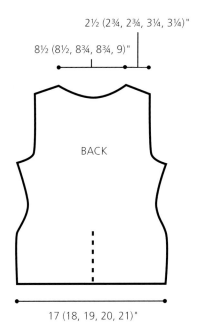

2½ (2¾, 2¾, 3¼, 3¼)"

8½ (8½, 8¾, 8¾, 9)"

BACK

17 (18, 19, 20, 21)"

14 (14½, 15, 15½, 16)"

6 (6½, 7, 7¼, 7½)"

SLEEVE

17"

7½ (7½, 8, 8½, 8½)"

Rep inc row every 4th row 13 (14, 15, 15, 16) times more—70 (72, 76, 78, 80) sts. Work even until piece measures 17"/43cm, end with a WS row.

CAP SHAPING
Bind off 5 sts at beg of next 2 rows.
Next (dec) row (RS) K2, ssk, work to last 4 sts, end k2tog, k2.
Next row Purl.
Rep dec row every RS row 18 (19, 21, 22, 23) times more—22 sts.
Work 3 rows even and bind off loosely.

FINISHING
FRONT LOWER EDGE TRIM
With RS facing and size 5 (3.75mm) needle, pick up 1 st for every cast-on st along lower edge. Knit 3 rows. Bind off. Rep for back lower edge.
Sew front to back at shoulders. Sew side seams, join trims where they meet.

NECKLINE
With RS facing and size 5 (3.75mm) circular needle, beg at right shoulder, pick up 57 sts along back neck, pick up 38 sts along left front to center, pick up 1 st at center neck and mark this st, pick up 38 sts to right shoulder—134 sts. Pm and join.
Next (dec) rnd Purl to 1 st before marked st, sl 2 tog knitwise, k1, p2sso, purl to end.
Knit 1 rnd.
Next rnd Rep dec rnd.
Bind off.

SLEEVE LOWER EDGE TRIM
With RS facing and size 5 (3.75mm) needle, beg at side edge, pick up 1 st for every cast-on st along lower edge, pick up 1 st in corner, then pick up 8 sts along slit opening. Knit 1 row.
Bind off on next row; AT THE SAME TIME, M1 at corner. Work on the other side, picking up first along slit opening. Join trims where they meet at top of slit. Sew sleeve seams. Sew sleeve caps into armholes.

BOWS (MAKE 5)
Cut an 8"/20.5cm length of satiny ribbon and fold to form 4"/10cm wide bow, tucking raw end to inside. Sew at center to hold layers in place. Cut a short length of velvet ribbon and wrap the bow at center, sewing at back. Sew bows in place at tops of pleats and at tops of sleeve slits. ■

Short-Sleeved Cardigan

page 62

SIZES
To fit sizes Small (Medium, Large, X-Large, XX-Large). Shown in size Medium.

MEASUREMENTS
Bust at underarm, including ½"/1.5cm buttonband: 36½ (38½, 42½, 46½, 50½)"/92.5 (98, 108, 118, 129)cm
Sleeve at upper arm:
13½ (14½, 15½, 15½, 16½)"/34.5 (37, 39.5, 39.5, 42)cm
Length from outer shoulder, including ½"/1.5cm trim:
25½ (26½, 26½, 27, 27½)"/65 (67.5, 67.5, 68.5, 70)cm
Length may vary slightly, depending on row gauge.

MATERIALS
• 8 (9, 10, 11, 12) 1¾oz/50g balls (each 137yd/125m) of Debbie Bliss/KFI *Baby Cashmerino* (merino wool/microfiber/cashmere) in #3 Light Lime (2)
• One pair each sizes 4 and 5 (3.5 and 3.75mm) needles *or size to obtain gauge*
• One each sizes 4 and 5 (3.5 and 3.75mm) circular needles, 32" or 40"/80 or 100cm long
• Stitch markers
• Stitch holders
• 7 buttons, ¾"/20mm wide

GAUGES
• 19 sts and 28 rows to 4"/10cm over Lace Chart using size 5 (3.75) needles.
• 24 sts and 28 rows to 4"/10cm over k2, p2 rib using size 5 (3.75) needles.
Take time to save time—check your gauges.

STOCKINETTE STITCH (ST ST)
(over any number of sts)
Knit RS rows, purl WS rows.

K2, P2 RIB
(multiple of 4 sts plus 2)
Row 1 (RS) K2, *p2, k2; rep from *.
Row 2 P2, *k2, p2; rep from *.
Rep rows 1 and 2 for k2, p2 rib.

K1, P1 RIB
(over an odd number of sts)
Row 1 (RS) K1, *p1, k1; rep from *.
Row 2 P1, *k1, p1; rep from *.
Rep rows 1 and 2 for k1, p1 rib.

NOTE
End row 1 of Lace Chart (p. 135) by working last 2 sts with ssk, instead of SK2P.

BODY
With size 5 (3.75mm) circular needle, cast on 193 (209, 233, 257, 281) sts. Work back and forth, do *not* join.
Row 1 (RS) K1 (edge st: keep in St st), place marker (pm), work row 1 of Lace Chart over 23 sts, ending ssk instead of SK2P, pm, work row 1 of k2, p2 rib over 50 (58, 70, 82, 94) sts, pm, work first st of Lace Chart, work 22-st rep twice over 45 sts, ending ssk instead of SK2P, pm, work row 1 of k2, p2 rib over 50 (58, 70, 82, 94) sts, pm, work row 1 of Lace Chart over 23 sts, ending ssk instead of SK2P, pm, end k1 (edge st: keep in St st).
Work even in pats as established until 126 rows are complete, piece measures approx 18"/45.5cm from beg.
Place side markers at center of 50 (58, 70, 82, 94)-st ribbed sections, dividing each section into two equal 25 (29, 35, 41, 47)-st sections.

SEPARATE FOR BACK AND FRONTS
Next row (RS) Cont in pats as established, work to 6 (6, 6, 8, 8) sts before first side marker, bind off 6 (6, 6, 8, 8) sts [(43 (47, 53, 57, 63) sts on front], remove marker, bind off 6 (6, 6, 8, 8) sts, then work as established in pats to 2nd side marker, turn.

Place front sts to separate holders and work on back only.

BACK ARMHOLE SHAPING
Bind off 6 (6, 6, 8, 8) sts, work as established to end of back, turn—83 (91, 103, 111, 123) sts on back.
Next (dec) row (RS) K1, ssk, work to last 3 sts, k2tog, k1.
Next row (WS) P2, work to last 2 sts, p2.
Rep the last 2 rows 4 (6, 9, 10, 13) times more, for a total of 5 (7, 10, 11, 14) decs each side above bind-off; AT THE SAME TIME, work until 143 rows have been completed in Lace chart, (4 reps of pat, minus 1 row), so end with a RS row.
Next row (WS) Cont armhole decs if necessary and work rib as established to lace section, sl marker, p45; AT THE SAME TIME, inc 9 (13, 13, 9, 9) sts evenly spaced in this section—54 (58, 58, 54, 54) sts in this section, sl marker, rib to end.
Next row (RS) Work row 1 of k2, p2 rib as established over *all* sts, remove markers. After armhole shaping is complete, work even until armhole measures 5½ (6½, 6½, 7, 7½)"/14 (16.5, 16.5, 18, 19) cm, end with a WS row—82 (90, 94, 98, 102) sts.

BACK NECK SHAPING
Mark center 36 (36, 38, 40, 44) sts.
Next row (RS) Work in rib for 23 (27, 29, 29, 30) sts, join a 2nd ball of yarn and bind off center 36 (36, 36, 40, 42) sts, work in rib to end.
Working both sides at once, bind off 3 sts from each neck edge 4 times; AT THE SAME TIME, when armhole measures 7 (8, 8, 8½, 9)"/18 (20.5, 20.5, 21.5, 23)cm, end with WS row—11 (15, 17, 17, 18) sts each side. Be sure to spread ribbed section above armhole shaping to 13½ (15, 15½, 16, 17)"/34.5(38, 39.5, 40.5, 43)cm to get correct armhole depth.

SHAPE SHOULDERS
Bind off 5 (7, 9, 9, 9) sts from each shoulder edge once, then 6 (8, 8, 8, 9) sts once.

LEFT FRONT
Next row (RS) Rejoin yarn to work left front sts and bind off 6 (6, 6, 8, 8) sts at armhole edge, work to end—43 (47, 53, 57, 63) sts.
Next row (WS) Work even as established.
Dec row (RS) K1, ssk, work in rib to end.
Next row (WS) Work to last 2 sts, end p2.
Rep last 2 rows 4 (6, 9, 10, 13) times more,

Note: This chart is used for this design as well as the three that follow.

STITCH KEY

☐ k on RS, p on WS

⊟ p on RS, k on WS

⊡ yo

◩ k2tog

◪ ssk

◩ sl1, k1, pass sl st over k st, return st to LHN, pass next st over, return to RHN

◩ sl1, k2tog, pass sl st over k st

◪ work as ssk on last rep of row 1

for a total of 5 (7, 10, 11, 14) decs above bind-off; AT THE SAME TIME, when 143 rows have been completed in Lace Chart (4 reps minus 1 row), end with a RS row.
Next row (WS) Cont armhole decs if necessary and work in rib as established to lace section, sl marker, p24; AT THE SAME TIME, inc 4 (4, 3, 4, 3) sts evenly spaced—28 (28, 27, 28, 27) sts in this section, sl marker, work in rib to end.
Next row (RS) Work row 1 of k2, p2 rib as established over *all* sts, remove markers. Work in rib for 1"/2.5cm more, end with a RS row—42 (44, 46, 50, 52) sts, after armhole decs are complete.

FRONT NECK SHAPING
Bind off 12 (12, 12, 14, 14) sts, work in rib to end.
Cont to shape neck by binding off 3 sts from neck edge twice, 2 sts 4 (3, 3, 4, 4) times, and 1 st 5 (5, 5, 5, 6) times—11 (15, 17, 17, 18) sts rem.
Work even until armhole measures 7 (8, 8, 8½, 9)"/18 (20.5, 20.5, 21.5, 23)cm, end with a WS row.

SHOULDER SHAPING
From shoulder edge, bind off 5 (7, 9, 9, 9) sts once, then 6 (8, 8, 8, 9) sts once.

RIGHT FRONT
Rejoin yarn to right front 43 (47, 53, 57, 63) sts. Work same as for left front, but reverse shaping and omit the 6-st armhole bind-off, which has already been worked.

SLEEVES
With size 5 (3.75mm) needles, cast on 82 (86, 94, 94, 98) sts. Work in k2, p2 rib for 6 (6, 6½, 6½, 6½)"/15 (15, 16.5, 16.5, 16.5)cm, end with a WS row.

CAP SHAPING
Bind off 6 (6, 6, 8, 8) sts at beg of next 2 rows—70 (74, 82, 78, 82) sts.
Next (dec) row (RS) K1, ssk, rib to last 3 sts, k2tog, k1—68 (72, 80, 76, 80) sts.
Next row (WS) P2, work in rib to last 2 sts, p2.
Rep last 2 rows 17 (19, 21, 22, 23) times more, for a total of 18 (20, 22, 23, 24) decs each side—34 (34, 38, 32, 34) sts.

LACE CHART

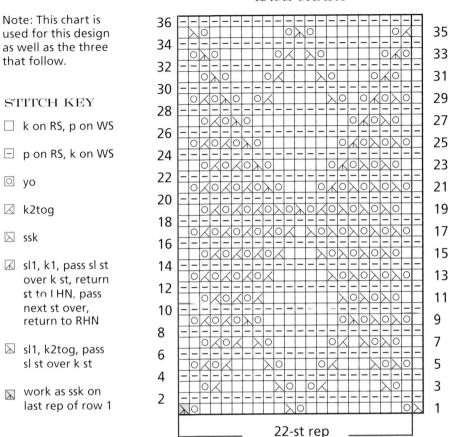

22-st rep

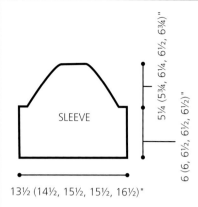

13½ (14½, 15½, 15½, 16½)"

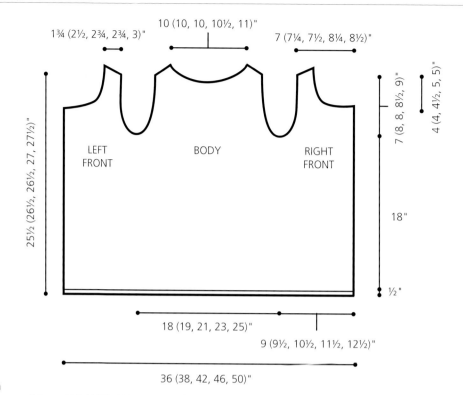

10 (10, 10, 10½, 11)"

1¾ (2½, 2¾, 2¾, 3)"

7 (7¼, 7½, 8¼, 8½)"

7 (8, 8, 8½, 9)"

4 (4, 4½, 5, 5)"

LEFT FRONT   BODY   RIGHT FRONT

25½ (26½, 26½, 27, 27½)"

18"

½"

18 (19, 21, 23, 25)"

9 (9½, 10½, 11½, 12½)"

36 (38, 42, 46, 50)"

Bind off 2 (2, 3, 2, 2) sts at beg of next 2 rows, then 3 (3, 4, 2, 3) sts at beg of next 2 rows. Bind off rem 24 sts.

FINISHING
Sew shoulder seams. Sew sleeve caps into armholes. Sew sleeve seams.

BOTTOM TRIM
With RS facing and size 4 (3.5mm) circular needle, pick up 233 (241, 257, 273, 289) sts along bottom edge of sweater. Work in k1, p1 rib for ½"/1.5cm. Bind off in rib.

NECKLINE TRIM
With RS facing and size 4 (3.5mm) needles, pick up 175 (175, 175, 177, 179) sts evenly around neckline. Work in k1, p1 rib for ½"/1.5cm. Bind off in rib.

LEFT FRONT BUTTONBAND
With RS facing and size 4 (3.5mm) needles, pick up 113 (117, 117, 119, 121) sts evenly along left front edge. Knit 5 rows. Bind off.

RIGHT FRONT BUTTONHOLE BAND
Place markers for buttonholes, the first at 2"/5cm from bottom edge, the last at ½"/1.5cm below neckline, and 5 more evenly spaced between.
With RS facing and size 4 (3.5mm) needles, pick up 113 (117, 117, 119, 121) sts evenly along right front edge.
Next (buttonhole) row (WS) *Knit to marker, bind off 3 sts; rep from * 6 times more, knit to end.
Knit next row, casting on 3 sts above 3 bound-off sts for each buttonhole. Knit 3 rows more. Bind off.
Sew buttons to left front opposite buttonholes. ∎

Ribbed Yoke Cardigan   ◼◼◼◻

page 61

SIZES
To fit Small (Medium, Large, X-Large, XX-Large). Shown in size Large.

MEASUREMENTS
Bust at underarm, including ½"/1.5cm buttonband:
35½ (39, 42, 46, 50)"/90 (99, 106.5, 117, 127)cm
Sleeve at upper arm:
13½ (14½, 15½, 15½, 16½)"/34.5 (37, 39.5, 39.5, 42)cm
Length from outer shoulder, including ½"/1.5cm trim:
25 (26½, 27, 28, 29)"/63.5 (67.5, 68.5, 71, 73.5)cm
Length may vary slightly, depending on row gauge.

MATERIALS
• 9 (10, 12, 13, 14) 1¾oz/50g balls (each 137yd/125m) of Debbie Bliss *Baby Cashmerino* (merino wool/microfiber/cashmere) in #026 Seafoam (2)
• One pair each sizes 4 and 5 (3.5 and 3.75mm) needles *or size to obtain gauge*
• One each sizes 4 and 5 (3.5 and 3.75mm) circular needles, 32" or 40"/80 or 100cm long
• 5 buttons, ¾"/20mm wide
• Stitch markers
• Stitch holders

GAUGES
• 19 sts and 32 rows to 4"/10cm over lace pat using size 5 (3.75mm) needles.
• 24 sts and 32 rows to 4"/10cm over k2, p2 rib using size 5 (3.75mm) needles.
Take time to save time—check your gauges.

STOCKINETTE STITCH (ST ST)
(over any number of sts)
Knit RS rows, purl WS rows.

K2, P2 RIB

(multiple of 4 sts plus 2)
Row 1 (RS) K2, *p2, k2; rep from *.
Row 2 P2, *k2, p2; rep from *.
Rep rows 1 and 2 for k2, p2 rib.

NOTE

End row 1 of Lace Chart (p. 135) by working last 2 sts with ssk, instead of SK2P.

BODY

With size 5 (3.75mm) circular needle, cast on 179 (201, 223, 245, 267) sts. Work back and forth, do *not* join.
Row 1 (RS) K1 (edge st: keep in St st), work first st of Lace Chart, work 22-st rep 8 (9, 10, 11, 12) times, ending last rep with ssk instead of SK2P, k1 (edge st: keep in St st). Work even as established for 107 rows (3 chart reps minus 1 row), ending with RS row. Piece measures approx 13½"/34cm.
Next row (WS) Purl, inc 31 (29, 27, 29, 31) sts evenly spaced across—210 (230, 250, 274, 298) sts.

BEGIN RIB PATTERN

Work row 1 of k2, p2 rib.
Next row (WS) Work 53 (57, 62, 69, 75) sts in rib for left front, place marker (pm), work 104 (116, 126, 136, 148) sts in rib for back, pm, work 53 (57, 62, 69, 75) sts in rib for right front.
Cont in rib as established for 4 (4½, 5, 5½, 6)"/10 (11.5, 12.5, 14, 15)cm from end of Lace Chart.
Note When taking this measurement, be sure to stretch rib to the bust measurement of 35 (38½, 41½, 45½, 49½)"/89 (98, 105.5, 115.5, 125.5)cm.

SEPARATE FOR BACK AND FRONTS

Next row (RS) Work in rib to 6 (6, 6, 8, 8) sts before first marker, bind off 6 (6, 6, 8, 8) sts—47 (51, 56, 61, 66) sts on front, remove marker, bind off 6 (6, 6, 8, 8) sts, work in rib to 2nd marker, turn. Place fronts on separate holders and work on back only.

BACK
ARMHOLE SHAPING

Bind off 6 (6, 6, 8, 8) sts, work in rib to end of back, turn—92 (104, 114, 120, 132) sts on back section.
Next (dec) row (RS) K1, ssk, work in rib to last 3 sts, k2tog, k1.
Next row (WS) P2, work in rib to last 2 sts, p2.
Rep last 2 rows 4 (6, 9, 10, 13) times more, for a total of 5 (7, 10, 11, 14) decs above bind-off—82 (90, 94, 98, 104) sts. Work even until armhole measures 5½ (6½, 6½, 7, 7½)"/14 (16.5, 16.5, 18, 19)cm.

BACK NECK SHAPING

Mark center 36 (36, 36, 40, 44) sts.
Next row (RS) Work in rib for 23 (27, 29, 29, 30) sts, join a 2nd ball of yarn and bind off center 36 (36, 36, 40, 44) sts, work in rib to end.

Working both sides at once, bind off 3 sts from each neck edge 4 times; AT THE SAME TIME, when armhole measures 7 (8, 8, 8½, 9)"/18 (20.5, 20.5, 21.5, 23)cm, end with a WS row—11 (15, 17, 17, 18) sts.

SHAPE SHOULDERS

Bind off 5 (7, 9, 9, 9) sts from each shoulder edge once, then 6 (8, 8, 8, 9) sts once.

LEFT FRONT

Next row (RS) Rejoin yarn to work left front sts and bind off 6 (6, 6, 8, 8) sts at armhole edge, work to end—47 (51, 56, 61, 66) sts.
Next row (WS) Work even.
Next (dec) row (RS) K1, ssk, work in rib to end.
Next row (WS) Work in rib to last 2 sts, end p2.
Rep last 2 rows 4 (6, 9, 10, 13) times more, for a total of 5 (7, 10, 11, 14) decs above bind-off—42 (44, 46, 50, 52) sts; AT THE SAME TIME, when front rib section measures 7 (8½, 8½, 9, 10)"/18 (21.5, 21.5, 23, 25.5)cm, beg neck shaping as foll:

NECK SHAPING

Bind off 12 (12, 12, 14, 14) sts, rib to end. Cont to shape neck by binding off 3 sts from neck edge twice, 2 sts 4 (3, 3, 4, 4) times, 1 st 5 (5, 5, 5, 6) times—11 (15, 17, 17, 18) sts rem.

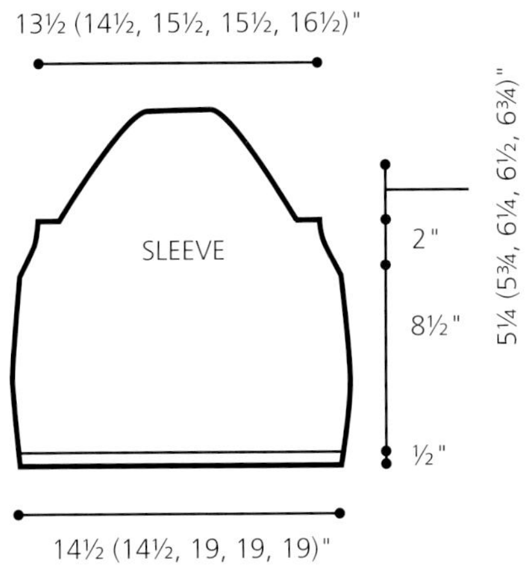

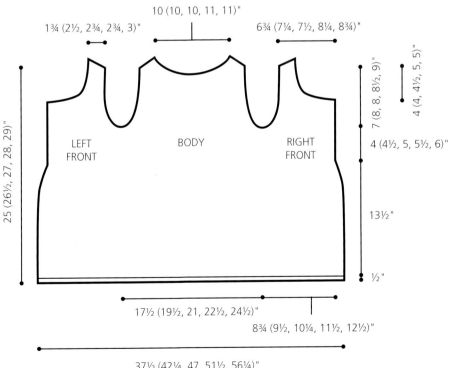

10 (10, 10, 11, 11)"

1¾ (2½, 2¾, 2¾, 3)" 6¾ (7¼, 7½, 8¼, 8¾)"

LEFT FRONT   BODY   RIGHT FRONT

25 (26½, 27, 28, 29)"

7 (8, 8, 8½, 9)"

4 (4, 4½, 5, 5)"

4 (4½, 5, 5½, 6)"

13½"

½"

17½ (19½, 21, 22½, 24½)"

8¾ (9½, 10¼, 11½, 12½)"

37½ (42¼, 47, 51½, 56¼)"

13½ (14½, 15½, 15½, 16½)"

SLEEVE

2"

8½"

½"

5¼ (5¾, 6¼, 6½, 6¾)"

14½ (14½, 19, 19, 19)"

Work even until armhole measures 7 (8, 8, 8½, 9)"/18 (20, 20, 21.5, 23)cm, end with a WS row.

SHOULDER SHAPING
From shoulder edge, bind off 5 (7, 9, 9, 9) sts once, and 6 (8, 8, 8, 9) sts once.

RIGHT FRONT
Rejoin yarn to right front sts. Work same as for left front, but reverse shaping and omit the first armhole bind-off.

SLEEVES
With size 5 (3.75mm) needles, cast on 69 (69, 91, 91, 91) sts.
Row 1 (RS) K1 (edge st: keep in St st), work row 1 of Lace Chart for 3 (3, 4, 4, 4) reps, end k1 (edge st: keep in St st).
Work even in Lace Chart as established for 71 rows total, (2 reps minus 1 row), end with a RS row. Piece measures approx 8½"/21.5cm from beg.
Next row (WS) Purl, inc 13 (17, 3, 3, 7) sts evenly spaced across—82 (86, 94, 94, 98) sts. Change to k2, p2 rib and work until piece measures 10½"/26.5cm from beg, end with a WS row.

CAP SHAPING
Bind off 6 (6, 6, 8, 8) sts at beg of next 2 rows—70 (74, 82, 78, 82) sts.
Next (dec) row (RS) K1, ssk, work in rib to last 3 sts, k2tog, k1—68 (72, 80, 76, 80) sts.
Next row (WS) P2, work in rib to last 2 sts, p2.
Rep last 2 rows 17 (19, 21, 22, 23) times more, for a total of 18 (20, 22, 23, 24) decs each side—34 (34, 38, 32, 34) sts.
Bind off 2 (2, 3, 2, 2) sts at beg of next 2 rows, then 3 (3, 4, 2, 3) sts at beg of next 2 rows. Bind off rem 24 sts.

FINISHING
Sew shoulder seams. Sew sleeve caps into armholes. Sew sleeve seams.

SLEEVE TRIM
With RS facing and size 4 (3.5mm) needles, pick up 69 (69, 91, 91, 91) sts along bottom edge of sleeve. Knit 3 rows. Bind off. Rep for second sleeve.

BOTTOM TRIM
With RS facing and size 4 (3.5mm) circular needle, pick up 179 (201, 223, 245, 267) sts along bottom edge of sweater.

Knit 3 rows. Bind off.

NECKLINE TRIM
With RS facing and size 4 (3.5mm) needles, pick up 165 (165, 165, 169, 169) sts evenly around neckline. Work in k1, p1 rib for ¾"/2cm. Bind off in rib.

LEFT FRONT BUTTONBAND
With RS facing and size 4 (3.5mm) needles, pick up 118 (124, 126, 130, 134) sts evenly along left front edge. Knit 5 rows. Bind off.

RIGHT FRONT BUTTONHOLE BAND
Place markers for buttonholes, the first at ½"/1.5cm above lace pat, the last at ½"/1.5cm below neckline, and 3 more evenly spaced between.
With RS facing and size 4 (3.5mm) needles, pick up 118 (124, 126, 130, 134) sts evenly along right front edge.
Next (buttonhole) row (WS) *K to marker, bind off 3 sts; rep from * 4 times more, k to end.
Knit next row, casting on 3 sts above 3 bound-off sts for each buttonhole. Knit 3 rows more. Bind off.
Sew buttons to left front opposite buttonholes. ∎

Collared Cardigan ◼◼◼◻

page 63

SIZES
To fit size Small (Medium, Large, X-Large, XX-Large). Shown in size X-Large.

MEASUREMENTS
BUST AT UNDERARM:
35 (38, 42, 46, 50)"/89 (96.5, 106.5, 117, 127)cm
SLEEVE AT UPPER ARM:
13½ (14½, 15½, 15½, 16½)"/34.5 (37, 39.5, 39.5, 42)cm
LENGTH FROM OUTER SHOULDER, INCLUDING ½"/1.5cm TRIM:
27 (28, 28, 28½, 29)"/68.5 (71, 71, 72.5, 73.5)cm
Length may vary slightly, depending on row gauge.

MATERIALS
• 13 (14, 16, 17, 18) 1¾oz/50g balls (each 137yd/125m) of Debbie Bliss *Baby Cashmerino* (merino wool/microfiber/cashmere) in #57 Blue Grey ②
• One pair each sizes 6 and 7 (4 and 4.5mm) needles *or size to obtain gauge*
• Size 6 (4mm) circular needle, 32" or 40"/80 or 100cm long

• 9 buttons, ⅝"/15mm wide
• Stitch markers

GAUGES
• 19 sts and 34 rows to 4"/10cm over lace pat using size 7 (4.5mm) needles.
• 24 sts and 32 rows to 4"/10cm over k2, p2 rib using size 7 (4.5mm) needles.
• 22 sts and 30 rows to 4"/10cm over garter rib using size 7 (4.5mm) needles.
Take time to save time—check your gauges.

STOCKINETTE STITCH (ST ST)
(over any number of sts)
Knit RS rows, purl WS rows.

K2, P2 RIB
(multiple of 4 sts plus 2)
Row 1 (RS) K2, *p2, k2; rep from *.
Row 2 P2, *k2, p2; rep from *.
Rep rows 1 and 2 for k2, p2 rib.

RIB PANEL
(worked over 14 sts)
Row 1 (RS) P2, *k2, p2; rep from *.
Row 2 K2, *p2, k2; rep from *.
Rep rows 1 and 2 for rib panel.

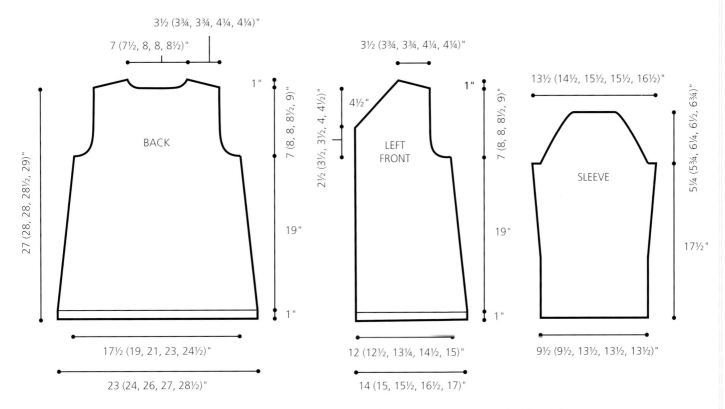

Schematic measurements:

BACK:
- 3½ (3¾, 3¾, 4¼, 4¼)"
- 7 (7½, 8, 8, 8½)"
- 1"
- 7 (8, 8½, 9)"
- 19"
- 1"
- 27 (28, 28, 28½, 29)"
- 17½ (19, 21, 23, 24½)"
- 23 (24, 26, 27, 28½)"

LEFT FRONT:
- 3½ (3¾, 3¾, 4¼, 4¼)"
- 1"
- 4½"
- 2½ (3½, 3½, 4, 4½)"
- 7 (8, 8½, 9)"
- 19"
- 1"
- 12 (12½, 13¼, 14½, 15)"
- 14 (15, 15½, 16½, 17)"

SLEEVE:
- 13½ (14½, 15½, 15½, 16½)"
- 5¼ (5¾, 6¼, 6½, 6¾)"
- 17½"
- 9½ (9½, 13½, 13½, 13½)"

GARTER RIB
(multiple of 4 sts plus 3)
Row 1 (RS) K3, *p1, k3; rep from *.
Row 2 Purl.
Rep rows 1 and 2 for garter rib.

NOTE
End row 1 of Lace Chart (p. 135) by working last 2 sts with ssk, instead of SK2P.

BACK
With size 7 (4.5mm) needle, cast on 134 (142, 150, 158, 166) sts. Purl 1 WS row.
Next row (RS) Work row 1 of garter rib over 19 sts, place marker (pm), work row 1 of rib panel over 14 sts, pm, work row 1 of garter rib over 27 (31, 35, 39, 43) sts, pm, work row 1 of rib panel over center 14 sts, pm, work row 1 of garter rib over 27 (31, 35, 39, 43) sts, pm, work row 1 of rib panel over 14 sts, pm, work row 1 of garter rib over 19 sts.
Work even for 9 (7, 9, 9, 9) rows more, end with a WS row.
Next (dec) row (RS) Work to first 2 sts of second garter rib section, ssk, work to last 2 sts of 3rd garter rib section, k2tog, work to end—124 (140, 148, 156, 164) sts.
Keeping in pat, rep dec row after 9 (7, 9, 9, 9) rows more, then every 10th (8th, 10th, 10th, 10th) row after for a total of 13 (15, 13, 11, 11) decs each side, 26 (30, 26,

22, 22) decs total—108 (112, 124, 136, 144) sts.
Work even until piece measures 19"/48.5cm from beg, end with a WS row.

ARMHOLE SHAPING
Bind off 7 (7, 8, 9, 10) sts at beg of next 2 rows.
Next (dec) row (RS) K1, ssk, work to last 3 sts, end k2tog, k1.
Next row Work as established.
Rep last 2 rows 7 (5, 10, 11, 12) times more, for a total of 8 (6, 11, 12, 13) decs each side—78 (86, 86, 94, 98) sts.
Work even until armhole measures 2 ½ (3½, 3 ½, 4, 4 ½)"/6.5 (9, 9, 10, 11.5)cm, end with a RS row.

RIBBED YOKE SECTION
Work as established to first of the center two garter rib sections, work 12 (16, 22, 28, 32) sts and at the same time inc 2 (2, 4, 2, 2) sts evenly spaced—18 (18, 26, 30, 34) sts, work center 14 rib panel sts as established, then work 12 (16, 22, 28, 32) sts and at the same time inc 2 (2, 4, 2, 2) sts evenly spaced—18 (18, 26, 30, 34) sts, work as established to end—82 (90, 94, 98, 102) sts.
Work in rib as established across all sts.
Work even until armhole measures 7 (8, 8, 8½, 9)"/18 (20.5, 20.5, 21.5, 23)cm,

end with a WS row.

SHAPE SHOULDERS AND BACK NECK
Mark center 22 (24, 28, 28, 30) sts.
Bind off 7 (8, 8, 8, 9) sts, work to center marked sts and join a 2nd ball of yarn, bind off center marked sts, work to end.
Working both sides at the same time with separate balls of yarn, bind off 7 (8, 8, 8, 9) sts at beg of next 3 shoulder edges, then 6 (6, 7, 9, 8) sts on last 2 shoulder edges; AT THE SAME TIME, bind off from each neck edge 5 sts twice.

LEFT FRONT
With size 7 (4.5mm) needle, cast on 80 (84, 88, 92, 96) sts. Purl 1 WS row.
Next row (RS) Work row 1 of garter rib over 19 sts, pm, work row 1 of rib panel over 14 sts, pm, work row 1 of garter rib over 23 (27, 31, 35, 39) sts, pm, work row 1 of Lace Chart over 23 sts, end k1 (St st edge st).
Work even for 9 (7, 9, 9, 9) rows more, end with a WS row.
Next (dec) row (RS) Work to first 2 sts of second garter rib section, ssk, work as established to end—79 (83, 87, 91, 95) sts.
Keeping in pat, rep dec row after 9 (7, 9, 9, 9) rows more, then every 10th (8th, 10th, 10th, 10th) row after for a total of 12 (15, 13, 11, 11) decs—67 (69, 75, 81, 85) sts.

Work even until piece measures 19"/48.5cm from beg, end with a WS row.

ARMHOLE SHAPING
Bind off 7 (7, 8, 9, 10) sts at beg of next RS row—59 (62, 67, 72, 75) sts.
Work WS row as established.
Next (dec) row (RS) K1, ssk, work as established to end.
Next row Work as established.
Rep last 2 rows 7 (5, 10, 11, 12) times more, for a total of 8 (6, 11, 12, 13) decs—52 (56, 56, 60, 62) sts.
Work even until armhole measures 2½ (3½, 3½, 4, 4½)"/6.5 (9, 9, 10, 11.5)cm, end with a RS row.
Next row (WS) Purl across lace and garter rib sections [32 (36, 42, 48, 52) sts in these two sections combined] to rib panel; AT THE SAME TIME, inc 4 (4, 4, 8, 10) sts evenly spaced in these two sections, work in rib as established to end—56 (60, 60, 68, 72) sts.
Next row (RS) Work in rib as established across all sts.

FRONT NECKLINE SHAPING
At beg of WS rows, bind off 3 (3, 3, 4, 4) sts 11 (11, 11, 10, 11) times, then 3 (4, 4, 3, 2) sts once.

Cont in rib as established until piece measures same as back to shoulder, end with a WS row—20 (23, 23, 25, 26) sts.

SHAPE SHOULDER
From RS shoulder edge, bind off 7 (8, 8, 8, 9) sts twice, then 6 (7, 7, 9, 8) sts on RS row.

RIGHT FRONT
Work same as for left front, reversing placement of patterns and all shaping.

SLEEVES
With larger needles, cast on 58 (58, 82, 82, 82) sts.
Work in k2, p2 rib for 3"/7.5cm, end with a RS row.
Purl next row, dec 9 (9, 13, 13, 13) sts evenly spaced—49 (49, 69, 69, 69) sts.

LACE BORDER
Next row K1 (edge st. keep in St st), work row 1 of Lace Chart for 2 (2, 3, 3, 3) reps wide, over 45 (45, 67, 67, 67) sts, ending ssk instead of SK2P, pm, end k1 (edge st: keep in St st).
Work even in Lace Chart until all 35 rows are complete, end with a RS row.
Purl 1 WS row, inc 6 sts evenly spaced—63 (67, 71, 75, 79) sts.

GARTER RIB SECTION
Next row (RS) Work row 1 of garter rib over 63 (67, 71, 75, 79) sts.
Work even in pat for 9 rows more, end with a WS row.
Next (inc) row (RS): K2, M1, work to last 2 sts, M1, end k2—65 (69, 73, 77, 81) sts.
Keeping first 2 and last 2 sts in St st, working incs into pat, work for 11 more rows, end with a WS row.
Rep inc row on next row, then every 12th row 3 more times, for a total of 5 incs each side—73 (77, 81, 85, 89) sts.
Work even until sleeve measures 16"/40.5cm, end with a RS row.
Next row Purl, inc 9 (9, 13, 9, 9) sts evenly spaced—82 (86, 94, 94, 98) sts.

UPPER SLEEVE
Work even in k2, p2 rib until sleeve measures 17½"/44.5cm, end with a WS row.

CAP SHAPING
Bind off 6 (6, 6, 8, 8) sts at beg of next 2 rows—70 (74, 82, 78, 82) sts.
Next (dec) row (RS) K1, ssk, work in

rib to last 3 sts, k2tog, k1—68 (72, 80, 76, 80) sts.
Next row (WS) P2, work in rib to last 2 sts, p2.
Rep last 2 rows 17 (19, 21, 22, 23) times more, for a total of 18 (20, 22, 23, 24) decs each side—34 (34, 38, 32, 34) sts.
Bind off 2 (2, 3, 2, 2) sts at beg of next 2 rows, then 3 (3, 4, 2, 3) sts at beg of next 2 rows. Bind off rem 24 sts.

FINISHING
Sew shoulder seams. Sew sleeve caps into armholes. Sew sleeve and side seams.

BOTTOM TRIM
With RS facing and size 6 (4mm) circular needle, pick up 271 (283, 299, 315, 331) sts along bottom edge of sweater. Knit 9 rows. Bind off.

LEFT FRONT BUTTONBAND
With RS facing and size 6 (4mm) needles, pick up 122 (126, 126, 128, 130) sts evenly along left front edge. Knit 5 rows. Bind off.

RIGHT FRONT BUTTONHOLE BAND
Place markers for buttonholes, the first at 5"/12.5cm bottom edge, the last at ½"/1.5cm below neckline, and 7 more evenly spaced between.
With RS facing and size 6 (4mm) needles, pick up 122 (126, 126, 128, 130) sts evenly along right front edge.
Next (buttonhole) row (WS) *Knit to marker, bind off 2 sts; rep from * 8 times more, knit to end.
Next row Knit, casting on 2 sts above 2 bound-off sts for each buttonhole. Knit 3 rows more. Bind off.

NECKLINE TRIM
With RS facing and size 6 (4mm) needles, pick up 141 (143, 145, 145, 147) sts evenly around neckline. Knit 1 row, purl 1 row. Bind off knitwise on WS.

COLLAR
With size 7 (4.5mm) needles, cast on 166 (166, 170, 170, 170) sts. Work in k2, p2 rib for 9"/23cm. Bind off in rib. Sew collar to neckline behind and to bottom of the neckline trim.

Overlapping the lace panels at center front, sew buttons to left front, to left side of lace panel, opposite buttonholes. ■

Peplum Cardi

page 65

SIZES
To fit size Small (Medium, Large, X-Large, XX-Large). Shown in size Medium.

MEASUREMENTS
Bust at underarm, including
1"/2.5cm buttonband:
34 (37½, 42, 46, 50)"/86.5
(95, 106.5, 117, 127)cm
Sleeve at upper arm:
13½ (14½, 15½, 15½, 16½)"/34.5
(37, 39.5, 39.5, 42)cm
Length from outer shoulder, including
½"/1.5cm lower trim:
23½ (24½, 24½, 25, 25½)"/59.5
(62, 62, 63.5, 65)cm
Length may vary slightly, depending
on row gauge.

MATERIALS
• 8 (9, 9, 10, 11) 1¾oz/50g balls
(each 137yd/125m) of Debbie Bliss *Baby Cashmerino* (merino wool/microfiber/
cashmere) in #202 Light Blue **2**
• One pair each sizes 6 and 7 (4 and
4.5mm) needles *or size to obtain gauge*
• One each sizes 6 and 7 (4 and 4.5mm)
circular needles, 32" or 40"/80 or
100cm long

• Six buttons, ¾"/20mm wide

GAUGES
• 19 sts and 34 rows to 4"/10cm over
Lace Chart using size 7 (4.5mm) needles.
• 24 sts and 32 rows to 4"/10cm over k2,
p2 rib using size 7 (4.5mm) needles.
• 22 sts and 30 rows to 4"/10cm over
garter rib using size 7 (4.5mm) needles.
*Take time to save time—check your
gauges.*

STOCKINETTE STITCH (ST ST)
(over any number of sts)
Knit RS rows, purl WS rows.

K2, P2 RIB
(multiple of 4 sts plus 2)
Row 1 (RS): K2, *p2, k2; rep from *.
Row 2 P2, *k2, p2; rep from *.
Rep rows 1 and 2 for k2, p2 rib.

GARTER RIB
(multiple of 4 sts plus 3)
Row 1 (RS) K3, *p1, k3; rep from *.
Row 2 Purl.
Rep rows 1 and 2 for garter rib.

NOTE
End row 1 of Lace Chart (p. 135) by working last 2 sts with ssk, instead of SK2P.

BODY
With size 7 (4.5mm) circular needle, cast
on 179 (201, 223, 245, 267) sts. Do
not join. Working back and forth, purl
1 row.

BEG LACE PATTERN
Note This sweater begins at the halfway
point of the Lace Chart, so beg with row
19 (RS) as described below.
Row 1 (RS) K1 (edge st: keep in St st),
work first st of chart, work row 19 of chart
over 22-st rep 8 (9, 10, 11, 12) times,
k1 (edge st: keep in St st).
Work even until 1 1/2 reps, or 55 lace
rows (19–36, then 1–36, then row 1)
are completed, piece measures approx
6½"/16.5cm from beg, end with a
RS row.
Next row (WS) Purl, dec 9 (19, 13, 11, 9)
sts evenly spaced across—170 (182, 210,
234, 258) sts.

BEGIN WAISTLINE
Work row 1 of k2, p2 rib over all sts.
Cont in rib for 3"/7.6cm (piece measures

approx 9½"/24cm from beg), end with a
RS row.
Next row (WS) Purl, inc 11 (15, 11, 11, 11)
sts evenly spaced—181 (197, 221, 245,
269) sts.

SET UP PATTERNS
Place markers (pm) on either side of
center 23 sts.
Next row (RS) K1 (St st edge st), work row
1 of Lace Chart over 23 sts, pm, work 55
(63, 75, 87, 99) sts in garter rib to marker,
pm, work row 1 of Lace Chart over center
23 sts, pm, work 55 (63, 75, 87, 99) sts in
garter rib, pm, work row 1 of Lace Chart
over 23 sts, end k1 (St st edge st).
Next row Work as established.
Place markers for "side seams."
Next row (RS) K1 (St st edge st), cont
Lace Chart over 23 sts, sl marker, work
22 (24, 31, 37, 43) sts in garter rib, pm
("side seam" marker), cont in garter rib to
center, cont Lace Chart over center 23 sts,
sl marker, work 33 (39, 44, 50, 56) sts in
garter rib, pm ("side seam" marker), cont
in garter rib to next marker, sl marker,
cont Lace Chart over 23 sts, end k1
(St st edge st).
Work even until piece measures
16½"/42cm from beg, end with a WS row.

SEPARATE FOR BACK AND FRONTS
Next row (RS) Work as established to 5
(6, 6, 8, 8) sts before first "side seam"
marker, bind off 5 (6, 6, 8, 8) sts, remove
marker, bind off 5 (6, 6, 8, 8) sts more,
work to 2nd "side seam" marker, turn.
Place front sts on separate holders to be
worked later.

BACK
ARMHOLE SHAPING
Bind off 5 (6, 6, 8, 8) sts, work to end of
back, turn—79 (89, 99, 107, 119) sts rem
on back section.
Next (dec) row (RS) K1, ssk, work in rib
to last 3 sts, k2tog, k1.
Next row (WS) P2, work in rib to last
2 sts, p2.
Rep last 2 rows 2 (4, 7, 9, 13) times
more—73 (79, 83, 87, 91) sts; AT THE
SAME TIME, when 73 rows of Lace Chart
are completed (2 reps plus 1 row), end
Lace Chart.

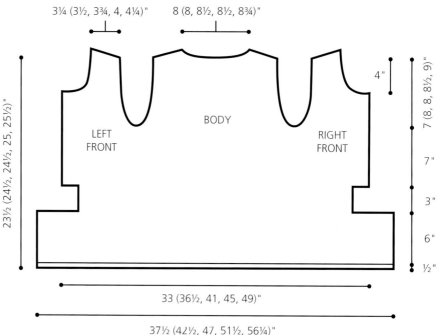

Measurements on body diagram:
3¼ (3½, 3¾, 4, 4¼)"   8 (8, 8½, 8½, 8¾)"

4 "

LEFT FRONT   BODY   RIGHT FRONT

23½ (24½, 24½, 25, 25½)"

7 (8, 8, 8½, 9)"

7 "

3 "

6 "

½ "

33 (36½, 41, 45, 49)"

37½ (42½, 47, 51½, 56¼)"

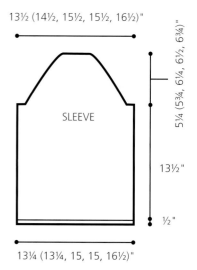

Sleeve diagram:
13½ (14½, 15½, 15½, 16½)"

SLEEVE

5¼ (5¾, 6¼, 6½, 6¾)"

13½ "

½ "

13¼ (13¼, 15, 15, 16½)"

Next row (WS) Purl, inc 13 (11, 11, 11, 11) sts evenly spaced—86 (90, 94, 98, 102) sts. Change to k2, p2 rib and work even until armhole measures 7 (8, 8, 8½, 9)"/18 (20.5, 20.5, 21.5, 23)cm, ending with a WS row.

BACK NECK SHAPING
Mark center 28 (28, 30, 30, 32) sts.
Next row (RS) Bind off 7 (7, 8, 8, 9) sts, work to center marked sts, join a 2nd ball of yarn and bind off center marked sts, work to end.
Working both sides at once, bind off 7 (7, 8, 8, 9) sts from next shoulder edge, then 6 (7, 7, 8, 8) sts on last 2 shoulder edges; AT THE SAME TIME, bind off 5 sts from each neck edge twice.

LEFT FRONT
Next row (RS) Rejoin yarn to the 46 (48, 55, 61, 67) left front sts and bind off 5 (6, 6, 8, 8) sts at armhole edge, work to end.
Next row (WS) Purl.
Next (dec) row (RS) K1, ssk, work to end.
Next row (WS) Work to last 2 sts, end p2.
Rep last 2 rows 2 (4, 7, 9, 13) times more—38 (37, 41, 43, 45) sts; AT THE SAME TIME, when 73 rows of Lace Chart are completed (2 reps plus 1 row), end Lace Chart.
Next row (WS) Purl, inc 4 (9, 9, 11, 13) sts evenly spaced—42 (46, 50, 54, 58) sts.
Change to k2, p2 rib and work for 2

(2½, 3, 3½, 4)"/5 (6.5, 7.5, 9, 10)cm, end with a RS row.

NECKLINE SHAPING
Bind off 7 (9, 9, 11, 11) sts at beg of row, work in rib to end. Cont to bind off at neck edge, 3 sts 2 (2, 3, 3, 5) times, then 2 sts 3 (3, 3, 3, 2) times, then 1 st 4 (4, 4, 4, 3) times—19 (21, 22, 24, 25) sts.
Work even until armhole measures 7 (8, 8, 8½, 9)"/18 (20, 20, 21.5, 23)cm, end with a WS row.

SHOULDER SHAPING
Bind off at beg of RS rows, 7 (7, 8, 8, 9) sts 1 (3, 1, 3, 1) times, then 6 (0, 7, 0, 8) sts 2 times.

RIGHT FRONT
Rejoin yarn to right front sts. Work same as for left front, but reverse shaping and *omit* the 5 (6, 6, 8, 8)-st armhole bind-off.

SLEEVES
With size 7 (4.5mm) needles, cast on 63 (63, 71, 71, 79) sts.

ESTABLISH PATTERNS
Next row (RS) K2 (edge sts: keep in St st), work row 1 of garter rib over 7 (7, 11, 11, 15) sts, work row 1 of Lace Chart over 45 sts (2 reps), work row 1 of garter rib over 7 (7, 11, 11, 15) sts, end k2 (edge sts: keep

in St st). Work even in pats as established until 36 rows of chart are completed.

CHANGE PATTERNS
Next row (RS) K2 (St st edge sts), work row 1 of garter rib over 59 (59, 67, 67, 75) sts, end k2 (St st edge sts).
Work as established until sleeve measures 11"/28cm, end with a RS row.
Next row (WS) Purl, inc 19 (23, 23, 23, 19) sts evenly spaced across—82 (86, 94, 94, 98) sts.
Change to k2, p2 rib and work until sleeve measures 13½"/34.5cm, end with a WS row.

CAP SHAPING

Cont in rib as established and bind off 6 (6, 6, 8, 8) sts at beg of next 2 rows—70 (74, 82, 78, 82) sts.

Next (dec) row (RS) K1, ssk, work in rib to last 3 sts, k2tog, k1.

Next row (WS) P2, work in rib to last 2 sts, p2.

Rep last 2 rows 17 (19, 21, 22, 23) times more—34 (34, 38, 32, 34) sts.

Bind off 2 (2, 3, 2, 2) sts at beg of next 2 rows, then 3 (3, 4, 2, 3) sts at beg of next 2 rows.

Bind off rem 24 sts.

FINISHING

Sew shoulder seams. Sew sleeve caps into armholes.

SLEEVE TRIM

With size 6 (4mm) needles and RS facing, pick up 55 (55, 63, 63, 71) sts evenly along cast-on edge. Knit 3 rows. Bind off. Sew sleeve seams.

BOTTOM TRIM

With RS facing and size 6 (4mm) circular needle, pick up 179 (201, 223, 245, 267) sts along bottom edge of sweater. Knit 3 rows. Bind off.

NECKLINE TRIM

With RS facing and size 6 (4mm) needles, pick up 146 (146, 150, 150, 150) sts evenly around neckline. Work in k1, p1 rib for ½"/1.5cm. Bind off in rib.

LEFT FRONT BUTTONBAND

With RS facing and size 6 (4mm) needles, pick up 116 (122, 124, 128, 132) sts evenly along left front edge. Knit 7 rows. Bind off.

RIGHT FRONT BUTTONHOLE BAND

Place markers for buttonholes, the first at ½"/1.5cm above lower lace pat, the last at ½"/1.5cm above upper lace pat, and 4 more evenly spaced between.

With RS facing and size 6 (4mm) needles, pick up 116 (122, 124, 128, 132) sts evenly along right front edge.

Next (buttonhole) row (WS) *K to marker, bind off 3 sts; rep from * 5 times more, k to end.

Knit next row, casting on 3 sts above 3 bound-off sts for each buttonhole. Knit 5 rows more. Bind off.

Sew buttons to left front opposite buttonholes. ▦

Dropped Shoulder Lace ◼◼◼◻

page 71

SIZES

To fit sizes X-Small/Small (Medium, Large/X-Large). Shown in size Medium.

MEASUREMENTS

Bust at underarm:
approx 47 (52, 59)"/119.5 (132, 149.5)cm
Length to outer shoulder:
26 (27, 28)"/66 (68.5, 71)cm
Sleeve at upper arm:
13 (13, 14)"/33 (33, 35.5)cm

MATERIALS

• 10 (11, 13) 1¾oz/50g hanks (each 175yd/159m) of Koigu *KPM* (merino wool) in #3003 Shades of Lilac ❶
• One pair size 5 (3.75mm) needles *or size to obtain gauge*
• Size 4 (3.5mm) circular needle, 16"/40cm long
• Stitch markers
• Tapestry needle

GAUGES

• 25 sts and 40 rows to 4"/10cm over Madeira cascade pat using size 5 (3.75mm) needles.
• 26 sts and 37 rows to 4"/10cm over Viennese horseshoe pat using size 5 (3.75mm) needles.

Take time to save time—check your gauges.

STOCKINETTE STITCH (ST ST)

(over any number of sts)
Knit RS rows, purl WS rows.

LACE LADDER

(multiple of 4 sts)
Row 1 (RS) *Ssk, [yo] twice, k2tog; rep from *.
Row 2 *P1, (p1, k1) into double yo, p1; rep from *.
Rep rows 1 and 2 for lace ladder.

MADEIRA CASCADE PATTERN

(multiple of 20 sts plus 5)
Row 1 (RS) Purl.
Row 2 Knit.
Row 3 K2, *k1, yo, k8, SK2P, k8, yo; rep from *, end k3.
Row 4 and all WS rows through row 18 Purl.
Row 5 K2, *k2, yo, k7, SK2P, k7, yo, k1; rep from *, end k3.
Row 7 K2, k2tog, *yo, k1, yo, k6, SK2P, k6, yo, k1, yo, SK2P; rep from * to last 4 sts, end last rep yo, ssk, k2 instead of yo, SK2P.
Row 9 K2, *k4, yo, k5, SK2P, k5, yo, k3; rep from *, end k3.
Row 11 K2, *k1, yo, SK2P, yo, k1, yo, k4, SK2P, k4, yo, k1, yo, SK2P, yo; rep from *, end k3.
Row 13 K2, *k6, yo, k3, SK2P, k3, yo, k5; rep from *, end k3.
Row 15 K2, k2tog, *yo, k1, yo, SK2P, yo, k1, yo, k2, SK2P, k2, [yo, k1, yo, SK2P] twice; rep from * to last 4 sts, end last rep yo, ssk, k2 instead of yo, SK2P.
Row 17 K2, *k8, yo, k1, SK2P, k1, yo, k7; rep from *, end k3.
Row 19 K2, *[k1, yo, SK2P, yo] 5 times; rep from *, end k3.
Row 20 Knit.
Rep rows 1–20 for Madeira cascade pat.

VIENNESE HORSESHOE PATTERN

(multiple of 20 sts plus 2)
Row 1 (WS) and all WS rows Purl, working (k1, p1) into each double yo of the previous row.
Row 2 K1, yo, *ssk, k2, yo, ssk, k1, yo, k2tog, p2, ssk, yo, k1, k2tog, yo, k2, k2tog, [yo] twice; rep from *, end last rep yo, k1 instead of [yo] twice.
Row 4 P2, *[yo, ssk, k2] twice, p2, [k2, k2tog, yo] twice, p2; rep from *.
Row 6 P2, *k1, yo, ssk, k2, yo, ssk, k1, p2,

141

k1, k2tog, yo, k2, k2tog, yo, k1, p2;
rep from *.

Row 8 P2, *ssk, [yo] twice, ssk, k2, yo, ssk,
p2, k2tog, yo, k2, k2tog, [yo] twice, k2tog,
p2; rep from *.

Row 10 P2, *ssk, [yo] twice, k2tog, k3, yo,
ssk, k2tog, yo, k3, ssk, [yo] twice, k2tog,
p2; rep from *.

Row 12 P2, *ssk, [yo] twice, k2tog, k1,
k2tog, yo, k4, yo, ssk, k1, ssk, [yo] twice,
k2tog, p2; rep from *.

Row 14 P2, *ssk, [yo] twice, [k2tog] twice,
yo, k6, yo, [ssk] twice, [yo] twice, k2tog,
p2; rep from *.

Row 16 P2, *ssk, yo, k1, k2tog, yo, k2,
k2tog, [yo] twice, ssk, k2, yo, ssk, k1, yo,
k2tog, p2; rep from *.

Row 18 P2, *[k2, k2tog, yo] twice, p2, [yo,
ssk, k2] twice, p2; rep from *.

Row 20 P2, *k1, k2tog, yo, k2, k2tog, yo,
k1, p2, k1, yo, ssk, k2, yo, ssk, k1, p2; rep
from *.

Row 22 P2, *k2tog, yo, k2, k2tog, [yo]
twice, k2tog, p2, ssk, [yo] twice, ssk, k2,
yo, ssk, p2; rep from *.

Row 24 K1, *k2tog, yo, k3, ssk, [yo] twice,
k2tog, p2, ssk, [yo] twice, k2tog, k3, yo,
ssk; rep from *, end k1.

Row 26 K3, *yo, ssk, k1, ssk, [yo] twice,
k2tog, p2, ssk, [yo] twice, k2tog, k1, k2tog,
yo, k4; rep from *, end last rep k3.

Row 28 K4, *yo, [ssk] twice, [yo] twice,
k2tog, p2, ssk, [yo] twice, [k2tog] twice, yo,

k6; rep from *, end last rep k4.
Rep rows 1–28 for Viennese horseshoe pat.

MARRIAGE LINES PATTERN
(panel of 7 sts)
Row 1 (RS) K1, yo, k2tog, k4.
Row 2 and all WS rows Purl.
Row 3 K2, yo, k2tog, k3.
Row 5 K3, yo, k2tog, k2.
Row 7 K4, yo, k2tog, k1.
Row 9 K5, yo, k2tog.
Row 11 K4, ssk, yo, k1.
Row 13 K3, ssk, yo, k2.
Row 15 K2, ssk, yo, k3.
Row 17 K1, ssk, yo, k4.
Row 19 Ssk, yo, k5.
Row 20 Purl.
Rep rows 1–20 for marriage lines pat.

K2, P2 CHECK
(multiple of 4 sts plus 2)
Rows 1 and 2 K2, *p2, k2; rep from *.
Rows 3 and 4 P2, *k2, p2; rep from *.
Rep rows 1–4 for k2, p2 check.

FRONT
With size 5 (3.75mm) needles, cast on 157
(177, 197) sts.
Next row (RS) P6, place marker (pm),
work row 1 of Madeira cascade pat over
145 (165, 185) sts, pm, p6.
Next row (WS) K6, sl marker, work row 2 of
Madeira cascade pat over 145 (165, 185)

sts, sl marker, end k6.
Next row (RS) K2 (St st edge sts), pm,
work row 1 of lace ladder over 4 sts, sl
marker, work row 3 of Madeira cascade pat
over 145 (165, 185) sts, sl marker, work
row 1 of lace ladder over 4 sts, pm, end k2
(St st edge sts).
Work in pats as established until 2 reps of
Madeira cascade pat are complete
(40 rows), end with a WS row.
Next row (RS) K2 (edge sts), sl marker,
work lace ladder over 4 sts, sl marker, p145
(165, 185), sl marker, work lace ladder over
4 sts, sl marker, end k2 (edge sts).
Next row (WS) Work 6 sts as established,
sl marker, k145 (165, 185) to last 6 sts;
AT THE SAME TIME, dec 3 sts evenly
spaced, sl marker, work rem 6 sts as
established—154 (174, 194) sts.
Next row (RS) Work 6 sts as established, sl
marker, work row 1 of Viennese horseshoe
pat over 142 (162, 182) sts, sl marker, work
rem 6 sts as established.
Work even in pats as established until piece
measures 21 (22, 23)"/53.5 (56, 58.5)cm
above Madeira cascade pat.

SHOULDER AND FRONT
NECKLINE SHAPING
Mark center 18 (22, 26) sts.
Change to k2, p2 check and bind off 4 sts
at beg of next 4 rows.
Next row (RS) Bind off 4 sts, work in pat as
established to center 18 (22, 26) sts, join
a 2nd ball of yarn and bind off 18 (22, 26)
sts, work as established to end.
Keeping in pat and working both sides at
the same time, bind off 4 sts at next WS
shoulder edge, then 4 sts from each
shoulder edge 10 (12, 14) more times; AT
THE SAME TIME, bind off from each neck
edge 2 sts 5 times, then 1 st 6 times.

BACK
Work same as for front to shoulder—154
(174, 194) sts.

SHOULDER AND BACK
NECKLINE SHAPING
Working in k2, p2 check, bind off 4 sts
at beg of next 18 (22, 26) rows—82
(86, 90) sts.
Next row (RS) Bind off 4 sts, work in pat as
established to center 18 (22, 26) sts, join
a 2nd ball of yarn and bind off center 18
(22, 26) sts, work as established to end.
Keeping in pat and working both sides
at the same time, bind off 4 sts at next

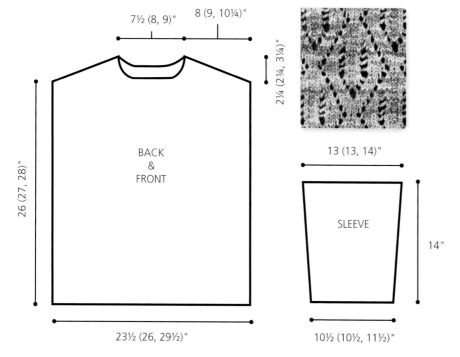

7½ (8, 9)"   8 (9, 10¼)"

2¼ (2¾, 3¼)"

BACK & FRONT

26 (27, 28)"

23½ (26, 29½)"

13 (13, 14)"

SLEEVE

14"

10½ (10½, 11½)"

WS shoulder edge, then 4 sts from each shoulder edge 3 more times; AT THE SAME TIME, bind off 8 sts from each neck edge 2 times.

SLEEVES
With size 5 (3.75mm) needles, cast on 69 sts.
Next row (RS) K2 (St st edge sts), work in Madeira cascade pat over center 65 sts, end k2 (St st edge sts).
Work in Madeira cascade pat for 2 reps (40 rows), then work RS row 1.
Next row (WS) Knit; AT THE SAME TIME, dec 2 (dec 2, inc 5) sts evenly spaced—67 (67, 74) sts.
Next row (RS) K2 (St st edge sts), work in marriage lines pat over 63 (63, 70) sts, end k2 (St st edge sts).
Work even for 9 rows more, end with a WS row.
Next (inc) row (RS) K2, M1, work in pat to last 2 sts, M1, end k2—69 (69, 76) sts.
Keeping edge sts in St st, working incs into pat, rep inc row after 9 rows more, then every 10th row for a total of 10 incs each side—87 (87, 94) sts.
Work even until sleeve measures 14"/35.5cm. Bind off.

FINISHING
Sew front to back at shoulders.

NECKLINE EDGE
With RS facing and size 4 (3.5mm) circular needle, beg at right shoulder, pick up 64 (70, 76) sts evenly spaced along back neck to shoulder, then 86 (92, 98) sts along front neck to beg—150 (162, 174) sts. Place marker and join.
Next rnd *K1, p1; rep from *.
Rep last rnd until rib measures ¾"/2cm, bind off.
Measure 6½ (6½, 7)"/16.5 (16.5, 18)cm down from shoulder on front and back, both sides. Sew sleeve tops between markers, centering at shoulder seam.
Sew side and sleeve seams.
Weave in ends. ■

Textured Raglan Pullover

page 76

SIZES
To fit sizes Small (Medium, Large, X-Large, XX-Large). Shown in size Large.

MEASUREMENTS
Bust at underarm:
35 (39, 43, 47, 51)"/89
(99, 109, 119.5, 129.5)cm
Length from center back:
24½ (25, 25½, 26, 26½)"/62
(63.5, 64.6, 66, 67)cm
Sleeve at upper arm:
12½ (13, 14, 15, 16)"/31.5
(33, 35.5, 38, 40.5)cm

MATERIALS
• 11 (12, 13, 14, 15) 1¾oz/50g balls
(each 120yd/132m) of Classic Elite
Magnolia (merino wool/silk) in #5457
Blue Iris (MC) 🔵
• 1 ball in #5448 Forget-Me-Not (CC)
• One pair size 6 (4mm) needles *or size to
obtain gauge*
• Size 5 (3.75mm) circular needle,
24"/60cm long
• Stitch markers
• Cable needle (cn)

GAUGES
• 21 sts and 30 rows to 4"/10cm over
garter rib using size 6 (4mm) needles.
• Lace panel = 2"/5cm using size 6
(4mm) needles.
• Cable/lace panel = 1½"/4cm using
size 6 (4mm) needles.

Take time to save time—check your gauges.

STOCKINETTE STITCH (ST ST)
(over any number of sts)
Knit RS rows, purl WS rows.

REVERSE STOCKINETTE STITCH (REV ST ST)
(over any number of sts)
Purl RS rows, knit WS rows.

GARTER RIB
(multiple of 5 sts plus 4)
Row 1 (RS) K4, *p1, k4; rep from *.
Row 2 Purl.
Rep rows 1–2 for garter rib.

K2, P2 RIB
(multiple of 4 sts plus 2)
All rnds K2, *p2, k2; rep from *.

P1, K1 RIB
(multiple of 2 sts)
All rnds *P1, k1; rep from *.

TWIST RIB
(over 26 sts)
Rnd 1 P2, *[RT] 3 times, p2; rep from *.
Rnd 2 P2, *k6, p2; rep from *.
Rnd 3 P2, *k1, [RT] 2 times, k1, p2;
rep from *.
Rnd 4 P2, *k6, p2; rep from *.
Rep rnds 1–4 for twist rib.

STITCH GLOSSARY
RT (right twist) K2tog, leave on needle,
then knit the first st again, slip both sts
from needle.
LT (left twist) Skip 1 st and knit into back
of 2nd st, then knit in front of the skipped
st, slip both sts from needle.

NOTES
1) All st counts are based on cable/lace
panel being on a 10-st row. If counting on
a 12-st row, remember to add those sts.
2) The lace panel is over 12 sts. See chart.
3) The cable/lace panel is over 10 sts,
changing to 12 sts and back to 10 sts.
See chart.

BACK
With size 6 (4mm) needles and MC, cast on
106 (116, 126, 136, 146) sts. Purl WS row.
Next row (RS) K6 (edge sts: keep in St st),
place marker (pm), work cable/lace panel
over 10 sts, pm, work in garter rib over 19

(24, 29, 34, 39) sts, pm, p1 (keep single st
in rev St st), pm, work lace panel over 12
sts, pm, work cable/lace panel over center
10 sts, pm, work lace panel over 12 sts,
pm, p1 (keep single st in rev St st), pm,
work in garter rib over 19 (24, 29, 34, 39)
sts, pm, work cable/lace panel over 10 sts,
pm, end k6 (edge sts: keep in St st).
Work even in pats until piece measures
19"/48cm, end with a WS row.
Shape armholes (RS) Bind off 6 sts at beg
of next 2 rows—94 (104, 114, 124, 134)
sts. Work 2 rows as established.
For ease of decreasing, remove outer markers at each end, the ones that divide cable/
lace panels from adjacent garter rib pat.
Next (dec) row (RS) Work to last st of first
cable/lace panel, then p2tog tbl this last
st with first st in garter rib section, then
work as established to last st of *last* garter
rib section (13 sts rem), then p2tog last st
with first st of last cable/lace panel, work as
established to end.
Next row (WS) Work in pats as
established, keeping outer cable/lace
panels intact, working one less st in each
garter rib section.
Work 2 rows even.
Rep the last 4 rows 8 (9, 10, 11, 12) times
more—76 (84, 92, 100, 108) sts. Bind off.

FRONT
Work same as for back, ending the piece
with 6 rows less than the back—80 (88, 96,
104, 112) sts. Bind off.

RIGHT SLEEVE
DEEP CUFF
With size 6 (4mm) needles and MC, cast on
80 sts. Purl 1 WS row.
Next row (RS) K2 (edge sts: keep in St st),
pm, work cable/lace panel over 10 sts, pm,
[work lace panel over 12 sts, pm, work
cable/lace panel over 10 sts, pm] 3 times,
end k2 (edge sts: keep in St st).
Work even until 49 rows (28 row repeat,
plus 21 rows) are complete, end with a
RS row—80 sts. (This is a 12-st row of the
cable/lace panel—88 sts.)

UPPER SLEEVE
Next (dec) row (WS) P2 (edge sts), work
cable/lace panel as established, sl marker
(sm), work lace panel over 12 sts as established, sm, then, removing center 2 markers, purl center 36 sts; AT THE SAME TIME,
dec 10 sts evenly spaced (now 26 sts in this
section), sm, work lace panel over 12 sts as

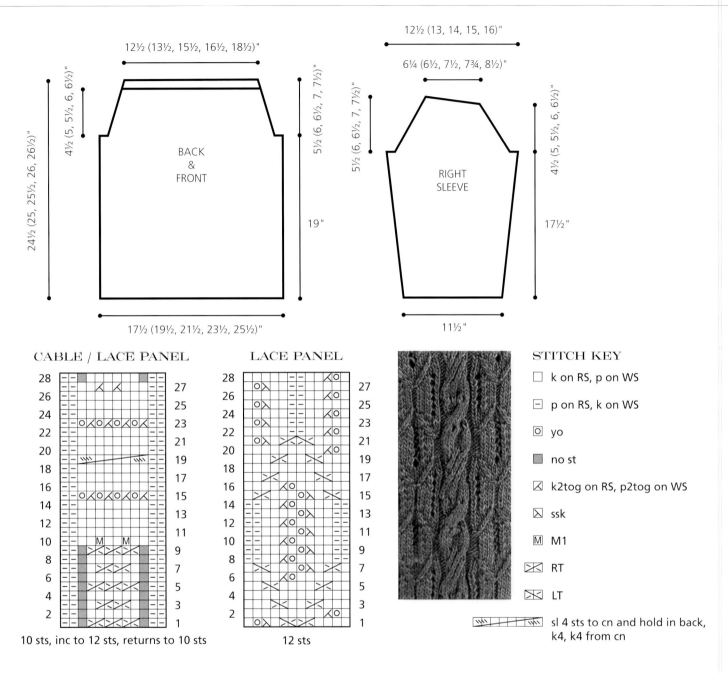

CABLE / LACE PANEL

10 sts, inc to 12 sts, returns to 10 sts

LACE PANEL

12 sts

STITCH KEY

☐ k on RS, p on WS

⊟ p on RS, k on WS

☐ yo

▨ no st

☒ k2tog on RS, p2tog on WS

☒ ssk

Ⓜ M1

⧓ RT

⧓ LT

▭▭▭▭ sl 4 sts to cn and hold in back, k4, k4 from cn

established, sm, work cable/lace panel as established, sm, end p2 (edge sts)—78 sts.
Next row (RS) Work 26 sts as established, sm, p1 (keep single st in rev St st), work next 24 sts in garter rib, p1 (keep single st in rev St st), sm, work rem 26 sts in pats as established.
Work even for 7 more rows as established.
Next (inc) row (RS) Work 25 sts as established (end with a purl st), sm, M1, work to next marker, M1, sm, work rem 25 sts in pats as established.
Working incs into garter rib, rep inc row every 22nd (16th, 10th, 8th, 6th) row 2 (4, 7, 9, 12) times more—76 (80, 86, 90, 96) sts.

Work even until sleeve measures 17½"/44.5cm, end with a WS row.

RAGLAN CAP SHAPING
Bind off 2 edge sts, plus sts for cable/lace panel at beg of next 2 rows—52 (56, 62, 66, 72) sts.
Work 2 rows even, keeping first 2 sts and last 2 sts in rev St st.
Next (dec) row (RS) P2, work lace panel over 12 sts, sm, p2tog tbl next st with first st in garter rib section, then work as established to last st of next garter rib section, then p2tog last st with next purl st, sm, work lace panel over 12 sts, end p2.

Next row (WS) Work in pats as established, keeping outer lace panel intact, working one less st in each garter rib section.
Work 2 rows even. Rep the last 4 rows 7 (8, 9, 10, 11) times more, end with a WS row—36 (38, 42, 44, 48) sts.

SHAPE TOP
Bind off 11 (12, 13, 14, 15) sts, cont to work dec at end of row.
Work WS row as established. Rep last 2 rows. Bind off rem 12 (12, 14, 14, 16) sts on last RS row.

LEFT SLEEVE
Work same as for right sleeve, reversing shaping by beg top of cap shaping one row later.

FINISHING
Sew fronts to back at raglan lines. Sew sleeve and side seams.

NECKLINE
With RS facing, locate back right shoulder seam. To the right of this seam (in top of sleeve) at beg of lace panel, beg to pick up for neck edge as foll:

With RS facing, circular needle and CC, over the lace panel (at right back sleeve top) and cable/lace panel, pick up 26 sts, pm, then pick up 54 (58, 62, 66, 70) sts along back neck to beg of cable/lace panel at left-hand side of back, over the cable/lace panel and lace panel, pm, pick up 26 sts, over the garter rib section in center of sleeve top, pm, pick up 10 (14, 14, 18, 22) sts, pm, over the lace panel and cable/lace panel, pick up 26 sts, pm, then pick up 54 (58, 62, 66, 70) sts along front neck to beg of cable/lace panel at left-hand side of front, pm, over the cable/lace panel and lace panel, pick up 26 sts, pm, over the garter rib section in center of sleeve top to end, pick up 10 (14, 14, 18, 22) sts—232 (248, 256, 272, 288) sts. Join and pm for beg of rnd.

SET UP PATTERNS
Next rnd Work row 1 of twist rib over 26 sts, sm, work k2, p2 rib over 54 (58, 62, 66, 70) sts, sm, work row 1 of twist rib over 26 sts, sm, work k2, p2 rib over 10 (14, 14, 18, 22) sts, sm, work row 1 of twist rib over 26 sts, sm, work k2, p2 rib over 54 (58, 62, 66, 70) sts, sm, work row 1 of twist rib over 26 sts, sm, work k2, p2 rib over 10 (14, 14, 18, 22) sts to end.
Work 3 more rnds even.

Note Remove markers when necessary to work following decs.
Next (dec) rnd Undo the last st of previous rnd and p2tog with next st in k2, p2 section.
Next rnd *Work in k2, p2 rib to last st, then p2tog this last st with next st in twist rib section, work in twist rib to last st, then p2tog with next st in k2, p2 rib section; rep from * to end (8 total decs)—224 (240, 248, 264, 280) sts.
Work 1 rnd even.
Rep the last 2 rows 3 times more—200 (216, 224, 240, 256) sts.
Next (dec) rnd *P2tog, [k2tog] 3 times, p2tog twice, work k2, p2 rib over back (front) sts and dec 1 at center, sm, p2tog, [k2tog] 3 times, p2tog twice, sm, work center sleeve sts as established and dec 1, sm; rep from * once more—144 (160, 168, 184, 200) sts.
Work in p1, k1 rib for ½"/1.5cm.
Bind off. ▪

Lace Yoke Pullover
◼◼◻◻

page 79

SIZES
To fit sizes Small (Medium, Large, X-Large). Shown in size Medium.

MEASUREMENTS
Bust at underarm:
approx 35 (41, 46, 51)"/89 (104, 116.5, 129.5)cm
Length from back neck:
25½ (26½, 27½, 28½)"/64.5 (67, 70, 72.5)cm
Sleeve width at upper arm:
13 (14, 15, 16)"/33 (35.5, 38, 40.5)cm
Lower yoke circumference:
approx 47 (50, 53, 56)"/119 (127, 134.5, 142)cm

MATERIALS
• 7 (8, 9, 11) 1¾oz/50g skeins (each 221yd/202m) of Quince & Co. *Finch* (wool) in #112 Pomegranate ⬤**1**
• One pair size 6 (4mm) needles *or size to obtain gauge*
• One each sizes 5 and 6 (3.75 and 4mm) circular needles, 24"/60cm long
• Stitch markers
• Tapestry needle

GAUGES
• 24 sts and 34 rows to 4"/10cm over eyelet pat using size 6 (4mm) needles.
• Each 19-st rep of border lace measures 3"/7.5cm wide using size 6 (4mm) needles.

Take time to save time—check your gauges.

STOCKINETTE STITCH (ST ST)
(over any number of sts)
Knit RS rows, purl WS rows.

BORDER LACE PATTERN (IN ROWS)
(multiple of 19 sts)
Note Rows 7 and 8 have multiples of 21 sts, but return to original 19 by end of pattern.
Row 1 (RS) *P4, k2tog, k3, yo, k1, yo, k3, ssk, p4; rep from *.
Row 2 *K4, p11, k4; rep from *.
Row 3 *P3, k2tog, k3, yo, k3, yo, k3, ssk, p3; rep from *.
Row 4 *K3, p13, k3; rep from *.
Row 5 *P2, k2tog, k3, yo, k1, yo, SK2P, yo, k1, yo, k3, ssk, p2; rep from *.
Row 6 *K2, p15, k2; rep from *.
Row 7 *P1, k2tog, k3, yo, k3, yo, k1, yo, k3, yo, k3, ssk, p1; rep from *.
Row 8 *K1, p19, k1; rep from *.
Row 9 *K2tog, k4, yo, SK2P, yo, k3, yo, SK2P, yo, k4, ssk; rep from *.
Row 10 Purl.
Rep rows 1–10 for border lace pat.

BORDER LACE PATTERN (IN THE ROUND)
To convert the border lace pattern to a circular one for the yoke of the sweater,

simply work the reverse of the sts given for WS rows: Knit when it says p, purl when it says k.

EYELET PATTERN
(multiple of 8 sts plus 7)
Row 1 (RS) Knit.
Row 2 and all other WS rows Purl.
Row 3 K2, yo, SK2P, yo, *k5, yo, SK2P, yo; rep from *, end k2.
Row 5 K3, yo, ssk, *k6, yo, ssk; rep from *, end k2.
Row 7 Knit.
Row 9 K1, *k5, yo, SK2P, yo; rep from *, end k6.
Row 11 K7, *yo, ssk, k6; rep from *.
Row 12 Purl.
Rep rows 1–12 for eyelet pat.

MID-YOKE BORDER PATTERN
(multiple of 13 sts)
Rnd 1 *P4, k5, p4; rep from *.
Rnds 2, 4, 6, and 8 Knit the yo's and k sts and p the p sts.
Rnd 3 *P3, k2tog, k1, yo, k1, yo, k1, ssk, p3; rep from *.
Rnd 5 *P2, k2tog, k1, yo, k3, yo, k1, ssk, p2; rep from *.
Rnd 7 *P1, k2tog, k1, yo, k5, yo, k1, ssk, p1; rep from *.
Rnd 9 *K2tog, k1, yo, k7, yo, k1, ssk; rep from *.
Rep rnds 1–9 for mid-yoke border pat.

BACK
LOWER BORDER
With size 6 (4mm) needles, cast on 118 (137, 156, 175) sts. Purl 1 WS row if long-tail method was used.
Keeping first and last 2 sts in St st, work in border lace pat over center 114 (133, 152, 171) sts until 79 rows are complete (7 reps plus 9 rows), end with RS row.
Next row (WS) Purl, dec 11 (14, 17, 20) sts evenly spaced—107 (123, 139, 155) sts.

CHANGE PATTERN
Next row K2 (edge sts: keep in St st), place marker (pm), work row 1 of eyelet pat over center 103 (119, 135, 151) sts, pm, end k2 (edge sts: keep in St st).
Work even in pat *except* rep only rows 1–6 of eyelet pat until back measures 19"/48cm total, end with a WS row.

ARMHOLE SHAPING
Keeping in pat as established, bind off 6 sts at beg of next 2 rows.

Next (dec) row (RS) K2, ssk, work to last 4 sts, end k2tog, k2.
Next row Purl.
Rep last 2 rows 4 times more—85 (101, 117, 133) sts.
Bind off very loosely.

FRONT
Work same as for back to armhole,

19"/48cm, end with a WS row—107 (123, 139, 155) sts.

ARMHOLE AND FRONT SHAPING
Mark center 41 (43, 45, 47) sts.
Next row (RS) Bind off 6 sts at beg of row, work to center marked sts, join a 2nd ball of yarn and bind off center 41 (43, 45, 47) marked sts very loosely, then work to end.

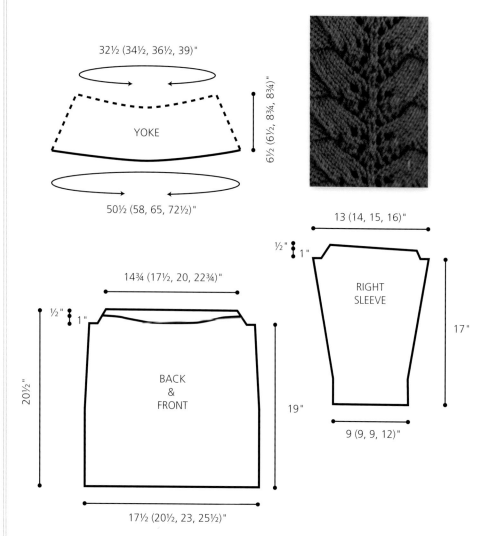

32½ (34½, 36½, 39)"

YOKE

6½ (6½, 8¾, 8¾)"

50½ (58, 65, 72½)"

14¾ (17½, 20, 22¾)"

½" 1"

20½"

BACK
&
FRONT

17½ (20½, 23, 25½)"

13 (14, 15, 16)"

½" 1"

RIGHT
SLEEVE

17"

19"

9 (9, 9, 12)"

Next row (WS) Working both sides at the same time with separate balls of yarn, bind off 6 sts at beg of this WS row, work to beg of 2nd section, bind off 6 (8, 10, 12) sts very loosely, work to end.
Next row (RS) K2, ssk, work to 2nd section, bind off 6 (8, 10, 12) sts very loosely, work to last 4 sts, end k2tog, k2.
Cont to bind off 6 (8, 10, 12) sts at each neck edge very loosely twice more, and dec 1 st at each armhole edge as established twice more, then bind off rem 6 (7, 8, 9) sts on each side very loosely.

RIGHT SLEEVE
With size 6 (4mm) needles, cast on 61 (61, 61, 80) sts. Purl 1 WS row if long-tail method was used.
Next row (RS) K2 (edge sts: keep in St st), pm, work in border lace pat over center 57 (57, 57, 76) sts, end k2 (edge sts: keep in St st). Work as established until 29 rows

are complete (2 reps plus 9 rows), end with RS row.
Next row (WS) Purl, dec 2 (2, 2, 5) sts evenly spaced—59 (59, 59, 75) sts.

CHANGE PATTERNS
Next row K2 (edge sts: keep in St st), work row 1 of eyelet pat over center 55 (55, 55, 71) sts, end k2 (edge sts: keep in St st). Rep rows 1–12 of eyelet pat 3 times, then rep rows 1–6 for remainder of sleeve; AT THE SAME TIME, work even until 10 (8, 10, 12) rows are complete, end with a WS row.
Next (inc) row (RS) K2, M1, work as established to last 2 sts, M1, end k2. Working incs into pat when possible, rep inc row every 12th (8th, 10th, 10th) row 9 (12, 9, 10) times more, then every 6th row 0 (0, 6, 0) times—79 (85, 91, 97) sts. Work even until sleeve measures 17"/43cm, end with a WS row.

ARMHOLE SHAPING
Bind off 6 sts at beg of next 2 rows.
Next (dec) row (RS) K2, ssk, work to last 4 sts, end k2tog, k2.
Purl WS row as established.
Rep last 2 rows twice more—61 (67, 73, 79) sts.
Next row (RS) Bind off 14 (15, 17, 18) sts very loosely, work as established to last 4 sts, end k2tog, k2.
Next row Purl.
Rep last 2 rows twice more.
Next row (RS) Bind off rem 16 (19, 19, 22) sts very loosely.

LEFT SLEEVE
Work same as for right sleeve, beg bind-offs and decs at top of sleeve one row later, on a WS row.

YOKE
With RS facing so you can see the seam, sew front and back to sleeves along decrease lines, using 1 st from each piece for your seam.
Mark center front and center back. Measure along top bound-off edges of sleeves and find center point of the angled edge and mark it.
With RS facing, beg at marker at right sleeve top and with size 5 (3.75mm) circular needle, pick up 71 (76, 81, 85) sts evenly spaced to center back, then 72 (76, 80, 86) sts to center left sleeve top, then 71 (76, 81, 85) sts to center front, then 71 (76, 81, 86) sts to end—285 (304, 323, 342) sts. Place marker for beg of rnd. Change to size 6 (4mm) circular needle. Work in border lace pat in the rnd for 3 reps (30 rnds).
Next (dec) rnd Knit, and dec 6 sts evenly and symmetrically in each 19-st section of pattern—195 (208, 221, 234) sts. Work mid-yoke border pat a total of 2 (2, 3, 3) times.

NECKLINE TRIM
Bind off loosely but do not cut strand. At beg of rnd, pick up 1 st for every bound-off st. Work in rnds of k1, p1 rib for 1"/2.5cm. Bind off.

FINISHING
Sew side and sleeve seams.
Weave in ends. ∎

Center Cable Pullover ■■□□

page 83

SIZES
To fit sizes Small (Medium, Large, 1X, 2X).
Shown in size Medium.

MEASUREMENTS
Bust at underarm:
37 (40, 43, 47, 51)"/94
(101.5, 109, 119, 129.5)cm
Length to outer shoulder:
25 (25½, 26, 26½, 27)"/63.5
(65, 66, 67, 68.5)cm
Sleeve at upper arm:
11½ (13, 14¼, 15½, 16½)"/29
(33, 36, 39.5, 42)cm

MATERIALS
• 6 (7, 8, 9, 10) 3½oz/100g hanks
(each 218yd/199m) of Plymouth Yarn
Company *Worsted Merino Superwash*
(wool) in #37 watermelon (4)
• One pair size 8 (5mm) needles OR SIZE
TO OBTAIN GAUGE
• One size 7 (4.5mm) circular needle,
24"/60cm long
• Cable needle (cn)
• Stitch markers

GAUGES
• 18 sts and 28 rows to 4"/10cm over
double seed st using size 8 (5mm) needles.
• One cable panel: 24 sts wide to
3½"/9cm.
Take time to save time—check your gauges.

STITCH GLOSSARY
pfb Purl in front and back of st—1 st
increased.
4-st RC Sl 2 sts to cn and hold to *back*, k2,
k2 from cn.
4-st LC Sl 2 sts to cn and hold to *front*, k2,
k2 from cn.
4-st RPC Sl 2 sts to cn and hold to *back*, k2,
p2 from cn.
4-st LPC Sl 2 sts to cn and hold to *front*, p2,
k2 from cn.

DOUBLE SEED STITCH
(multiple of 4 sts)
Row 1 (RS) *K2, p2; rep from * to end.
Row 2 Rep row 1.
Row 3 *P2, k2; rep from * to end.
Row 4 Rep row 3.
Rep rows 1–4 for double seed st.

BACK
With size 8 (5mm) needles, cast on 88
(96, 104, 112, 120) sts.
Row 1 (RS) K2, p4, *k4, p4; rep from *,
end k2.
Row 2 P2, k4, *p4, k4; rep from *, end p2.
Rep rows 1 and 2 for k4, p4 rib until
piece measures 3"/7.5cm from beg,
end with a RS row.
Inc row (WS) Purl 34 (38, 42, 46, 50),
[pfb, p3] twice, p4, [pfb, p3] twice, purl to
end—92 (100, 108, 116, 124) sts.

BEG BODY PATS
Row 1 (RS) K2 (selvedge sts), work row 1
of double seed st over next 32 (36, 40, 44,
48) sts, place marker (pm), work row 1 of
cable panel over center 24 sts, pm, work
row 1 of double seed st over 32 (36, 40,
44, 48) sts, k2 (selvedge sts).
Row 2 (WS) P2 (selvedge sts), work row
2 of double seed st to marker, sl marker,
work row 2 of cable panel over center 24
sts, sl marker, work double seed st to last
2 sts, p2 (selvedge sts).
Cont in pats as established until piece measures 17½"/44.5cm from beg.

SHAPE ARMHOLE
Bind off 4 (5, 5, 6, 6) sts at beg of next
2 rows, 0 (0, 2, 2, 3) sts at beg of

next 0 (0, 2, 2, 2) rows.
Dec row (RS) K1, ssk, work in pat to last
3 sts, k2tog, k1.
Next row (WS) P2, work in pat to
last 2 sts, p2.
Rep last 2 rows 3 (5, 7, 9, 10) times
more—76 (78, 78, 80, 84) sts.
Work even until armhole measures 5½
(6, 6½, 7, 7½)"/14 (15, 16.5, 18, 19)cm,
end with a WS row.

SHAPE NECK AND SHOULDER
Next row (RS) Work 25 (25, 25, 26, 28) sts,
join a 2nd ball of yarn and bind off center
26 (28, 28, 28, 28) sts, work to end.
Working both sides at once with separate
balls of yarn, bind off 3 sts from each neck
edge 4 times; AT THE SAME TIME, when
armhole measures 7 (7½, 8, 8½, 9)"/18
(19, 20.5, 21.5, 23)cm, shape shoulder by
binding off from each lower edge 5 (5, 5,
4, 6) sts once then 4 (4, 4, 5, 5) sts twice.

FRONT
Work as for back until armhole measures
3 (3½, 4, 4½, 5)"/7.5 (9, 10, 11.5, 12.5)cm.

SHAPE NECK
Next row (RS) Work 27 (27, 27, 28, 30) sts,
join a 2nd ball of yarn and bind off center
22 (24, 24, 24, 24) sts, work to end.
Working both sides at once, bind off 2
sts from each neck edge 7 times; AT THE
SAME TIME, when armhole measures
same as back to shoulder, shape shoulder
as on back.

SLEEVES
With size 8 (5mm) needles, cast on 48
(48, 56, 56, 56) sts. Work in k4, p4 rib as
on back for 6"/15cm, end with a RS row.
Dec row (WS) Purl, dec 4 (4, 4, 2, 0) sts
evenly spaced across—44
(44, 52, 54, 56) sts.
Next row (RS) K2, work double seed st to
last 2 sts, k2.
Next row (WS) P2, work double seed st to
last 2 sts, p2.
Rep last 2 rows once more.
Inc row (RS) K2, M1, work double seed st
to last 2 sts, M1, k2.
Working inc sts into double seed st, rep
inc row every 20th (12th, 12th, 10th, 8th)
row 3 (6, 5, 7, 8) times more—52 (58, 64,
70, 74) sts.
Work even until piece measures
18½"/47cm from beg.

SHAPE CAP
Bind off 4 (5, 5, 6, 6) sts at beg of next 2 rows.
Dec row (RS) K1, ssk, work in pat to last 3 sts, k2tog, k1.
Next row (WS) P2, work in pat to last 2 sts, p2.
Rep last 2 rows 14 (16, 18, 20, 22) times more. Bind off rem 14 (14, 16, 14, 16) sts.

FINISHING
Sew shoulder seams.

NECKBAND
With RS facing and circular needle, pick up and k 56 (58, 58, 58, 58) sts along back neck and 69 (72, 72, 72, 72) sts along front neck—125 (130, 130, 130, 130) sts. Join and pm for beg of rnd.
Rnd 1 *K3, p2; rep from * around.
Cont in k3, p2 rib for 1½"/4cm.
Bind off in rib. Set in sleeves. Sew side and sleeve seams. ■

STITCH KEY
☐ k on RS, p on WS
— p on RS, k on WS
4-st RC
4-st LC
4-st RPC
4-st LPC

CABLE PANEL

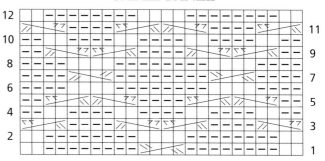

24 sts

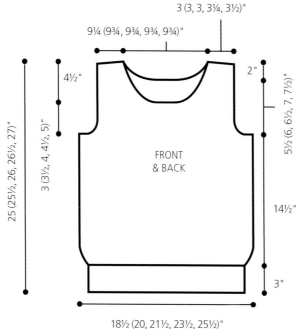

FRONT & BACK

3 (3, 3, 3¼, 3½)"
9¼ (9¾, 9¾, 9¾, 9¾)"
4½"
2"
5½ (6, 6½, 7, 7½)"
25 (25½, 26, 26½, 27)"
3 (3½, 4, 4½, 5)"
14½"
3"
18½ (20, 21½, 23½, 25½)"

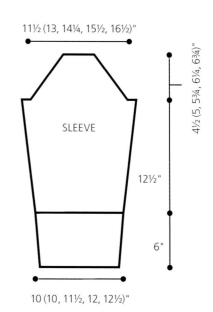

SLEEVE

11½ (13, 14¼, 15½, 16½)"
4½ (5, 5¾, 6¼, 6¾)"
12½"
6"
10 (10, 11½, 12, 12½)"

Side-to-Side Cardigans

page 89 | *page 91*

SIZES
To fit sizes Small (Medium, Large, X-Large).
Long Dolman Cardi shown in size Large.
Short Sleeveless Cardi shown in size Small.

MEASUREMENTS
Bust at underarm: 36 (42, 48, 54)"/91.5
(106.5, 122, 137)cm
Length from center back:
LONG DOLMAN CARDI
25 (25, 26, 27)"/63.5 (63.5, 66, 68.5)cm
SHORT SLEEVELESS CARDI
18 (18,18½,18½)"/45.5 (45.5, 47, 47)cm

MATERIALS
LONG DOLMAN CARDI
• 10 (11, 13, 15) 1¾oz/50g balls
(each 128yd/116m) of Classic Elite *Ava*
(wool/viscose/metallized polyester) in
#6881 Olive Gold (**3**)
• Seven ¾"/20mm buttons

SHORT SLEEVELESS CARDI
• 5 (6, 7, 7) 1¾oz/50g balls (each
137yd/125m) of Classic Elite *Soft Linen*
(wool/linen/baby alpaca) in #2203
Dove Gray (**3**)
• Seven ½"/13mm buttons

BOTH CARDIS
• One pair each sizes 4, 5, and 6 (3.5, 3.75,
and 4mm) needles *or size to obtain gauge*
• Cable needle (cn)

GAUGES
• 22 sts and 32 rows to 4"/10cm over lace
and seed st using size 6 (4mm) needles.
• 20 sts and 32 rows to 4"/10cm
over yoke pat using size 6 (4mm) needles.
*Take time to save time—check your
gauges.*

STOCKINETTE STITCH (ST ST)
(over any number of sts)
Knit RS rows, purl WS rows.

REVERSE STOCKINETTE STITCH
(REV ST ST)
(over any number of sts)
Purl RS rows, knit WS rows.

SEED STITCH
(over 5 sts)
Every row K1, p1, k1, p1, k1.

SHORT ROW PLEATS
(20 sts—for left back and right front)
Row 1 (RS of rev St st pleat) Purl.
Row 2 (WS) K14, sl 1, bring yarn to front,
sl st back to LH needle, bring yarn to back,
turn work and purl to end of row, turn,
k14, with tip of RH needle, place wrap
on needle and knit it together with
wrapped st.
Rows 3, 5, 7, and 9 Purl.
Rows 4, 6, and 8 Knit.
Row 10 Work as for row 2.
Row 11 Purl.
Row 12 Knit.
Row 13 (RS of St st pleat) Knit.
Row 14 (WS) P14, sl 1, bring yarn to
back, sl st back to LH needle, bring yarn
to front, knit to end of row, turn, p14,
with tip of RH needle, place wrap on
needle and purl it together with
wrapped st.
Rows 15, 17, 19, and 21 Knit.
Rows 16, 18, and 20 Purl.
Row 22 Rep row 14.
Row 23 Knit.
Row 24 Purl.
Rep rows 1–24 for short row pleats (left
back and right front).

SHORT ROW PLEATS
(20 sts—for right back and left front)
Row 1 (RS of rev St st pleat) Purl.
Row 2 (WS) Knit.
Row 3 (RS) P14, sl 1, bring yarn to back,
sl st back to LH needle, bring yarn to front,
knit to end of row, turn, p14, with tip of
RH needle, place wrap on needle and purl

it together with wrapped st.
Rows 4, 6, 8, and 10 Knit.
Rows 5, 7, and 9 Purl.
Row 11 Work as for row 3.
Row 12 Knit.
Row 13 (RS of St st pleat) Knit.
Row 14 Purl.
Row 15 (RS) K14, sl 1, bring yarn to front,
sl st back to LH needle, bring yarn to back,
turn work and purl to end of row, turn, k14,
with tip of RH needle, place wrap on needle
and knit it together with wrapped st.
Rows 16, 18, 20, and 22 Purl.
Rows 17, 19, and 21 Knit.
Row 23 Rep row 15.
Row 24 Purl.
Rep rows 1–24 for short row pleats (right
back and left front).

LACE PANEL
(over 13 sts)
Row 1 (RS) K1, k2tog, yo, k1, yo, k6, ssk, k1.
Row 2 and all other WS rows Purl.
Row 3 K1, k2tog, k1, yo, k1, yo, k5, ssk, k1.
Row 5 K1, k2tog, k2, yo, k1, yo, k4, ssk, k1.
Row 7 K1, k2tog, k3, yo, k1, yo, k3, ssk, k1.
Row 9 K1, k2tog, k4, yo, k1, yo, k2, ssk, k1.
Row 11 K1, k2tog, k5, yo, k1, yo, k1,
ssk, k1.
Row 13 K1, k2tog, k6, yo, k1, yo, ssk, k1.
Row 15 K1, k2tog, k5, yo, k1, yo, k1,
ssk, k1.
Row 17 K1, k2tog, k4, yo, k1, yo, k2, ssk, k1.
Row 19 K1, k2tog, k3, yo, k1, yo, k3, ssk, k1.
Row 21 K1, k2tog, k2, yo, k1, yo, k4, ssk, k1.
Row 23 K1, k2tog, k1, yo, k1, yo, k5, ssk, k1.
Row 24 Purl.
Rep rows 1–24 for lace panel.

CENTER BACK CABLE
(over 6 sts)
Row 1 (RS) P1, k2, yo, k2tog, p1.
Row 2 K1, p2, yo, p2tog, k1.
Rows 3 and 5 Same as row 1.
Rows 4 and 6 Same as row 2.
Row 7 P1, sl 2 sts to cn and hold in *front*, k2,
then k2 from cn, p1.
Row 8 Same as row 2.
Rows 9, 11, 13, and 15 Same as row 1.
Rows 10, 12, 14, and 16 Same as row 2.
Rep rows 1–16 for center back cable.

YOKE PATTERN
(multiple of 6 sts plus 4)
Row 1 (RS) K4, *yo, ssk, k4; rep from *.
Rows 2 and 4 Purl.
Row 3 K4, *k2tog, yo, k4; rep from *.
Rep rows 1-4 for yoke pat.

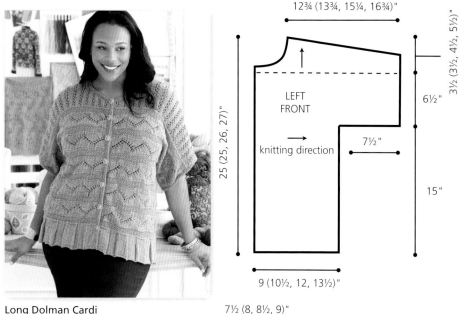

12¾ (13¾, 15¼, 16¾)"

3½ (3½, 4½, 5½)"

LEFT
FRONT

↑

knitting direction →

6½"

7½"

15"

25 (25, 26, 27)"

9 (10½, 12, 13½)"

Long Dolman Cardi

7½ (8, 8½, 9)"

12¾ (13¾, 15¼, 16¾)"

3½ (3½, 4½, 5½)"

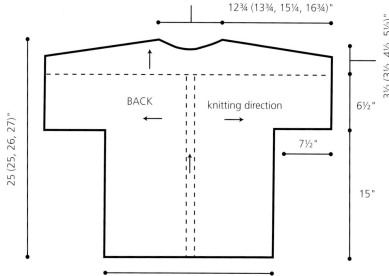

BACK

knitting direction →

←

↑

6½"

7½"

15"

25 (25, 26, 27)"

18 (21, 24, 27)"

Long Dolman Cardi

BACK
With size 6 (4mm) needles, cast on 6 sts.
Work center back cable for 21½"/52cm.
Bind off.

RIGHT BACK
With RS facing and size 6 (4mm) needles,
pick up 118 sts along side of cable, starting
at bottom.
Set-up row (WS) P2, [k1, p1, k1, p1, k1,
p13] 5 times, k1, p1, k1, p1, k1, p1, k20.

ESTABLISH PATTERNS
Next row Work short row pleats (for right
back) over 20 sts, work 1 st in St st,
[work seed st over 5 sts, work lace panel
over 13 sts] 5 times, work seed st over
5 sts, work 2 sts in St st.
Work in pats as established until piece
measures 9 (10 ½, 12, 13 ½)"/23
(26.5, 30.5, 34)cm, ending with row 24
of lace panel.

SLEEVE
Bind off 82 sts, cont rem 36 sts in pat as
established.
Work until sleeve measures
7½"/19cm. Bind off.

LEFT BACK
With RS facing and size 6 (4mm) needles,

pick up 118 sts along side of cable, starting
at the top.
Set-up row (WS) K20, p1, [k1, p1, k1, p1,
k1, p13] 5 times, k1, p1, k1, p1, k1, p2.

ESTABLISH PATTERNS
Next row Work 2 sts in St st, [work seed st
over 5 sts, work lace panel over 13 sts]
5 times, work seed st over 5 sts, work 1
st in St st, work short row pleats (for left
back) over next 20 sts.
Work in pats as established until piece
measures 9 (10½,12,13½)"/23 (26.5, 30.5,
34)cm, ending with row 23 of lace panel.

SLEEVE
Bind off 82 sts, cont rem 36 sts in pat
as established. Work until sleeve measures
7½"/19cm. Bind off.

BACK YOKE
With RS of back facing and size 6 (4mm)
needles, pick up 166 (178, 196, 208) sts
along top edge of back. Purl 1 WS row.
Work in yoke pat until yoke measures 2 (2,
3, 4)"/5 (5, 7.5, 10)cm, end with a WS row.

SHOULDER AND NECK SHAPING
Bind off 6 sts at beg of next 12 rows—94
(106, 124, 136) sts.
Mark center 18 (20, 24, 26) sts.
Next row (RS) Keeping in pat, bind off 7
(8, 10, 11) sts, work to center sts, join a
2nd ball of yarn and bind off center 18
(20, 24, 26) sts, work to end.
Working both sides with separate balls of
yarn, bind off 7 (8, 10, 11) sts at beg of
next 7 (5, 7, 5) shoulder edges, then 0 (9,
0, 12) sts at beg of next 0 (2, 0, 2) shoulder
edges; AT THE SAME TIME, bind off 5 sts at
each neck edge twice.

FRONT
LEFT FRONT
Cast on 118 sts. Work as for right back,
beg with set-up row.

LEFT FRONT YOKE
With RS facing and size 6 (4mm) needles,
pick up 82 (88, 100, 106) sts along top
edge of left front. Purl 1 WS row. Work in
yoke pat for ½ (½, 1½, 1½)"/1.5 (1.5, 4, 4)
cm, end with a RS row.

NECKLINE SHAPING
Keeping in pat, bind off from beg of WS
rows 3 sts 4 (5, 6, 5) times, then 2 sts 3
(2, 3, 4) times—64 (69, 76, 79) sts.

Work even until yoke measures 3 (3, 3½, 3½)"/7.5 (7.5, 9, 9)cm, end with a WS row.

SHOULDER SHAPING
Bind off 6 sts at beg of the next 6 RS rows—28 (33, 40, 45) sts. Bind off 7 (8, 10, 11) sts at beg of the next 4 (3, 4, 3) RS rows, then 0 (9, 0, 10) sts on the last RS row.

RIGHT FRONT
Cast on 118 sts. Work as for left back, beg with set-up row.

RIGHT FRONT YOKE
Work same as for left front yoke, except beg neckline shaping on the following RS row.

FINISHING
Sew shoulder seams.

ARMHOLE TRIM
With RS facing and size 5 (3.75mm) needles, pick up 90 (96, 102, 108) sts evenly spaced along sleeve edge. Knit 5 rows. Bind off. Rep for second sleeve. Sew side and sleeve seams.

LEFT FRONT BUTTONBAND
With RS facing and size 4 (3.5mm) needles, pick up 4 (4, 7, 7) sts along yoke edge, then 1 st for every st in front edge to end—122 (122, 125, 125) sts. Knit 4 rows. Bind off.

RIGHT FRONT BUTTONHOLE BAND
With RS facing and size 4 (3.5mm) needles, beg at lower edge, pick up 1 st for every st in front edge to yoke, then pick up 4 (4, 7, 7) sts along yoke edge to end—122 (122, 125, 125) sts.
Note The top buttonhole is worked in the neckline trim.
Next (buttonhole) row (WS) *K12 (12, 15, 15), bind off 3 sts; rep from * until there are 6 buttonholes worked, knit to end. Knit 3 rows. Bind off.

NECKLINE TRIM
With RS facing and size 4 (3.5mm) needles, pick up 114 (118, 122, 128) sts evenly around neckline.
Next row (WS) K to last 6 sts, bind off 3 sts, k to end.
Knit 4 rows. Bind off.
Sew buttons to left front buttonband, opposite buttonholes. ∎

Short Sleeveless Cardi

Short Sleeveless Cardi
BACK
With size 6 (4mm) needles, cast on 6 sts. Work center back cable for 15"/38cm. Bind off.

RIGHT BACK
With RS facing and size 6 (4mm) needles, pick up 82 sts along side of cable, starting at the bottom.
Set-up row (WS) P2, [k1, p1, k1, p1, k1, p13] 3 times, k1, p1, k1, p1, k1, p1, k20.

ESTABLISH PATTERN
Work short row pleats (for right back) over 20 sts, work 1 in St st, [work seed st over 5 sts, work lace panel over 13 sts] 3 times, work seed st over 5 sts, work 2 sts in St st. Work in pats as established until piece measures 9 (10½,12,13½)"/23 (26.5, 30.5, 34)cm, ending with row 24 of lace panel. Bind off.

LEFT BACK
With RS facing and size 6 (4mm) needles, pick up 82 sts along side of cable, starting at the top.
Set-up row (WS) K20, p1, [k1, p1, k1, p1, k1, p13] 3 times, k1, p1, k1, p1, k1, p2.

ESTABLISH PATTERNS
Work 2 sts in St st, [work seed st over 5 sts, work lace panel over 13 sts] 3 times, work seed st over 5 sts, work 1 st in St st, work short row pleats over next 20 sts. Work in pats as established until piece

measures 9 (10½, 12, 13½)"/23 (26.5, 30.5, 34)cm, ending with row 24 of lace panel. Bind off.

BACK YOKE
With RS of back facing and size 6 (4mm) needles, pick up 94 (106, 124, 136) sts along top edge of back. Purl WS row. Work in yoke pat until yoke measures 3 (3, 3½, 3½)"/7.5 (7.5, 9, 9)cm, end with a WS row.

SHOULDER SHAPING
Mark center 18 (20, 24, 26) sts.
Next row (RS) Keeping in pat, bind off 7 (8, 10, 11) sts, work to center sts, join a 2nd ball of yarn and bind off center 18 (20, 24, 26) sts, work to end.
Working both sides with separate balls of yarn, bind off 7 (8, 10, 11) sts at beg of next 7 (5, 7, 5) shoulder edges, then 0 (9, 0, 12) sts at beg of next 0 (2, 0, 2) shoulder edges; AT THE SAME TIME, bind off at each neck edge 5 sts twice.

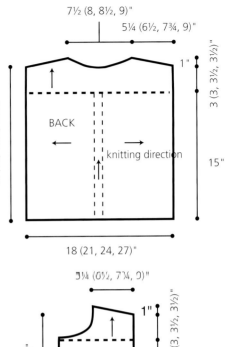

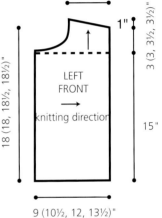

FRONT

LEFT FRONT
With size 6 (4mm) needles, cast on 82 sts. Work as for right back, beg with set-up row.

LEFT FRONT YOKE
With RS facing and size 6 (4mm) needles, pick up 46 (52, 64, 68) sts along top of left front. Purl 1 WS row. Work in yoke pat for ½ (½, 1, 1)"/1.5 (1.5, 2.5, 2.5)cm, end with a RS row.

NECKLINE SHAPING
Keeping in pat, bind off from beg of WS rows 3 sts 4 (5, 6, 5) times, then 2 sts 3 (2, 3, 4) times—28 (33, 40, 45) sts. Work even until yoke measures 3 (3, 3½, 3½)"/ 7.5 (7.5, 9, 9)cm, end with a WS row.

SHOULDER SHAPING
Bind off 7 (8, 10, 11) sts at beg of next 4 (3, 4, 3) RS rows, then 0 (9, 0, 12) sts on last RS row.

RIGHT FRONT
With size 6 (4mm) needles, cast on 82 sts. Work as for left back, beg with set-up row.

RIGHT FRONT YOKE
Work same as for left front yoke, but beg neckline shaping on the following RS row.

FINISHING
Sew shoulder seams.

ARMHOLE TRIM
Place markers 8 (8½, 9, 9½)"/20.5 (21.5, 23, 24)cm down from shoulders on front and back. With RS facing and size 5 (3.75mm) needles, pick up 90 (96, 102, 108) sts evenly spaced between markers. Knit 5 rows. Bind off. Rep for second side. Sew side seams.

LEFT FRONT BUTTONBAND
With RS facing and size 4 (3.5mm) needles, pick up 3 (3, 6, 6) sts along yoke edge, then 1 st for every st in front edge to end—85 (85, 88, 88) sts. Knit 3 rows. Bind off.

RIGHT FRONT BUTTONHOLE BAND
With RS facing and size 4 (3.5mm) needles, beg at lower edge, pick up 1 st for every st in front edge to yoke, then pick up 3 (3, 6, 6) sts along yoke edge to end—85 (85, 88, 88) sts.
Next (buttonhole) row (WS) K3, (k2tog, yo, ssk), *k6, (k2tog, yo, ssk); rep from * until there are 7 buttonholes worked, knit to end.
Next row (RS) Knit, except work (k1, p1) into each yo of the previous row. Knit 1 row. Bind off.

NECKLINE TRIM
With RS facing and size 5 (3.75mm) needles, pick up 110 (113, 119, 115) sts evenly around neckline. Knit 1 row, purl 1 row, bind off knitwise. Sew buttons to left front buttonband, opposite buttonholes. ∎

Ribbed Cardigans ◼◼◼◻

page 95 *page 97*

SIZES
To fit sizes Small (Medium, Large, X-Large, XX-Large). Both cardigans shown in size Small.

MEASUREMENTS
TEXTURED RIB CARDI
Bust at underarm:
37 (41, 46, 50, 55)"/94 (104, 116.5, 127, 139.5)cm
Length to back neck:
26½ (27, 27½, 28, 28½)"/67.5 (68.5, 70, 71, 72.5)cm

Sleeve width at upper arm:
12 (13, 14, 15, 16)"/ 30.5 (33, 35.5, 38, 40.5)cm

EYELET RIB CARDI
Bust at underarm:
42 (47½, 52, 58, 63)"/106.5 (120.5, 134.5, 147, 160)cm
Length to back neck:
23½ (24, 24½, 25, 25½)"/59.5 (61, 62, 63.5, 64.5)cm
Sleeve at upper arm:
14¾ (16, 17, 18½, 18½)"/37.5 (40.5, 43, 47, 47)cm

MATERIALS
TEXTURED RIB CARDI
• 13 (14, 16, 18, 20) 1¾oz/50g hanks (each 109yd/100m) of Knit One Crochet Too *Brae Tweed* (merino wool/llama/donegal wool/bamboo) in #392 Russet (A) ▣
• One separating zipper, 14"/36cm long, medium weight, with metal teeth
• Dressmaker pins
• Sewing needle and thread for zipper

EYELET RIB CARDI
• 13 (14, 16, 18, 19) 1¾oz/50g balls (each 98yd/90m) of Louisa Harding *Akiko* (merino wool/alpaca) in #003 Twig (B) = 4>
• 13 buttons, ⅝"/15mm wide

BOTH CARDIS
• One pair each sizes 5 and 7 (3.75 and 4.5mm) needles *or size to obtain gauge*
• Cable needle (cn)
• Stitch markers
• Tapestry needle

GAUGES
• 25 sts and 30 rows to 4"/10cm over textured rib with A using size 7 (4.5mm) needles
• 22 sts and 26 rows to 4"/10cm over Eyelet Rib with B using size 7 (4.5mm) needles *Take time to save time—check your gauges.*

STOCKINETTE STITCH (ST ST)
(over any number of sts)
Knit RS rows, purl WS rows.

K2, P2 RIB
(multiple of 4 sts plus 2)
Row 1 K2, *p2, k2; rep from *.
Row 2 P2, *k2, p2; rep from *.
Rep rows 1–2 for k2, p2 rib.

TEXTURED RIB
(multiple of 7 sts plus 3)
Row 1 (RS) P3, *k2, p1, k1, p3; rep from *.
Row 2 K the knit sts and p the purl sts.
Row 3 P3, *k1, p1, k2, p3; rep from *.
Row 4 Same as row 2.

Textured Rib Cardi

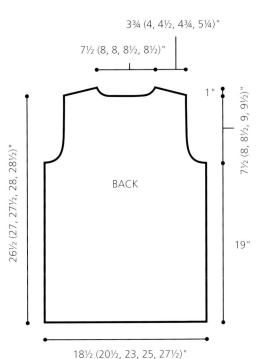

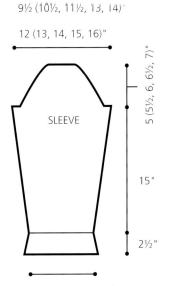

CABLE CHART

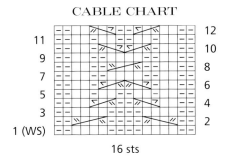

16 sts

Rep rows 1–4 for textured rib.

EYELET RIB
(multiple of 7 sts plus 2)
Row 1 (RS) P2, *k2tog, yo, k1, yo, ssk, p2; rep from *.
Row 2 K2, *p5, k2; rep from *.
Row 3 P2, *k5, p2; rep from *.
Row 4 K2, *p5, k2; rep from *.
Rep rows 1-4 for eyelet rib.

STITCH GLOSSARY
RT (right twist) K2tog, leave on needle, then knit the first st again, slip both sts from needle.
LT (left twist) Skip 1 st and knit into back of 2nd st, then k into front of the skipped st, slip both sts from needle.

STITCH KEY

☐ k on RS, p on WS

⊟ p on RS, k on WS

sl 2 sts to cn and hold in front, p1, k2 from cn

sl 1 st to cn and hold in back, k2, p1 from cn

sl 2 sts to cn and hold in front, k2, k2 from cn

sl 2 sts to cn and hold in back, k2, k2 from cn

Textured Rib Cardi
BACK
With size 7 (4.5mm) needles, cast on 119 (133, 147, 161, 175) sts.
Next row (RS) K2 (St st edge sts), work in textured rib over center 115 (129, 143, 157, 171) sts, end k2 (St st edge sts). Work even until back measures 19"/48cm, end with a WS row. (Before measuring, spread piece out to measurements from schematics.)

ARMHOLE
Bind off 6 (6, 8, 8, 10) sts at beg of next 2 rows.
Next (dec) row (RS) K1, ssk, work as established in rib to last 3 sts, end k2tog, k1.

Next row (WS) P2, work in pat to last 2 sts, end p2.
Rep last 2 rows 5 (9, 11, 15, 17) times more—95 (101, 107, 113, 119) sts. Work even until armhole measures 7½ (8, 8½, 9, 9½)"/19 (20.5, 21.5, 23, 24)", end with a WS row. (Before measuring, spread piece out to measurements from schematics.)

SHOULDER AND NECK SHAPING
Mark center 27 (31, 31, 33, 33) sts.
Next row Bind off 8 (9, 10, 10, 11) sts, work to center sts, join a 2nd ball of yarn and bind off center 27 (31, 31, 33, 33) sts, work to end.
Working both sides at the same time, bind off 8 (9, 10, 10, 11) sts at beg of next 5

(1, 1, 5, 5) shoulder edges, then 0 (8, 9, 0, 0) sts at beg of next 4 shoulder edges; AT THE SAME TIME, bind off from each neck edge 5 sts twice.

LEFT FRONT

With size 7 (4.5mm) needles, cast on 63 (70, 77, 84, 91) sts.

Next row (RS) K2 (St st edge sts), work in textured rib over center 59 (66, 73, 80, 87) sts, end k2 (St st edge sts).
Work even for 3"/7.5cm, end with a WS row.

Cable set-up row Work to last 19 sts, place marker (pm), p2, RT, work next 3 sts as established, p1, p2tog, work next 3 sts as established, LT, p2, pm, end k2 (St st edge sts)—62 (69, 76, 83, 90) sts.

Next row (WS) P2 (St st edge sts), sl marker (sm), work WS row 1 of Cable Chart over 16 sts, sm, work as established to end.
Work even until front measures 14"/35.5cm, end with a WS row.
(Before measuring, spread piece out to measurements from schematics.)

SHAPE V-NECK

Note For ease of working band later, pm at end of next row for beg of V-neck shaping.
Next (dec) row (RS) Work to 2 sts before marker, k2tog, sm, work as established to end.
Next row (WS) P2, sm, work cable as established over 16 sts, sm, p1 (keep this st in St st), work in textured rib as established to last 2 sts, end p2 (edge sts).
Work 2 rows even.
Rep last 4 rows for a total of 20 (22, 22, 23, 23) decs at neckline edge; AT THE SAME TIME, when front measures same as back to armhole, end with a WS row.

ARMHOLE SHAPING

Next row Bind off 6 (6, 8, 8, 10) sts at beg of row and cont neckline shaping at end of row as established.
Next row (WS) Work as established.
Next (dec) row (RS) K1, ssk, work as established to end.
Next row Work as established.
Rep last 2 rows 5 (9, 11, 15, 17) times more—30 (31, 34, 36, 39) sts after all decs.
Cont until armhole depth measures 7½ (8, 8½, 9, 9½)"/19 (20.5, 21.5, 23. 24)cm, end with a WS row.

SHOULDER SHAPING

Bind off 8 (9, 10, 10, 11) sts at beg of first RS row, then 11 (11, 12, 13, 14) sts at beg of next 2 RS rows.
Note There are more sts on front shoulders than back to accommodate the cable.

RIGHT FRONT

Work same as for left front, reversing placement of patterns and all shaping. Beg armhole and shoulder shaping one row later than for left front.

SLEEVES

With size 7 (4.5mm) needles, cast on 49 (49, 56, 56, 63) sts.
Next row (RS) K2 (St st edge sts), work in textured rib over center 45 (45, 52, 52, 59) sts, end k2 (St st edge sts).
Work even for 5 more rows, end with a WS row.
Next (inc) row (RS) K2, M1, work to last 2 sts, M1, end k2.
Keeping edge sts in St st, and working incs into textured rib, rep inc row every 6th row 13 (15, 15, 18, 18) times more—77 (81, 88, 94, 101) sts.
Work even until sleeve measures 15"/38cm, end with a WS row. (Before measuring, spread piece out to measurements from schematics.)

CAP SHAPING

Bind off 6 (6, 8, 8, 10) sts at beg of next 2 rows.
Next (dec) row (RS) K1, ssk, work as established to last 3 sts, end k2tog, k1.
Next row (WS) P2, work in pat to last 2 sts, end p2.
Rep last 2 rows 17 (19, 21, 23, 24) times more.
Bind off 3 (3, 2, 3, 3) sts at beg of next 2 rows.
Bind off rem 23 (23, 24, 24, 25) sts on last RS row.

SLEEVE LOWER EDGE

With RS facing, pick up 46 (46, 54, 54, 58) sts evenly along lower edge.
Row 1 (RS) Beg with p2, work in k2, p2 rib for 1"/2.5cm, end with RS row.
Row 2 and all even-numbered (WS) rows Purl.
Row 3 K1, *yo, ssk, k2; rep from *, end k1.
Row 5 K2, *yo, ssk, k2; rep from *.
Row 7 K3, *yo, ssk, k2; rep from *, end k1 instead of k2.
Bind off purlwise on next RS row.

FINISHING

Sew fronts to back at shoulders. Sew sleeve and side seams. Sew sleeve caps into armholes, easing in any fullness.

FRONT BAND

With size 5 (3.75mm) needles, cast on 9 sts.
Next row (RS) K2, p1, [k1, p1] twice, end k2.
WS row P2, k1, [p1, k1] twice, end p2.

Rep these 2 rows until band is same number of rows as left front to marker for V-neck shaping, leave sts on needle. With RS facing, sew band to left front edge, using 1 seam st from each piece, matching 2 rows for 2 rows.
Resume knitting until band reaches shoulder. With RS facing, sew band to left front edge to shoulder. When band reaches shoulder, place marker on band.
Resume knitting until band, from shoulder, measures 7½ (8, 8, 8½, 8½)"/19 (20.5, 20.5, 21.5, 21.5)cm slightly stretched. Leave sts on needle, and with RS facing, sew edge of this section of band to back neck evenly.
Cont to knit band until there are the same number of rows from shoulder to beg of V-neck shaping on right front edge. Sew edge of band to V-neck shaping, cont knitting until band is the same number of rows to bottom edge. Sew rem band to right front.
Pin zipper in place from lower edge to beg of neckline shaping. Sew from lower edge upward, in the purl rib next to the 2 edge sts, on each side. ■

Eyelet Rib Cardi
BACK

With size 7 (4.5mm) needles, cast on 118 (132, 146, 160, 174) sts.
Next row (RS) K2 (St st edge sts), work in eyelet rib over center 114 (128, 142, 156, 170) sts, end k2 (St st edge sts).
Work even until back measures 16"/40.5cm, end with a WS row. (Before measuring, spread piece out to measurements from schematics.)

ARMHOLE SHAPING

Bind off 6 (6, 8, 8, 10) sts at beg of next 2 rows.
Next (dec) row (RS) K1, ssk, work as established in rib to last 3 sts, end k2tog, k1.

Eyelet Rib Cardi

EYELET CABLE CHART

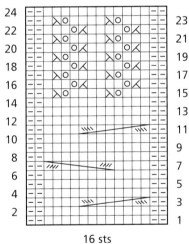

16 sts

Measurements on schematics:

BACK
4¼ (4½, 5, 5¼, 6)"
8½ (9, 9, 9½, 9½)"
1"
7½ (8, 8½, 9, 9½)"
23½ (24, 24½, 25, 25½)"
16"
21 (23¾, 26, 29, 31½)"

LEFT FRONT
4¼ (4½, 5, 5¼, 6)"
1"
4½ (5, 5½, 6, 6½)"
7½ (8, 8½, 9, 9½)"
16"
10½ (11¾, 13, 14½, 15½)"

SLEEVE
6¾ (7, 7½, 7¾, 8)"
6"
14¾ (16, 17, 18½, 18½)"

STITCH KEY

☐ k on RS, p on WS

⊟ p on RS, k on WS

⊙ yo

⊠ k2tog on RS, p2tog on WS

⊠ ssk

sl 2 sts to cn and hold in front, k2, k2 from cn

sl 2 sts to cn and hold in back, k2, k2 from cn

sl 4 sts to cn and hold in front, k4, k4 from cn

sl 4 sts to cn and hold in back, k4, k4 from cn

Next row (WS) P2, work in pat to last 2 sts, end p2.
Rep last 2 rows 5 (9, 11, 15, 17) times more—94 (100, 106, 112, 118) sts. Work even until armhole measures 7½ (8, 8½, 9, 9 ½)"/19 (20.5, 21.5, 23. 24)cm, end with a WS row. (Before measuring, spread piece out to measurements from schematics.)

SHOULDER AND NECK SHAPING
Mark center 26 (30, 30, 32, 32) sts. Bind off 8 (9, 10, 10, 11) sts, work to

center sts, join 2nd ball of yarn and bind off center 26 (30, 30, 32, 32) sts, work to end. Working both sides at the same time, bind off 8 (9, 10, 10, 11) sts at beg of next 5 (1, 1, 5, 5) shoulder edges, then 0 (8, 9, 0, 0) sts at beg of next 4 shoulder edges; AT THE SAME TIME, bind off 5 sts from each neck edge twice.

LEFT FRONT
With size 7 (4.5mm) needles, cast on 62 (69, 76, 83, 90) sts.
Next row (RS) K2 (St st edge sts), work in

eyelet rib over center 58 (65, 72, 79, 86) sts, end k2 (St st edge sts).
Work even for 3"/7.5cm, end with a RS row.
Next row (WS) P2, place marker (pm), k2, p12, k2, pm, work as established to end.

ESTABLISH EYELET CABLE CHART
Next row K2 (St st edge sts), work as established over 42 (49, 56, 63, 70) sts to marker, sm, work row 1 of Eyelet Cable Chart over 16 sts, sm, end k2 (St st edge sts).

Work even until front measures 16"/40.5cm, end with a WS row.

ARMHOLE SHAPING
Next row (RS) Bind off 6 (6, 8, 8, 10) sts at armhole edge.
Next row Work as established.
Next (dec) row (RS) K1, ssk, work as established to end.
Next row (WS) Work as established in pat to last 2 sts, end p2.
Rep last 2 rows 5 (9, 11, 15, 17) times more—50 (53, 56, 59, 62) sts.
Work until armhole measures 3"/7.5cm, end with a RS row.

NECKLINE SHAPING
Next row (WS) Bind off 16 (16, 16, 17, 17) sts, work to end.
Work 1 RS row.
Keeping in pat, bind off 2 sts from neck edge 5 (6, 6, 6, 6) times—24 (25, 28, 30, 33) sts.
Work even until armhole measures 7½ (8, 8½, 9, 9½)"/19 (20.5, 21.5, 23. 24)cm, end with a WS row. (Before measuring, spread piece out to measurements from schematics.)

SHOULDER SHAPING
Bind off 8 (9, 10, 10, 11) sts at beg of the next 3 (1, 1, 3, 3) RS rows, then 0 (8, 9, 0, 0) sts at beg of next 2 RS rows.

RIGHT FRONT
Work same as for left front, reversing all shaping and pattern placement and begin Eyelet Cable Chart with row 15. Beg armhole, neckline, and shoulder shaping one row later than for left front.

SLEEVES
With size 7 (4.5mm) needles, cast on 83 (90, 97, 104, 104) sts.
Next row (RS) K2 (St st edge sts), work in eyelet rib over center 79 (86, 93, 100, 100) sts, end k2 (St st edge sts).
Work even for 6"/15cm, end with a WS row.

CAP SHAPING
Bind off 6 (6, 8, 8, 10) sts at beg of next 2 rows.
Next (dec) row (RS) K1, ssk, work as established in rib to last 3 sts, end k2tog, k1.
Next row (WS) P2, work in pat to last 2 sts, end p2.

Rep last 2 rows 20 (20, 21, 22, 24) times more.
Bind off 3 (3, 3, 4, 4) sts at beg of next 2 rows, then 0 (3, 3, 4, 0) sts at beg of next 2 rows. Bind off rem 23 (24, 25, 26, 26) sts on last RS row.

FINISHING
Sew fronts to back at shoulders.

NECKLINE TRIM
With RS facing and smaller needle, beg at right front edge, pick up 45 (47, 49, 51, 53) sts along neck edge to shoulder, then 49 (51, 51, 53, 53) sts along back neck, then 45 (47, 49, 51, 53) sts to left front edge—139 (145, 149, 155, 159) sts.
Next row (WS) P2 (St st edge sts), k1, *p1, k1; rep from * to last 2 sts, end p2 (St st edge sts).
Next row (RS) K2 (St st edge sts), p1, *k1, p1; rep from * to last 2 sts, end k2 (St st edge sts).
Rep last 2 rows once more, then bind off in rib.

LEFT FRONT BUTTONBAND
With RS facing, pick up 94 sts evenly spaced. Knit 4 rows. Bind off on WS.

RIGHT FRONT BUTTONHOLE BAND
With RS facing, pick up 94 sts evenly spaced.
Next row (WS) K2, *(k2tog, yo, ssk), k3; rep from * 12 times more, end k4 instead of k3.
Next row (RS) Knit, and knit into the front and the back of each yo.
Knit 2 rows. Bind off on WS.

Sew sleeve seams. Sew caps into armhole, easing in any fullness. Sew buttons opposite buttonholes.
To reinforce back neck and shoulders, take a strand of firm yarn and sew through the shoulder seams and the ridge formed by picked-up sts, backstitching occasionally. Weave in all ends. Steam lightly. ■

Button-Back Sweaters

page 99   *page 102*

SIZES
To fit sizes Small (Medium, Large, X-Large). Sweater with pockets shown in size Medium; sweater with darts shown in size Small.

MEASUREMENTS
Bust at underarm, buttoned:
40 (43, 46, 49)"/10.5 (109, 117, 124.5)cm
Length from outer shoulder, including 1"/2.5cm trim:
22¼ (23, 23¾, 24½)"/56.5 (58, 60, 62)cm
Sleeve at upper arm:
12½ (13¾, 15½, 17)"/31.5 (35, 39.5, 43)cm

MATERIALS
BUTTON-BACK SWEATER WITH POCKETS
• 9 (9, 10, 12) 1¾oz/50g hanks (each 160yd/146m) of The Fibre Company/Kelbourne Woolens *Savannah* (wool/cotton/linen/soya) in Denim ⬛

BUTTON-BACK SWEATER WITH DARTS
• 9 (9, 10, 12) hanks in Marigold

BOTH SWEATERS
• One pair each sizes 6 and 7 (4 and 4.5mm) needles *or size to obtain gauge*
• Four ¾"/20mm buttons
• Stitch markers
• Tapestry needle

GAUGES
• 21 sts and 32 rows to 4"/10cm over basketweave pat using size 7 (4.5mm) needles.
• 29-st lace pattern: 5½"/14cm wide.

Take time to save time—check your gauges.

NOTES
1) Lower garter st trims are picked up and worked after pieces are complete.
2) Make front first.

Button-Back Sweater with Pockets
FRONT
With size 7 (4.5mm) needles, cast on 41 (49, 57, 65) sts.

Next row (RS) Work 6 (10, 14, 18) sts in basketweave pat foll chart, place marker (pm), work center 29 sts in lace pat foll chart, pm, work rem 6 (10, 14, 18) sts in basketweave pat foll chart

Keeping in pat sts as established, working inc sts in basketweave pat, cast on 2 sts at beg of next 32 rows—105 (113, 121, 129) sts. Pm each side of last row to indicate beg of side seams. Work even in pats until front measures 10"/25.5cm from markers.

ARMHOLE SHAPING
Bind off 5 (5, 6, 6) sts at beg of next 2 rows. Work even for 2 rows.

Next (dec) row (RS) K1, ssk, work as established to last 3 sts, end k2tog, k1. Keeping first and last 2 sts of every row in St st, work even for 3 rows.
Rep dec row. Work 1 WS row.
Rep last 2 rows 7 (9, 10, 12) times more—77 (81, 85, 89) sts.
Work even until armhole measures 4¼ (5, 5¾, 6½)"/11 (12½, 14.5, 16.5)cm, end with a WS row.

NECK SHAPING
Mark center 27 sts.

Next row Work as established to first marker, join a 2nd ball of yarn, bind off center 27 sts, work to end.
Working both sides at the same time with separate balls of yarn, bind off 2 sts from each neck edge 5 times—15 (17, 19, 21) sts each side.
Work even until armhole measures 7¼ (8, 8¾, 9½)"/18.5, 20.5, 22, 24)cm, end with a WS row.

SHOULDER SHAPING
Bind off 5 (6, 6, 7) sts from each shoulder twice, then 5 (5, 7, 7) sts once.

LOWER EDGE TRIM
With RS facing and size 6 (4mm) needles,

pick up 44 (48, 52, 56) sts along curve, 29 sts along lace pat, and 44 (48, 52, 56) sts along curve—117 (125, 133, 141) sts.
Knit 11 rows; AT THE SAME TIME, dec 1 st at each end of every RS row. Bind off.

LEFT POCKET
Locate row on left front that corresponds to last cast-on row for curved front and count 8 sts from center lace panel on this row. With yarn and crochet hook, pick up and k 10 sts toward side seam along front. Sl these sts to size 7 (4.5mm) needle so needle is pointing toward center of front.
Row 1 (WS) Purl.
Working in basketweave pat, cast on 2 sts at beg of next 8 rows—26 sts.

Inc 1 st each side on next row for St st edge st—28 sts.
Work in basketweave pat until pocket measures 3½"/9cm from picked-up row, end with WS row.
Mark center 10 sts.

Next row Work to first marker, join a 2nd ball of yarn and bind off center 10 sts, work to end.
Working both sides at the same time with separate balls, bind off 2 sts from center edge 4 times. Fasten off last st each side.

POCKET BORDER
With RS facing and size 6 (4mm) needles, pick up 32 sts evenly along pocket top.

LACE PATTERN

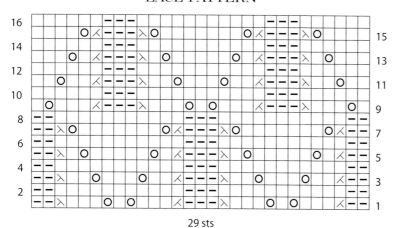

29 sts

BASKETWEAVE PATTERN

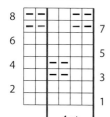

4-st

STITCH KEY

☐ k on RS, p on WS

− p on RS, k on WS

◯ yo ⟋ k2tog

⟍ ssk

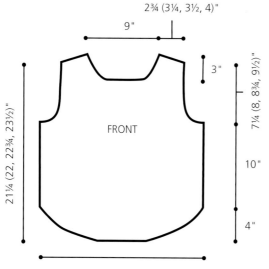

FRONT

9"

2¾ (3¼, 3½, 4)"

3"

7¼ (8, 8¾, 9½)"

10"

4"

21¼ (22, 22¾, 23½)"

20 (21½, 23, 24½)"

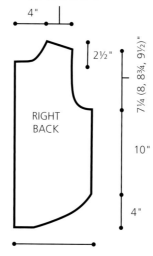

RIGHT BACK

4"

2¾ (3¼, 3½, 4)"

2½"

7¼ (8, 8¾, 9½)"

10"

4"

9½ (10¼, 11, 12)"

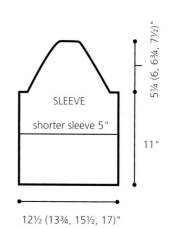

SLEEVE

shorter sleeve 5"

5¼ (6, 6¾, 7½)"

11"

12½ (13¾, 15½, 17)"

Next row (WS) Knit.
Next row (RS) K9, ssk, k10, k2tog, k9.
Next row (WS) K1, M1, work to last st, M1, k1.
Rep the last 2 rows 3 times more. Bind off. Sew sides of pocket to front.

RIGHT POCKET
Work as for left pocket, using the same method for placement.

RIGHT BACK
With size 7 (4.5mm) needles, cast on 18 (22, 26, 30) sts.
Work in basketweave pat for 2 rows. Keeping in pats as established, working new sts into basketweave pat, cast on 2 sts at beg of next 16 RS rows—50 (54, 58, 62) sts. Pm at beg of row to indicate beg of side seam. Work even in pat until front measures 10"/25.5cm from marker.

Piece should measure approx 14"/35.5cm from lowest edge.

ARMHOLE SHAPING
Bind off 5 (5, 6, 6) sts at beg of next RS rows. Work even for 3 rows.
Next (dec) row (RS) K1, ssk, work as established to end.
Keeping first 2 sts of every RS row in St st, rep dec row every 4th row once, then

every RS row 7 (9, 10, 12) times—36 (38, 40, 42) sts.
Work even until armhole measures 4¾ (5½, 6¼, 7)"/12 (14, 16, 18)cm, end with a RS row.

NECK SHAPING
Bind off 11 sts, work to end. Cont to shape neck, binding off 2 sts at beg of next 5 WS rows; AT THE SAME TIME, when armhole measures same as front to shoulder, bind off 5 (6, 6, 7) sts from shoulder edge twice, then 5 (5, 7, 7) sts once.

LOWER EDGE TRIM
With RS facing and size 6 (4mm) needles, pick up and k 56 (60, 64, 68) sts evenly spaced. K 11 rows; AT THE SAME TIME, dec 1 st at end of every RS row (at side edge). Bind off.

LEFT BACK
Work same as for right back, reversing all shaping.

SLEEVES
With size 7 (4.5mm) needles, cast on 65 (73, 81, 89) sts.
Next row (RS) Work 18 (22, 26, 30) sts in basketweave pat, pm, work center 29 sts in lace pat, pm, work rem 18 (22, 26, 30) sts in basketweave pat.
Cont in pats until sleeve measures 11"/28cm, end with a WS row.
(Note: For shorter sleeve, work to 5"/12.5cm before cap.)

CAP SHAPING
Bind off 5 (5, 6, 6) sts at beg of next 2 rows. Work even for 2 rows.
Next (dec) row (RS) K1, ssk, work as established to last 3 sts, end k2tog, k1.
Keeping first and last 2 sts of every row in St st, work WS row.
Rep last 2 rows 18 (21, 24, 27) times more—17 (19, 19, 21) sts. Bind off.

LOWER TRIM
With RS facing and size 6 (4mm) needles, pick up and k 55 (63, 71, 79) sts evenly spaced across lower edge. Knit 11 rows. Bind off.

FINISHING
Sew front to backs at shoulders.

NECKBAND
With size 6 (4mm) needles and RS facing, pick up and k 28 sts evenly along back neck edge, then 70 sts along front edge to shoulder, then 28 sts to end—126 sts. Knit 9 rows. Dec 8 sts evenly on next row. Knit 1 WS row. Bind off.

RIGHT BACK BUTTON BAND
Starting at neckline edge, with size 6 (4mm) needles and RS facing, pick up and k 106 (110, 114, 118) sts evenly along back edge. Knit 11 rows, then bind off.

LEFT BACK BUTTONHOLE BAND
Pick up and k sts in same way as right back band. Knit 1 WS row.
Next (buttonhole) row (RS) K28 (29, 30, 31), bind off 3 sts, *k21 (22, 23, 24), bind off 3 sts; rep from * 2 times more, then k3 to end.
Knit 9 rows. Bind off.

Sew side seams, joining trims where they meet. Sew sleeve seams. Sew sleeve cap into armhole. Sew buttons opposite buttonholes. ▪

Button-Back Sweater with Darts
FRONT
With size 7 (4.5mm) needles, cast on 41 (49, 57, 65) sts.
Next row (RS) Work 6 (10, 14, 18) sts in basketweave pat foll chart, place marker (pm), work center 29 sts in lace pat foll chart, pm, work rem 6 (10, 14, 18) sts in basketweave pat foll chart.
Keeping in pats as established, working new sts in basketweave pat as sts are increased, cast on 2 sts at beg of next 32 rows—105 (113, 121, 129) sts. Pm each side of last row to indicate beg of side seams.
Work even in pats until front measures 10"/25.5cm from markers.

ARMHOLE SHAPING
Bind off 5 (5, 6, 6) sts at beg of next 2 rows. Work even for 2 rows.
Next (dec) row (RS) K1, ssk, work as established to last 3 sts, end k2tog, k1.
Keeping first and last 2 sts of every row in St st, work even for 3 rows.
Rep dec row. Work WS row.
Rep last 2 rows 7 (9, 10, 12) times more—77 (81, 85, 89) sts.

Work even until armhole measures 4¼ (5, 5¾, 6½)"/11 (12¾, 14.5, 16.5)cm, end with a WS row.

NECK SHAPING
Mark center 27 sts.
Work as established to first marker, join a 2nd ball of yarn, bind off center 27 sts, work to end.
Working both sides at the same time with separate balls of yarn, bind off 2 sts from each neck edge 5 times—15 (17, 19, 21) sts each side.
Work even until armhole measures 7¼ (8, 8¾, 9½)"/18.5, 20.5, 22, 24)cm, end with a WS row.

SHOULDER SHAPING
Bind off 5 (6, 6, 7) sts from each shoulder twice, then 5 (5, 7, 7) sts once.

DART
Note Insert darts if desired, opposite your bust point.
Next row (RS) Work in pat to last 8 sts, yarn forward (yf), sl 1, yarn back (yb), sl st back to LH needle, turn.
Next row (WS) Work to last 8 sts, yf (if not there already), sl 1, yarn back (yb), sl st back to LH needle and turn.
Next row Work to last 16 sts, yf, sl 1, yb, sl st back to LH needle, turn.
Next row Work to last 16 sts, yf (if not there already), sl 1, yb, sl st back to LH needle and turn.
Next row Work to last 24 sts, yf, sl 1, yb, sl st back to LH needle, turn.
Next row Work to last 24 sts, yf (if not there already), sl 1, yb, sl st back to LH needle and turn.
*Work back over the entire row, working each wrapped st with the strand that surrounds it; turn and rep from *.
Dart measures approx 4½"/11.5cm wide.

Work remaining sweater as for Button-Back Sweater with Pockets, except with no pockets and work sleeves for 5"/12.5cm instead of 11"/28cm. ▪

Leaf-Embossed Skirt ◼◼◼▶

page 105

SIZES
To fit sizes Small (Medium, Large, X-Large).
Shown in size Small.

MEASUREMENTS
High-hip waistband:
approx 30 (36, 43, 49)"/76
(91.5, 108, 124.5)cm
Length, from below waistband to point:
approx 20"/51cm
Hips (approx 8½"/21.5cm below waist):
42 (46, 49, 53)"/106.5 (117, 124.5,
134.5)cm

MATERIALS
• 12 (14, 15, 17) 1¾oz/50g balls
(each 77yd/70m) of Filatura di Crosa/
Tahki•Stacy Charles *Zara Plus* (merino wool)
in #409 Lime Green ⬛④
• Two size 7 (4.5mm) circular needles,
24"/60cm and 32"/80cm long, *or size to
obtain gauge*
• Cable needle (cn)
• 1 (1¼, 1½, 1¾)yd/1 (1.25, 1.5, 1.75)m of
1"/2.5cm-wide waistband elastic
• Sewing needle and thread
• Tapestry needle

GAUGE
18 sts and 28 rnds to 4"/10cm in St st
using size 7 (4.5mm) needles.
*Take time to save time—check your
gauge.*

STOCKINETTE STITCH (ST ST)
(over any number of sts)
Knit every rnd.

REVERSE STOCKINETTE STITCH
(REV ST ST)
(over any number of sts)
Purl every rnd.

STITCH GLOSSARY
BKC (back knit cross) Sl 1 st to cn and hold
to *back*, k1, k1 from cn.
FKC (front knit cross) Sl 1 st to cn and hold
to *front*, k1, k1 from cn.
FPC (front purl cross) Sl 1 st to cn and hold
to *front*, p1, k1 from cn.
BPC (back purl cross) Sl 1 st to cn and hold
to *back*, k1, p1 from cn.
RT (right twist) K2tog, but do not sl st from
needle; insert RH needle between sts just
knit together and knit first st again; then sl
both sts from needle together.

LEAF PANEL
(begins over 35 sts)
Rnds 1–8 K10, p6, k3, p6, k10.
Rnd 9 K9, p6, BKC, k1, FKC, p6, k9.
Rnd 10 K8, p6, BPC, k3, FPC, p6, k8.
Rnd 11 K7, p6, BPC, p1, k3, p1, FPC, p6, k7.
Rnd 12 K6, p6, BPC, p2, k3, p2, FPC, p6, k6.
Rnd 13 K5, p6, BKC, p3, k3, p3, FKC, p6, k5.
Rnd 14 K4, p6, BPC, k1, p3, k3, p3, k1, FPC,
p6, k4.
Rnd 15 K3, p6, BPC, p1, k1, p3, k3, p3, k1,
p1, FPC, p6, k3.
Rnd 16 K2, p6, BPC, p2, k1, p3, k3, p3, k1,
p2, FPC, p6, k2.
Rnd 17 K1, p6, BKC, p3, yo, k1, yo, p3, k3,
p3, yo, k1, yo, p3, FKC, p6, k1.
Rnd 18 P6, BPC, k1, [p3, k3] 3 times, p3, k1,
FPC, p6.
Rnd 19 P5, BPC, p1, k1, p3, [k1, yo] twice,
k1, p3, k3, p3, [k1, yo] twice, k1, p3, k1,
p1, FPC, p5.
Rnd 20 P4, BPC, p2, k1, p3, k5, p3, k3, p3,
k5, p3, k1, p2, FPC, p4.
Rnd 21 P3, BPC, p3, k1, p3, k2, yo, k1, yo,
k2, p3, k3, p3, k2, yo, k1, yo, k2, p3, k1,
p3, FPC, p3.
Rnd 22 K the knit sts and the yo sts, and p
the purl sts.
Rnd 23 P3, yo, k1, yo, p4, k1, p3, ssk, k3,
k2tog, p3, k3, p3, ssk, k3, k2tog, p3, k1,
p4, yo, k1, yo, p3.
Rnd 24 Rep rnd 22.
Rnd 25 P3, [k1, yo] twice, k1, p4, k1, p3,
ssk, k1, k2tog, p3, k3, p3, ssk, k1, k2tog,
p3, k1, p4 [k1, yo] twice, k1, p3.

Rnd 26 Rep rnd 22.
Rnd 27 P3, k2, yo, k1, yo, k2, p4, yo, k1,
yo, p3, SK2P, p2, BPC, k1, FPC, p2, SK2P,
p3, yo, k1, yo, p4, k2, yo, k1, yo, k2, p3.
Rnd 28 Rep rnd 22, except p1 in st at top of
completed leaves.
Rnd 29 P3, ssk, k3, k2tog, p4, (k1, yo)
twice, k1, p5, BPC, p1, k1, p1, FPC, p5,
(k1, yo) twice, k1, p4, ssk, k3, k2tog, p3.
Rnd 30 Rep rnd 22.
Rnd 31 P3, ssk, k1, k2tog, p4, k2, yo, k1,
yo, k2, p4, BPC, p2, k1, p2, FPC, p4, k2,
yo, k1, yo, k2, p4, ssk, k1, k2tog, p3.
Rnd 32 Same as rnd 22.
Rnd 33 P3, SK2P, p4, ssk, k3, k2tog, p3,
BPC, p3, k1, p3, FPC, p3, ssk, k3, k2tog,
p4, SK2P, p3.
Rnd 34 Rep rnd 22, except p1 in st at top of
completed leaves.
Rnd 35 K1, p7, ssk, k1, k2tog, p3, yo, k1,
yo, p4, k1, p4, yo, k1, yo, p3, ssk, k1,
k2tog, p7, k1.
Rnd 36 K2, work as for rnd 22 to last 2 sts,
end k2.
Rnd 37 K3, p5, SK2P, p3, [k1, yo] twice, [k1,
p4] twice, [k1, yo] twice, k1, p3, SK2P, p5,
k3. Turn.
Note Cont to work back and forth in rows.
Row 38 (WS) P3, then k the knit sts and p
the purl sts and the yo sts and k1 in st at
top of completed leaves, until last 3 sts,
end p3—43 sts each panel.
Row 39 (RS) K2, ssk, p8, k2, yo, k1, yo, k2,
p4, yo, k1, yo, p4, k2, yo, k1, yo, k2, p8,
k2tog, k2—47 sts.
Row 40 (WS) K the knit sts and p the purl
sts and yo sts—47 sts.
Row 41 K2, ssk, p7, ssk, k3, k2tog, p4, [k1,
yo] twice, k1, p4, ssk, k3, k2tog, p7, k2tog,
k2—43 sts.
Row 42 (WS) Rep row 40—43 sts.
Row 43 (RS) K2, ssk, p6, ssk, k1, k2tog, p4,
k2, yo, k1, yo, k2, p4, ssk, k1, k2tog, p6,
k2tog, k2—39 sts.
Row 44 Rep row 40—39 sts.
Row 45 (RS) K2, ssk, p5, SK2P, p4, ssk, k3,
k2tog, p4, SK2P, p5, k2tog, k2—31 sts.
Row 46 Rep row 40, except k1 in st at top
of completed leaves—31 sts.
Row 47 (RS) K2, ssk, p9, ssk, k1, k2tog, p9,
k2tog, k2—27 sts.
Row 48 Rep row 40—27 sts.
Row 49 (RS) K2, ssk, p8, SK2P, p8, k2tog,
k2—23 sts.
Row 50 P3, k17, p3—23 sts.
Row 51 K2, ssk, p15, k2tog, k2—21 sts.
Row 52 P2, p2tog, k13, p2tog-tbl,
p2—19 sts.

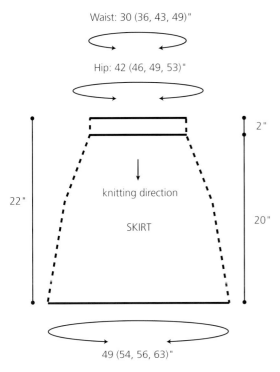

Waist: 30 (36, 43, 49)"

Hip: 42 (46, 49, 53)"

2"

knitting direction

SKIRT

22"

20"

49 (54, 56, 63)"

Row 53 K2, ssk, p11, k2tog, k2—17 sts.
Row 54 P2, p2tog, k9, p2tog-tbl, p2—15 sts.
Row 55 K2, ssk, p7, k2tog, k2—13 sts.
Row 56 P2, p2tog, k5, p2tog-tbl,
p2—11 sts.
Row 57 K2, ssk, p3, k2tog, k2—9 sts.
Row 58 P2, p2tog, k1, p2tog-tbl, p2—7 sts.
Bind off.

8-ST CABLE TWIST
Rnd 1 P2, k4, p2.
Rnd 2 P2, [RT] twice, p2.
Rnd 3 P2, k4, p2.
Rnd 4 P2, k1, RT, k1, p2.
Rep rnds 1–4 for 8-st cable twist.

12-ST CABLE TWIST
Rnd 1 P3, k6, p3.
Rnd 2 P3, [RT] 3 times, p3.
Rnd 3 P3, k6, p3.
Rnd 4 P3, k1, [RT] twice, k1, p3.
Rep rnds 1–4 for 12-st cable twist.

NOTE
The skirt is made in the round from the
top down.

SKIRT
With shorter circular needle, cast on 186
(210, 217, 245) sts. Pm and join to work in
the rnd, being careful not to twist sts.
Next rnd (est panels) *K4 (St st), p6
(rev St st), k3 (St st), p6 (rev St st), k4 (St st),

[23 sts for each Leaf Panel], place marker
(pm), work rnd 1 of 8-st (12-st, 8-st, 12-st)
cable twist, pm; rep from * 5 (5, 6, 6)
times more.
Work even as established for 7 more rnds.
Next (inc) rnd *K2, M1, k2, p6, k3, p6, k
to last 2 sts in last St st section, M1, k2, [25
sts for each Leaf Panel], work cable twist
as established; rep from * 5 (5, 6, 6) times
more—198 (222, 231, 259) sts (inc 2 sts in
each leaf panel).
Keeping in pats as established and
working incs into St st, rep inc rnd after 9
more rnds, then every 10th rnd, for a total
of 6 inc rnds (60 rnds completed)—258
(282, 301, 329) sts [35 sts each leaf panel].
Change to longer needle when necessary.
Piece measures approx 8½"/21.5cm.
Work even for 20 rnds more: piece should
measure approx 11"/28cm.
Note This would be a good place to adjust
the length of the skirt, if desired.

BEG LEAF PANEL
Next rnd *Work rnd 1 of leaf panel over
35 sts, sl marker (sm), work cable twist as
established, sm; rep from * 5 (5, 6, 6)
times more.

Work even until rnd 36 of leaf panel is
complete.

SEPARATE FOR POINTS
Next rnd *Work rnd 37 of leaf panel,
bind off 8 (12, 8, 12) sts of cable twist;
rep from * to end. Cut yarn. Turn.
Join yarn at end of last leaf panel of
prev rnd, and cont in pat over those sts
only through row 58. Bind off rem 7 sts.
Work rem 5 (5, 6, 6) leaf panels separately.

FINISHING
Weave in all ends.

WAISTBAND
With RS facing and circular needle, beg
at start of original rnd, pick up and k 134
(162, 194, 220) sts evenly spaced. Join and
work in St st for 2"/5cm.
Sew sts down to ridge formed by pick-up
rnd, leaving a 2"/5cm opening to thread
elastic through. Leave end hanging.

Cut elastic 31 (37, 44, 50)"/78.5 (94,
111.5, 127)cm long. Thread through
casing and overlap ends. Sew ends firmly,
close casing. ▪

Rib & Twist Shorts

page 106

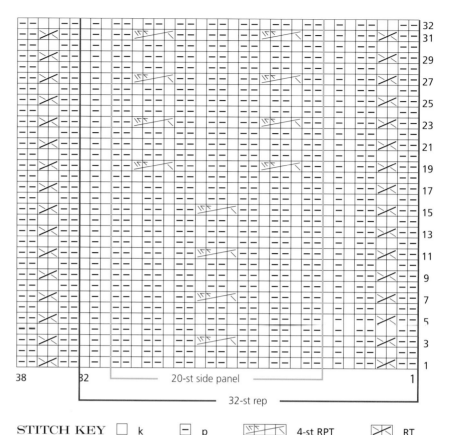

STITCH KEY

☐ k ⊟ p ⟍⟋ 4-st RPT ⟋⟍ RT

SIZES
To fit sizes Small (Medium, Large, X-Large).
Shown in size Small.

MEASUREMENTS
Waist: 26 (28, 30, 32)"/66 (71, 76, 81)cm
Hip: 33 (35½, 36½, 39)"/84 (90, 92.5, 99)cm
Thigh: 19 (20, 21, 21¾)"/48 (51, 53, 55)cm
Inseam: 10"/25.5cm

MATERIALS
• 4 (5, 5, 6) 3½oz/100g skeins
(each approx 215yd/197m) of Brown Sheep
Company *Cotton Fleece* (cotton/wool) in
#CW 760 Emperor's Robe ❸
• Two each sizes 5 and 6 (3.75mm
and 4mm) circular needle, both in 16" and
24"/40cm and 60cm lengths, *or size to
obtain gauge*
• Cable needle (cn)
• Stitch markers
• 1yd/1m of 1"/2.5cm-wide
waistband elastic
• Sewing needle and thread

GAUGES
• 20 sts and 28 rnds to 4"/10cm over St st
using size 6 (4mm) circular needle.
• Cable/rib panel over
20 sts = 2½"/6.5cm wide.
Take time to save time—check your gauges.

SHORT ROW WRAP & TURN (W&T)
on RS row (on WS row)
1) Wyib (wyif), sl next st purlwise.
2) Move yarn between the needles to the
front (back).
3) Sl the same st back to LH needle. Turn
work. One st is wrapped.
4) When working the wrapped st, insert
RH needle under the wrap and work it tog
with the corresponding st on needle to
close wraps.

STITCH GLOSSARY
4-st RPT Sl 3 sts to cn and hold to *back*, k1,
then sl the 2 p sts back to LH needle and
place the rem k st to front of work, then p2
from LH needle, k1 from cn.
RT K2tog and leave sts on LH needle, then
insert RH needle between 2 sts just ktog
and k first st again, then sl both sts from
LH needle.

LEFT LEG
With shorter size 5 (3.75mm) needle, cast
on 115 (121, 127, 133) sts. Join, being
careful not to twist sts, and place marker
(pm) for beg of rnd.
Note Beg of rnd is inseam of leg.
Rnd 1 [K1, p1] 3 (4, 6, 7) times, k1, pm;

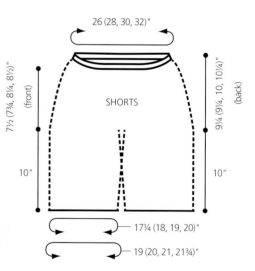

[work sts 1–32 of rib and cable chart] 3
times, then work sts 33–38 of cable chart,
pm; [k1, p1] 3 (5, 6, 8) times. The sts at beg
and end of rnd, before and after the chart,
are worked in k1, p1 rib. Cont to work in
this way until rnd 10 is completed.
Inc rnd 1 K1, p1, kfb, work in established
pat to last 2 sts, kfb, p1—2 sts inc'd.
Work 7 rnds even.
Inc rnd 2 K1, p1, (k1, p1) into next st, work
in established pat to last 2 sts, (p1, k1) into

next st, p1—2 sts inc'd.
Work 7 rnds even. Rep last 16 rnds twice more—127 (133, 139, 145) sts. Work even until 32-rnd rep has been completed twice. Rep rnds 1 and 2. Piece measures approx 9½"/24cm from beg, slightly stretched. Change to shorter size 6 (4mm) needle.

For sizes Medium and X-Large only
Move last st of previous rnd to beg of rnd.
Dec rnd [K5 (6, 6, 6), k2tog] 7 times, k5 (1, 4, 7), cont next 20 sts foll chart (side panel); [k5 (6, 6, 6), k2tog] 7 times, k4 (0, 3, 6)—113 (119, 125, 131) sts.
Next 3 rnds Work the first 47 (50, 53, 56) sts in St st (k every rnd), the next 20 sts foll chart, and the last 46 (49, 52, 55) sts in St st.
At beg of next rnd, sl the first 7 (7, 8, 8) sts to a st holder and the last 8 (8, 9, 9) sts to same st holder for 15 (15, 17, 17) sts for crotch. Sl the rem 98 (104, 108, 114) sts to longer size 6 (4mm) needle to leave on hold. Cut yarn.

RIGHT LEG
Work as for left leg up to dec rnd.

For sizes Small and Large only
Move first st of next rnd to end of previous rnd.
Dec rnd [K5 (6, 6, 6), k2tog] 7 times, k4

(0, 3, 6), cont next 20 sts foll chart (side panel); [k5 (6, 6, 6), k2tog] 7 times, k5 (1, 4, 7)—113 (119, 125, 131) sts.
Next 3 rnds Work the first 46 (49, 52, 55) sts in St st (k every rnd), the next 20 sts foll chart, and the last 47 (50, 53, 56) sts in St st.
At beg of next rnd, sl the first 7 (7, 8, 8) sts to a st holder and the last 8 (8, 9, 9) sts to same st holder for 15 (15, 17, 17) sts for crotch. Sl the rem 98 (104, 108, 114) sts to longer size 6 (4mm) needle to leave on hold. Cut yarn.

HIP
Reposition all 196 (208, 216, 228) sts onto longer size 6 (4mm) needle so that beg-of-rnd marker is placed after the 20-st side panel at right back. Rejoin yarn at this point. Note that the 20-st side panel will cont up the sides of the shorts to the waistband.
Rnd 1 *K79 (85, 89, 95) (back St st panel), cont 20-st cable panel, k77 (83, 87, 93) (front St st panel), cont 20-st cable panel. Mark center 3 sts on both front and back St st panels.
Work even (foll rnd 1) for 19 (21, 23, 25) rnds more OR until crotch measures approx 2¾ (3, 3½, 3¾)"/7 (7.5, 9, 9.5)cm.
Dec rnd *Work to 2 sts before center 3 marked sts, k2tog, sm, k3, sm, ssk; rep

Rep dec rnd every 3rd rnd 10 times more—152 (164, 172, 184) sts.
Work 2 rnds even.

BACK WAIST SHAPING
Note The back is elongated from the front just before the waistband using short-row shaping.
Short row 1 (RS) K to 1 st before the first 20-st side panel, w&t.
Short row 2 (WS) P to 1 st before the 20-st side panel, w&t.
Short row 3 (RS) K to 5 sts before the previous wrapped st, w&t.
Short row 4 (WS) P to 5 sts before the previous wrapped st, w&t.
Short rows 5, 7, and 9 Rep short row 3.
Short rows 6, 8, and 10 Rep short row 4.
Next rnd K around on all sts, closing up the wraps.
Knit 1 rnd even. Change to longer size 5 (3.75mm) needle and work in k1, p1 rib for 2¼"/6cm. Leave sts on hold.

FINISHING
Cut elastic to 27 (29, 31, 33)"/68.5 (73.5, 78.5, 84)cm. Overlap by 1"/2.5cm and sew into a circle, using thread. Fold the waistband over the elastic waistband to the WS and sew the sts on hold in place at the rib base, covering the waistband. Seam crotch sts. ▪

"Marbleized Paper" Skirt

page 115

SIZES
To fit sizes Small (Medium, Large, X-Large). Shown in size Medium.

MEASUREMENTS
Finished waist:
approx 26 (30, 34, 38)"/66 (76. 86. 96.5)cm
Hip (9"/23cm down from waist):
37 (42½, 48, 53)"/94 (108, 122, 134.5)cm
Length, from waistband to lower edge: approx 23"/58.5cm

MATERIALS
• 2 3½oz/100g hanks (each 308yd/281m) of Cascade *Venezia Sport* (merino wool/ mulberry silk) in #194 Rose (A) (**2**)
• 1 hank each in #193 Pink (B), #178 Sage (C), #179 Deep Turquoise (D), #192 Grape (E), #158 Burgundy (F), #191 Orange (G), and #177 Light Purple (H)
• Size 6 (4mm) circular needle, 24"/61cm long, *or size to obtain gauge*

• ¾"/2cm-wide flat elastic, 26 (30, 34, 38)"/66 (76, 86, 96.5)cm slightly stretched
• Stitch markers
• Sewing needle thread

GAUGE
27 sts and 32 rnds to 4"/10cm over Lace Charts with size 6 (4mm) needles.
Take time to save time—check your gauge.

K1, P1 RIB (IN THE RND)
(over an even number of sts)
All rnds *K1, p1; rep from *.

COLOR SEQUENCE
*4 rnds A, 2 rnds B, 6 rnds A, 4 rnds C, 6 rnds D, 4 rnds E, 2 rnds B, 8 rnds F, 4 rnds H, 4 rnds A, 2 rnds G, 6 rnds A. 8 rnds D, 6 rnds F, 2 rnds H, 4 rnds A, 2 rnds B, 6 rnds E, 6 rnds G; rep from * for color sequence.

CHART 1

o				⋏⋏	o				19
o				⋏		o			17
o			⋏			o			15
o		⋏				o			13
o	⋏⋏						o		11
o		⋏				o			9
o			⋏			o			7
o				⋏		o			5
o				⋏		o			3
o					⋏⋏	o			1

9 st rep

CHART 2

o					⋏⋏	o				23
o				⋏		o				21
o			⋏			o				19
o		⋏				o				17
o	⋏⋏						o			15
o	⋏					o				13
o		⋏				o				11
o			⋏			o				9
o				⋏		o				7
o				⋏		o				5
o					⋏		o			3
o					⋏⋏	o				1

10 st rep

CHART 3

o					⋏⋏	o					27
o					⋏		o				25
o				⋏			o				23
o			⋏				o				21
o		⋏					o				19
o	⋏⋏							o			17
o	⋏						o				15
o		⋏					o				13
o			⋏				o				11
o				⋏			o				9
o				⋏			o				7
o					⋏		o				5
o					⋏⋏	o					3
o						⋏⋏	o				1

11 st rep

CHART 4

o							⋏⋏	o				31
o						⋏		o				29
o					⋏			o				27
o				⋏				o				25
o			⋏					o				23
o		⋏						o				21
o	⋏							o				19
o	⋏⋏								o			17
o	⋏⋏								o			15
o		⋏						o				13
o			⋏					o				11
o				⋏				o				9
o					⋏			o				7
o					⋏⋏		o					5
o						⋏⋏		o				3
o							⋏⋏	o				1

12 st rep

CHART 5

o							⋏⋏	o					35
o						⋏		o					33
o					⋏			o					31
o				⋏				o					29
o			⋏					o					27
o		⋏						o					25
o	⋏							o					23
o	⋏⋏								o				21
o	⋏							o					19
o		⋏						o					17
o			⋏					o					15
o				⋏				o					13
o					⋏			o					11
o						⋏		o					9
o						⋏⋏		o					7
o							⋏⋏	o					5
o							⋏⋏	o					3
o								⋏⋏	o				1

13 st rep

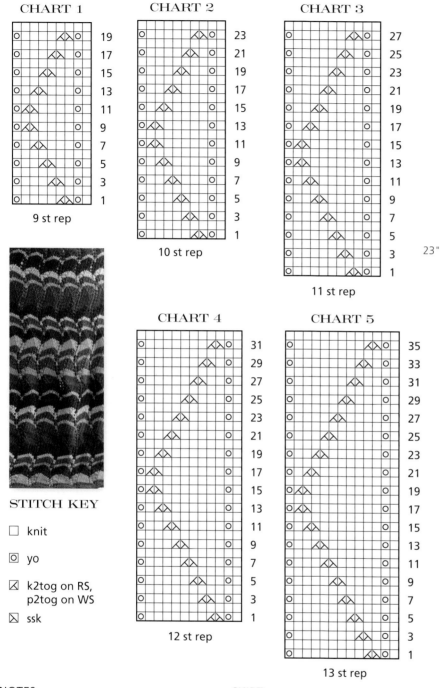

STITCH KEY

- ☐ knit
- ⊡ yo
- ⊠ k2tog on RS, p2tog on WS
- ⊠ ssk

Waist: 26 (30, 34, 38)"

Hip: 37 (42½, 48, 53)"

1½"

knitting direction ↓

SKIRT

23"

21½"

40 (46, 52, 57¾)"

NOTES

1) Read all rnds of each chart from right to left.

2) The skirt is worked in the rnd from top to bottom. The 86 rnds of the striped color sequence are worked at the same time as the changing Lace Charts, from beg of skirt to end. When the first 86 rnds are complete, return to the beg of the color sequence: You will probably not complete the second rep of color sequence.

SKIRT

With A, cast on 189 (216, 243, 270) sts. Place marker (pm) and join to work in the rnd, being careful not to twist sts. Beg color sequence and work Chart #1 21 (24, 27, 30) times around, dividing reps with markers. Work rnds 1–19 of Chart #1.
Next (inc) rnd (rnd 20 of chart) *K8, M1, k1; rep from * to end—210 (240, 270, 300) sts.
Cont color sequence as established, work

Chart #2 21 (24, 27, 30) times around. Work rnds 1–23 of Chart #2.
Next (inc) rnd (rnd 24 of chart) *K9, M1, k1; rep from * to end—231 (264, 297, 330) sts.
Cont color sequence as established, work Chart #3 21 (24, 27, 30) times around. Work rnds 1–27 of Chart #3.
Next (inc) rnd (rnd 28 of chart) *K10, M1, k1; rep from * to end—252 (288, 324, 360) sts.
Cont color sequence as established, work Chart #4 21 (24, 27, 30) times around. Work rnds 1–31 of Chart #4.
Next (inc) rnd (rnd 32 of chart) *K11, M1, k1; rep from * to end—273 (312, 351, 390) sts.
Cont color sequence, work Chart #5 21 (24, 27, 30) times around. Work rnds 1–36 of Chart #5 until skirt measures 21½"/54.5cm, or to desired length. Bind off loosely.

LOWER EDGE TRIM

With B and RS facing, pick up and k 1 st for every st along lower edge. Pm and join. Purl 3 rnds. Bind off.

FINISHING
Weave in all ends.

WAISTBAND
With RS facing, A and circular needle, beg at first raised "bump" of panel, *pick up and k 8 sts in solid St st section of panel, then cast on 4 sts over 3 st of lace section; rep from * across to end—252 (288, 324, 360) sts. Pm for beg of rnd. With A, work in rnds of k1, p1 rib for ¾"/2cm. Change to G. Work 3 rnds. Change to D and rib until band measures 3"/7.5cm.

Fold rib to WS and sew down st by st, leaving a 2"/5cm opening.

Cut elastic to desired length, slightly stretched, plus 1"/2.5cm for overlap.

Thread elastic through with the help of a pin at the end (anchor the other end with a pin in the fabric so it does not get lost in casing). Sew ends of elastic tog, overlapping 1"/2.5cm, then close up rem ribbed opening.

Tack upper St st pleats loosely to WS at base of ribbing.

Steam skirt lightly. ▪

Houndstooth Coat And Overvest

page 117

SIZES
To fit sizes Small (Medium, Large, X-Large, XX-Large). Shown in size Medium.

MEASUREMENTS
COAT
Finished bust, zippered:
39½ (43½, 47½, 51½, 55½)"/100
(110.5, 120.5, 130.5, 141)cm
Sleeve width at upper arm:
12 (13, 14, 15, 16)"/30.5
(33, 35.5, 38, 40.5)cm
Length from outer shoulder to
lower edge:
34½ (35, 35½, 36, 36½)"/87.5 (89,
90, 91.5, 92.5)cm

OVERVEST
Finished bust:
43½ (47 ½, 51½, 55½, 59½)"/110.5
(120.5, 130.5, 141, 151)cm
Length from outer shoulder to
lower back:
18½ (19, 19½, 20, 20½)"/47 (48, 49.5,
51, 52)cm

MATERIALS
FOR COAT AND OVERVEST, ALL SIZES
• 3 4oz/113g hanks (each 220yd/200m) of
Imperial Yarn *Columbia* (wool) each in #126
Spring Sage (A), #125 Canyon Shadow (C),
and #114 Dusty Rose (F) (4)
• 2 hanks each in #124 Pine Tree (B),
#101 Teal Heather (D), #08 Teal (E),
#21 Cactus Blossom (G)
• One pair each size 8 (5mm) and
9 (5.5mm) needles or size to obtain
given gauge.
• Size 8 (5mm) circular needle,
40"/100cm long
• Stitch markers
• Cable needle (cn)

FOR COAT
• One separating zipper, 25"/63.5cm,
medium weight, with metal teeth, in army
green: available from Zipperstop.com
• Dressmaker pins
• Sewing needle and thread for zipper

FOR OVERVEST
• 3 buttons, 1⅛"/28mm

GAUGE
16 sts and 18 rows to 4"/10cm
over houndstooth pats using size 9
(5.5mm) needles.
Take time to save time—check your gauge.

STOCKINETTE STITCH (ST ST)
(over any number of sts)
Knit RS rows, purl WS rows.

STITCH GLOSSARY
RT (right twist) K2tog, leave on needle,
then knit the first st again, slip both sts
from needle.
5-st FC (front cross) Sl 3 sts to cn and hold
to *front*, k2, sl last st from cn back to LH
needle and p it, k2 from cn.
5-st BC (back cross) Sl 3 sts to cn and hold
to *back*, k2, sl last st from cn back to LH
needle and p it, k2 from cn.
7-st FC (front cross) Sl 4 sts to cn and hold
to *front*, k3, sl last st from cn back to LH
needle and p it, k3 from cn.
7-st BC (back cross) Sl 4 sts to cn and hold
to *back*, k3, sl last st from cn back to LH
needle and p it, k3 from cn.
9-st FC (front cross) Sl 5 sts to cn and hold
to *front*, k4, sl last st from cn back to LH
needle and p it, k4 from cn.
9-st BC (back cross) Sl 5 sts to cn and
hold to *back*, k4, sl last st from cn back to

LH needle and p it, k4 from cn.
wrap st Sl next st purlwise, bring yarn
forward between needles, sl the same st
back to LH needle, turn work and bring
yarn forward between needles.

NOTES
1) The body of the coat is made of two side
pieces. These pieces are sewn at the center
back to a cable, which is worked separately.
2) Each side piece is divided for front and
back at the armhole, which falls at the
center of the pieces (see schematic).
3) Each piece starts in a different place in
the color sequence.
4) Carry yarns not in use loosely across back
of fabric, twisting when necessary to avoid
long floats. Twist yarn at edges.
5) Charts are worked in St st.

COLOR SEQUENCE
Rows 1–16 A-background (BG),
B-houndstooth (HT).
Rows 17–32 C-BG, D-HT.
Rows 33–40 A-BG, D-HT.
Rows 41–48 A-BG, E-HT.
Rows 49–56 F- BG, E-HT.
Rows 57–64 F-BG, D-HT.
Rows 65–72 C-BG, B-HT.
Rows 73–80 F-BG, B-HT.
Rows 81–88 F-BG, G-HT.
Rows 89–96 A-BG, G-HT.
Rows 97–104 C-BG, D-HT.
Rows 105–112 C-BG, E-HT.
Rows 113–120 A-BG, G-HT.
Rows 121–128 F-BG, G-HT.
Rep rows 1–128 for color sequence.

Coat
LEFT SIDE
With size 9 (5.5mm) needles and A, cast
on 96 (104, 112, 120, 128) sts. If long-tail
cast-on method was used, purl 1 WS row.
Next row (RS) Beg with row 1 of color
sequence, k1 in background (BG) color
(edge st: keep in St st and BG), beg with
5th (1st, 5th, 1st, 5th) st of Large
Houndstooth Chart and work over next 32
(36, 40, 44, 48) sts, k1 in BG color (divider
st: keep in St st and BG), place marker
(pm), beg with 1st of rep and work Small
Houndstooth Chart over next 24 sts, pm,
k1 in BG color (divider st: keep in St st and
BG), pm, work 1st row of Large
Houndstooth Chart over next 36
(40, 44, 48, 52) sts, pm, end k1 in BG
(edge st: keep in St st).
Work even in color sequence and charts

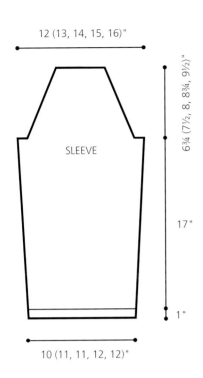

12 (13, 14, 15, 16)"

6¾ (7½, 8, 8¾, 9½)"

SLEEVE

17"

1"

10 (11, 11, 12, 12)"

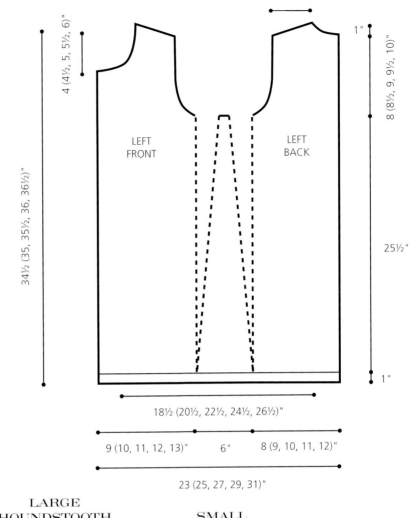

3¾ (4, 4¼, 4¼, 4½)"

4 (4½, 5, 5½, 6)"

1"

LEFT
FRONT

LEFT
BACK

34½ (35, 35½, 36, 36½)"

25½"

8 (8½, 9, 9½, 10)"

1"

18½ (20½, 22½, 24½, 26½)"

9 (10, 11, 12, 13)"   6"   8 (9, 10, 11, 12)"

23 (25, 27, 29, 31)"

for 15 rows, end with WS row.
Next (dec) row (RS) Work as established to first divider st, ssk this divider st tog with the next st of Small Houndstooth Chart, work to 1 st before next divider st, k2tog last st of Small Houndstooth Chart with divider st, work as established to end. Keeping in pats, and color sequence, rep dec row after 7 rows, then every 8th row after for a total of 11 decs each side of Small Houndstooth Chart—74 (82, 90, 98, 106) sts.
Work even until piece measures 25 ½"/64.5cm, end with a RS row.

DIVIDE FRONT AND BACK
Work to the divider st before the rem 2 sts in Small Houndstooth Chart, then bind off 4 sts, work to end.
Turn—33 (37, 41, 45, 49) sts in back section, 37 (41, 45, 49, 53) sts in front section.

LEFT BACK
ARMHOLE SHAPING
Cont in pat as established, bind off 2 sts at beg of next 1 (1, 2, 2, 2) WS rows—31 (35, 37, 41, 45) sts.
Next (dec) row (RS) Work in pat as established to last 2 sts, end k2tog.
Next row (WS) Work as established.
Rep last 2 rows 5 (7, 7, 9, 11) times more—25 (27, 29, 31, 33) sts.

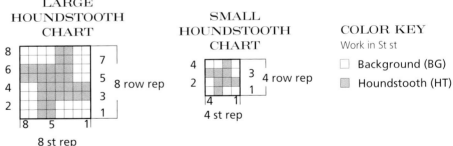

LARGE
HOUNDSTOOTH
CHART

8 row rep
8 st rep

SMALL
HOUNDSTOOTH
CHART

4 row rep
4 st rep

COLOR KEY
Work in St st

☐ Background (BG)

▨ Houndstooth (HT)

Work even until armhole measures 8 (8½, 9, 9½, 10)"/20.5 (21.5, 23, 24, 25.5)cm, end with a WS row.

NECK AND SHOULDER SHAPING
Bind off from neck edge (RS) 3 (3, 0, 5, 5) sts 2 (1, 0, 2, 3) times, then 4 sts 1 (2, 3, 1, 0) times; AT THE SAME TIME, from shoulder edge (WS), bind off 4 sts 3 (4, 3, 3, 3) times, then 3 (0, 5, 5, 6) sts once.

LEFT FRONT
Cont in color sequence as established, join yarns at beg of RS row.

Bind off 2 sts at beg of next 1 (1, 2, 2, 2) RS rows—35 (39, 41, 45, 49) sts.
Next row (WS) Work as established.
Next (dec) row (RS) Ssk, work in pat as established to end. Work WS row as established.
Rep last 2 rows 5 (7, 7, 9, 11) times more; AT THE SAME TIME, when armhole measures 4 (4½, 5, 5½, 6)"/10 (11.4, 12.5, 14, 15)cm, end with a RS row.

NECK AND SHOULDER SHAPING
Bind off from neck edge (WS) 4 (5, 6, 8, 9) sts once, then 2 sts 5 times.

Work even until armhole measures 8 (8½, 9, 9½, 10)"/20.5 (21.5, 23, 24, 25.5)cm, end with a WS row.
At beg of RS rows, work shoulder shaping as for left back.

RIGHT SIDE
With size 9 (5.5mm) needles and F, cast on 96 (104, 112, 120, 128) sts. If long-tail cast-on method was used, purl 1 WS row.
Next row (RS) Beg with row 73 of color sequence, k1 in BG color (edge st: keep in St st), beg with 1st row of Large Houndstooth Chart and work over next 36 (40, 44, 48, 52) sts, pm, k1 in BG color (divider st: keep in St st and BG), pm, beg with 1st row of Small Houndstooth Chart over next 24 sts, pm, k1 in BG color (divider st: keep in St st and BG), pm, beg with 1st row of Large Houndstooth Chart and work over next 32 (36, 40, 44, 48) sts, pm, (half rep of pattern will be at end—reverse of left side), end k1 in BG color (edge st: keep in St st).
Work same as for left side, working same decs at center of piece and reversing all shaping, beg neckline shaping one row before, on a RS row.

LEFT SLEEVE
With size 9 (5.5mm) needles and A, cast on 40 (44, 44, 48, 48) sts. If long-tail cast-on method was used, purl 1 WS row.
Next row (RS) Beg with row 1 of color sequence, k2 in BG color (edge sts: keep in St st), beg with 1st row of Large Houndstooth Chart and work over center 36 (40, 40, 44, 44) sts, end k2 in BG color (edge sts: keep in St st).
Work even in color sequence for 7 more rows, end with WS row.
Next (inc) row (RS) K2 (edge sts), M1, work to last 2 sts, M1, end k2 (edge sts).
Keeping in color sequence and working incs into chart pat, rep inc row after 15 rows, then every 16th (16th, 12th, 12th, 10th) row after for a total of 4 (4, 6, 6, 8) incs each side—48 (52, 56, 60, 64) sts.
Work even until sleeve measures 17"/43cm, or to desired length, end with WS row.
CAP SHAPING
Keeping in color sequence, discontinue edge sts for cap, bind off 4 (4, 5, 5, 5) sts at beg of next 2 rows—40 (44, 46, 50, 54) sts. Work 6 rows even.
Next (dec) row Ssk, work in pat as established to last 2 sts, end k2tog.

Next row (WS) Work as established.
Rep last 2 rows 10 (12, 13, 15, 17) times more—18 sts. Bind off on last RS row.

RIGHT SLEEVE
With size 9 (5.5mm) needles and F, cast on 40 (44, 44, 48, 48) sts. If long-tail cast-on method was used, purl 1 WS row.
Next row (RS) Beg with row 49 of color sequence, k2 in BG color (edge sts: keep in St st), beg with 1st row of Large Houndstooth Chart and work over center 36 (40, 40, 44, 44) sts, end k2 in BG color (edge sts: keep in St st).
Work shaping same as for left sleeve and cont in color sequence as established.

FINISHING
CENTER BACK CABLE
Note Cable begins at back neck edge, and widens gradually to lower edge.
With size 9 (5.5mm) needles, cast on 16 sts.

Section 1
Row 1 and all other WS rows K1, p14, k1.
Row 2 (RS) P1, [k2, p1] 4 times, k2, p1.
Row 4 P1, k2, [p1, FC] twice, p1.
Row 6 Rep row 2.
Row 8 P1, [BC, p1] twice, k2, p1.
Row 10 Rep row 2.
Rep rows 1–10 until piece measures approx 9–10"/23–25.5cm, ending with a row 3.
Next (inc) row (RS) P1, k2, M1, p1, sl next 3 sts to cn and hold to *front*, k2, M1, sl last st from cn back to LH needle and p it, k2 from cn, M1, p1, sl next 3 sts to cn and hold to *front*, k2, M1, sl last st from cn back to LH needle and p it, M1, k2 from cn, p1—21 sts.

Section 2 (over 21 sts)
Row 1 and all other WS rows K1, p19, k1.
Rows 2 and 4 (RS) P1, [k3, p1] 4 times, k3, p1.
Row 6 P1, [BC, p1] twice, k3, p1.
Rows 8 and 10 Rep rows 2 and 4.
Row 12 P1, k3, [p1, FC] twice, p1.
Row 14 Rep row 2.
Rep rows 1–14 until piece measures approx 18–20"/45.5–51cm, ending with a row 11.
Next (inc) row (RS) P1, k3, M1, p1, sl next 4 sts to cn and hold to *front*, k3, M1, sl last st from cn back to LH needle and p it, k3 from cn, M1, p1, sl next 4 sts to cn and hold in front, k3, M1, sl last st from cn back to LH needle and p it, M1, k3 from cn, p1—26 sts.

Section 3
Row 1 and all other WS rows K1, p24, k1.
Rows 2, 4, and 6 (RS) P1, [k4, p1] 4 times, k4, p1.
Row 8 P1, [BC, p1] twice, k4, p1.
Rows 10, 12, and 14 Rep row 2.
Row 16 P1, k4, [p1, FC] twice, p1.
Row 18 Same as row 2.
Rep rows 1–18 until piece measures same as center back edges.

Steam cable. Pin one edge of cable evenly to one side of center back, with narrow cast-on end at the top. With RS facing, sew cable in place. Rep on other side. Sew shoulder seams.

BODY LOWER EDGE TRIM
With RS facing, size 8 (5mm) circular needle and C, pick up and k 1 st for every cast-on st along lower edge to beg of back cable, then pick up and k 17 sts in cable, then 1 st for every cast-on st along edge to end. Knit 7 rows, then bind off with larger needle.

LOWER SLEEVE TRIM
With RS facing, size 8 (5mm) circular needle and C, pick up and k 1 st for every cast-on st along lower edge. Work same as for body.

NECKLINE TRIM
With RS facing, size 8 (5mm) needle and C, pick up and k 85 (93, 101, 109, 117) sts evenly along neckline edge. Knit 5 rows. Change to F and knit 2 rows. Change to G and knit 2 rows. Bind off.

LEFT FRONT EDGE TRIM
With RS facing, size 8 (5mm) needle and B, pick up and k 125 (129, 133, 137, 141) sts evenly along front edge, including trim at lower edge and neckline. Knit WS row, then bind off with larger needle. Rep on right front edge.
Pin zipper along front edges, with top "tab" extensions even with edge of top of neckline trim, leave the lower edge free. With needle and thread, baste in place, sewing in "dent" between trim and main fabric. Check the drape of zipper, then sew permanently.
Sew sleeve seams. Sew caps into armholes.

Overvest with Hood

BACK

With size 9 (5.5mm) needle and A, cast on 86 (94, 102, 110, 118) sts. If long-tail cast-on method was used, purl 1 WS row. Beg with row 33 of color sequence.
Next row (RS) K1 in BG color (edge st), pm, beg with first st of Small Houndstooth Chart and rep over next 84 (92, 100, 108, 116) sts, pm, k1 in BG color (edge st). Keeping in pat, work even for 8 pat rows, so end with WS.
Dec 1 st at each end of the next row and every 8th row after for a total of 4 decs each side—78 (86, 94, 102, 110) sts. Work even until piece measures 9"/23cm, end with a WS row.

ARMHOLE SHAPING

Keeping in pat, bind off 6 sts at beg of next 2 rows—66 (74, 82, 90, 98) sts.
Dec 1 st at each end of next row and every RS row after for a total of 6 decs each side above bind offs—54 (62, 70, 78, 86) sts. Work even until armhole measures 9 (9½, 10, 10½, 11)"/23 (24, 25.5, 26.5, 28)cm, end with a WS row.

SHOULDER AND NECK SHAPING

Mark center 20 (22, 20, 22, 20) sts.
Next row (RS) Bind off 2 (3, 4, 4, 5) sts, work to center 20 (22, 20, 22, 20) sts, join new balls of yarn and bind off center marked 20 (22, 20, 22, 20) sts, work as established to end.
Working both sides with separate skeins of yarn, bind off 2 (3, 4, 4, 5) sts from the next 5 shoulder edges, then 3 (3, 3, 6, 6) sts on last 2 shoulder edges, and at the same time, bind off from each neck edge 4 (4, 5, 5, 6) sts twice.

LEFT FRONT

Note Both fronts begin with the same color sequence.
With size 9 (5.5mm) needles and F, cast on 42 (46, 50, 54, 58) sts. If long-tail cast-on method was used, purl 1 WS row.
Beg with row 49 of color sequence.
Next row (RS) K1 in BG (edge st), pm, beg with first st of rep, work Small Houndstooth Chart over next 40 (44, 48, 52, 56) sts, pm, k1 in BG color (edge st). Keeping in pat, work even for 8 pat rows, so end with WS.
Dec 1 st at each end of the next row and every 8th row after once more, total of 2 decs at edge—40 (44, 48, 52, 56) sts.

Work even until piece measures 4½"/11.5cm, end with a WS row.

SHAPING ARMHOLE

Keeping in pat, bind off 6 sts at beg of next row—34 (38, 42, 46, 50) sts.
Dec 1 st at beg of next 6 RS rows—28 (32, 36, 40, 44) sts. Work even until armhole measures 5"/12.5cm, end with a RS row.

NECK AND SHOULDER SHAPING

Bind off 4 sts at beg of next 2 WS rows, then 2 sts at beg of next 5 (6, 6, 6, 6) WS rows, then 1 (0, 1, 2, 3) sts on the next WS row—9 (12, 15, 18, 21) sts. Work even until armhole measures 9 (9½, 10, 10½, 11)"/23 (24, 25.5, 26.5, 28)cm, end with a WS row.
Bind off 2 (3, 4, 4, 5) sts at beg of next 3 RS rows, then 3 (3, 3, 6, 6) sts on last RS row.

RIGHT FRONT

With size 9 (5.5mm) needles and F, cast on 42 (46, 50, 54, 58) sts. If long-tail cast-on method was used, purl 1 WS row.
Beg with row 49 of color sequence.
Keeping in pat as established, work same as for left front, reversing all shaping.

FINISHING

Sew fronts to back at shoulders.

SIDE CABLES (MAKE 2)

Note Cable panel is worked over 10 sts.
With size 9 (5.5mm) needles and D, cast on 10 sts.
Row 1 and all other WS rows K1, p8, k1.
Row 2 P1, k1, RT 3 times, k1, p1.
Row 4 P1, RT 4 times, p1.
Rep rows 1–4 for 4½"/11.5cm, same length as side of front. Bind off.
Sew cable to side of left front, then to side of matching back side at the same depth. Rep on other side.

BACK LOWER TRIM

With RS facing, size 8 (5mm) needles and C, pick up and k 1 st for every cast-on st along lower back. Knit 1 WS row, purl 1 RS row. Bind off knitwise.

LEFT FRONT LOWER TRIM

Beg at edge of cable, with RS facing, size 8 (5mm) needle and C, pick up and k 7 sts along bottom of cable, then 1 st for every cast-on st along lower back. Knit 1 WS row, purl 1 RS row. Bind off knitwise.

Rep for right front lower edge.

BACK SIDE TRIM

With RS facing, size 8 (5mm) needle and C, pick up and k 18 sts along lower side edge of back. Knit 1 WS row.
Bind off knitwise.

ARMHOLE TRIM

With RS facing, size 8 (5mm) needle and C, beg at cable, pick up and k 7 sts along top of cable, pick up 52 (56, 60, 64, 68) sts to shoulder, then 52 (56, 60, 64, 68) sts to beg—111 (119, 127, 135, 143) sts. Purl 1 row. Bind off knitwise.

NECKLINE TRIM

With RS facing, size 8 (5mm) needle and C, beg at right front, pick up and k 37 (38, 39, 40, 41) sts to shoulder, then 40 (42, 44, 46, 48) sts along back neck, then 37 (38, 39, 40, 41) sts to left front—114 (118, 122, 126, 130) sts. Knit 1 WS row, purl 1 RS row. Bind off knitwise.

LEFT FRONT BUTTONBAND

With RS facing, size 8 (5mm) needles and A, pick up and k 36 (38, 40, 42, 44) sts evenly along left front edge. Knit 5 rows. Bind off.

RIGHT FRONT BUTTONHOLE BAND

Work same as for left front band; AT THE SAME TIME, on first WS row, work buttonholes as foll: k3, [bind off 4 sts, k8] twice, bind off 4 sts, k to end.

HOOD

Note Hood is the same for all sizes.
With size 9 (5.5mm) needles and A, cast on 34 sts.
Next row (RS) K1 in BG color (St st edge st), pm, beg with first st of Large Houndstooth Chart and rep to last st, pm, k1 in BG (St st edge st).
Work in pat for 152 rows. Bind off. Piece should measure approx 32"/81cm.

HOOD TRIM

With RS facing, size 9 (5.5mm) needles and F, pick up and k 132 sts along one side of hood piece.
Knit 2 rows.
Next row (RS) K2, M1, k38, wrap next st, turn, knit WS to end.
Next row (RS) K2, M1, k30, wrap next st, turn, knit WS to end.
Next row (RS) K2, M1, k22, wrap next st,

turn, knit WS to end.
Next row (RS) K2, M1, k12 , wrap next st, turn, knit WS to end.
Next row (RS) K2, M1, k to last 2 sts, knitting each wrapped st tog with strand that surrounds it, M1, end k2—138 sts.
Next row (WS) K41, wrap next st, turn, knit RS to last 2 sts, M1, k2.
Next row (WS) K32, wrap next st, turn, knit RS to last 2 sts, M1, k2.
Next row (WS) K23, wrap next st, turn, knit RS to last 2 sts, M1, k2.
Next row (WS) K14, wrap next st, turn, knit RS to last 2 sts, M1, k2—142 sts.

Next row (WS) Knit to end, k each wrap st tog with strand that surrounds it.
Cont to inc 1 st each end of RS rows as established, knit 2 rows. Change to G and knit 2 rows. Bind off.

CENTER BACK HOOD
With size 9 (5.5mm) needles and F, cast on 30 (30, 32, 32, 34) sts.
Knit every row, work even until piece measures 2 (2, 1, 1, 1)"/5 (5, 2.5, 2.5, 2.5)cm, end with WS row.
Next (dec) row (RS) K2, ssk, work to last 4 sts, end k2tog, k2.

Knit 3 rows.
Rep last 4 rows 12 (12, 13, 13, 14) times more; AT THE SAME TIME, when F section measures 5"/12.5cm, change to A and cont for 3½"/9cm, change to D and cont to end—4 sts. Work even until piece measures 16"/40.5cm. Bind off.
Mark center of untrimmed edge of hood. Sew each side of center back piece evenly. Sew lower edge of hood along inner neck edge.
Sew buttons opposite buttonholes. ■

Resources

BERROCO, INC.
berroco.com

BROWN SHEEP COMPANY, INC.
brownsheep.com

CASCADE YARNS
cascadeyarns.com

CLASSIC ELITE YARNS
classiceliteyarns.com

COATS & CLARK
makeitcoats.com

DEBBIE BLISS
knittingfever.com

FILATURA DI CROSA
tahkistacycharles.com

IMPERIAL STOCK RANCH YARN
imperialyarn.com

THE FIBRE COMPANY
kelbournewoolens.com

KELBOURNE WOOLENS
kelbournewoolens.com

KNIT ONE, CROCHET TOO, INC.
knitonecrochettoo.com

KNITTING FEVER INC. (K.F.I.)
knittingfever.com

KOIGU WOOL DESIGNS
koigu.com

LOUISA HARDING
knittingfever.com

PLYMOUTH YARN CO.
plymouthyarn.com

QUINCE & CO.
quinceandco.com

ROWAN
knitrowan.com

TAHKI•STACY CHARLES, INC.
tahkistacycharles.com

Managing Editor: LAURA COOKE

Senior Editor: LISA SILVERMAN

Art Director: DIANE LAMPHRON

Yarn Editor: VANESSA PUTT

Supervising Patterns Editor:
CARLA SCOTT

Patterns Editor:
BARBARA KHOURI

Proofreader: CHRISTINA BEHNKE

Illustration: DEBORAH NEWTON

Technical Illustrations:
BARBARA KHOURI

Vice President: TRISHA MALCOLM

Publisher: CARRIE KILMER

Production Manager:
DAVID JOINNIDES

President: ART JOINNIDES

Chairman: JAY STEIN

**PHOTOGRAPHY
& ILLUSTRATION CREDITS**

Still-Life Photographer:
MARCUS TULLIS

Model Photographer:
JACK DEUTSCH

Fashion Stylist: JOANNA RADOW

Fashion Stylist's Assistant:
KATHERINE VILLALON

Hair and Makeup: SOKPHALLA BAN

Illustrations pp. 20-21 and p. 35:
KATE FRANCIS

*Photographs from
Vogue® Knitting:*
p. 86
PAUL AMATO
for LVARepresents.com

p. 86
left: ROSE CALLAHAN
center: PAUL AMATO
for LVARepresents.com
right: JACK DEUTSCH

p. 106
ROSE CALLAHAN

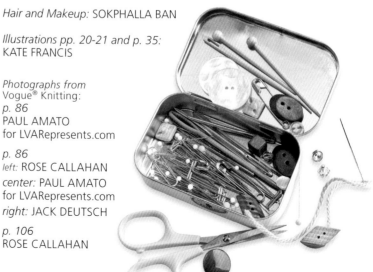